Praise for *Taxtopia*

"*Taxtopia*'s anonymous author has done the impossible – created a hilarious and deeply troubling exposé about how the world's shady tax system is exploited and proves what we always suspected – that our tax system is rigged against us. Read it and weep."
Geraint Anderson, author of *City Boy*

"A shocking, enraging, sometimes hilarious exposé of a tax system that lives down to all our worst fears of further enriching the wealthy at the expense of the little guys."
Piers Morgan

"Funny, clever and really quite brilliant. *Taxtopia* will make you furiously angry and possibly even filthy rich."
Tom Peck, *Independent*

"Very funny (and furious) . . . By the end of the book you may be spluttering with rage at the injustice of it all. Page after page shows how the rich are exploiting loopholes to reduce their tax bill . . ."
Telegraph

"Enormously readable . . . I would very much recommend reading *Taxtopia* because it's the most hilarious book about tax I've ever read!"
Siân Pattenden, The Bunker podcast

"Would I recommend the book? For readers of *Spear's* my answer is 'yes', and it may also be worth going back over some of the more interesting ideas with your accountant."
Spear's

MONEY MANIA

THE REBEL ACCOUNTANT

MONEY MANIA

WEALTH, POWER AND THE CULT OF ECONOMICS

monoray

First published in Great Britain in 2026 by Monoray, an imprint of
Octopus Publishing Group Ltd
Carmelite House
50 Victoria Embankment
London EC4Y 0DZ
www.octopusbooks.co.uk

An Hachette UK Company
www.hachette.co.uk

The authorized representative in the EEA is Hachette Ireland,
8 Castlecourt Centre, Dublin 15, D15 XTP3, Ireland (email: info@hbgi.ie)

Copyright © The Rebel Accountant 2026

Distributed in the US by Hachette Book Group
1290 Avenue of the Americas, 4th and 5th Floors
New York, NY 10104

Distributed in Canada by Canadian Manda Group
664 Annette St., Toronto, Ontario, Canada M6S 2C8

All rights reserved. No part of this work may be reproduced or utilized in any form or by any means, electronic or mechanical, including photocopying, recording or by any information storage and retrieval system, without the prior written permission of the publisher.

The Rebel Accountant asserts the moral right to be identified as the author of this work.

ISBN (Hardback): 978 1 80096 308 5
ISBN (Trade paperback): 978 1 80096 309 2
eISBN: 978 1 80096 311 5

A CIP catalogue record for this book is available from the British Library.

Typeset in 11.25/16pt Heldane Text by Six Red Marbles UK, Thetford, Norfolk

Printed and bound in Great Britain.

13 5 7 9 10 8 6 4 2

This **monoray** book was crafted and published by
Jake Lingwood, Sybella Stephens, Fraser Crichton, Mel Four and Sarah Parry.

This FSC® label means that materials used for
the product have been responsibly sourced.

CONTENTS

Introduction ... 1

1. Why I no longer trust live TV... ... 7
2. ...And why I no longer trust 19th-century economists ... 17
3. Why the tax on penguins might make sense, or could be the culmination of a Soviet plot ... 31
4. Why free trade might not be free (and we test the depth of a lake) ... 49
5. X-rated economics (in which we struggle with page one of the textbook) ... 63
6. The Third Most Famous Man in America ... 83
7. Is the entirety of modern economics one giant conspiracy? And is Deathless Soul Jelly a real thing? ... 103
8. The Dumbest Idea in the World (and other things they teach you at business school) ... 115
9. The secret cat and the un-secret society ... 133
10. The rise of neoliberalism, the Georgist civil war, and an unlikely vendor of plastic ducks ... 151
11. Is finance high? And will a simple equation lead to the end of the world? ... 171
12. The Iron Lady, the lettuce and the inequality machine ... 195
13. You are here ... 217

Notes ... 239

INTRODUCTION

"The purpose of studying economics is to learn how to avoid being deceived by economists."
Joan Robinson, economist

Shortly after the second election of Donald Trump, I discovered that I couldn't sit down. I hadn't forgotten how to or anything, I just felt a piercing stab of pain whenever I did, starting at my coccyx and running up my back. I'm not blaming Trump for this, by the way, I just thought it might help to place this unfortunate event in time.

The doctor I went to see explained that his radiators were broken and apologised that his room was so cold. He listened respectfully to my story, stood next to me, and prodded my spine a bit. As he did, I saw that the hoodie he was wearing said *Galenicals*.

"Is that, as in *Galen*?" I asked him.

"I think so," he said. "It was my medical school student society. It's my favourite jumper."

Not to sound alarmist, but this struck me as deeply worrying.

Galen, in case you've forgotten, was a philosopher and physician who amazed his contemporaries in second-century Alexandria with his knowledge of human anatomy. His insights were particularly impressive because, somewhat surprisingly, human dissection was illegal in the ancient Roman Empire, so Galen had figured out how humans fit together by cutting open animals – mostly pigs, but also the occasional unfortunate monkey.

Building on the work of his predecessor, Hippocrates (from whom doctors today get their Hippocratic Oath to *do no harm*), Galen announced that diseases were caused by one of the body's 'four humours' being out of balance. These humours were phlegm, black bile, yellow bile, and blood.

So, to cure disease, a doctor should get the affected humour back into balance. As phlegm is cold and wet, for instance, a patient with too much phlegm should wear a gold bracelet. Gold, you see, is representative of the sun, which is hot (and the gold itself is dry).

It was all deeply logical. As an example, if you have too much blood, you should cut your veins open to let the blood out. Oh, and semen is made in the brain (obviously).

The Romans thought he was a genius – so much so that his teachings were considered infallible for the best part of one and a half thousand years. If Galen said it was so, then it was. Indeed, when Leonardo da Vinci drew his own anatomical sketches of the human body in the late 1400s, he was so convinced by Galen's teaching that he ignored the evidence of his own eyes and drew tubes connecting the penis to the spine (as how else would the semen get to where it needed to be?).

Galen was intelligent, widely read, and a skilled surgeon, but his real talent was for self-promotion. He lectured widely, performed thrilling public dissections of live animals (more thrilling for the spectators than the animals), employed twenty scribes to write down his ideas and became personal physician to the Roman emperor Commodus (the one who killed Russell Crowe in *Gladiator*). He was almost single-handedly responsible for introducing bloodletting (of the medical kind) to Rome – a practice that continued throughout Europe well into the 19th century.

Now, before you start checking which book you've accidentally picked up, please be assured that this is not a book about Galen. You're holding the right book. *Moneymania* is a book about economics. It's about money – who has it, where it comes from, and where it goes. That means that this is also a book about wealth and power, and the people who have found novel ways to justify why they're the ones who should have it.

But if this is not a book about Galen, then why have I been banging on about him? It's not that Galen had a theory of money – though the original Hippocratic Oath begins with a promise to share your money with your teacher, which in Galen's time was . . . *Galen* – but rather because it demonstrates one of the key problems with the study of wealth.

In case you haven't realised it, what alarmed me about a doctor wearing a *Galenical* hoodie was that Galen was spectacularly wrong about almost everything. His assumptions, particularly that both personalities and health were determined by the four humours, were completely mistaken, as were his conclusions that purgatives and emetics and bloodletting would cure what ailed you.

And yet Galen's ideas persisted for *well over a thousand years*. It's easy to see why. No one else was cutting up animals with such obsessive attention to detail and describing what they saw. No one else had imperial patronage and an army of scribes. He knew more than anyone else, and the people whose opinions mattered believed in him. His theories seemed to make sense – *I do feel out of balance when I'm ill. I do feel better after puking. I do think less clearly when I'm horny.*

And more than that, sometimes – just sometimes – his treatments worked. Occasionally patients got better, and he made sure people heard about it. There's even a small degree of evidence that in a tiny number of cases bloodletting can work, by depriving bacteria of iron, and thus helping the body fight infection (not that Galen would have known this).

That may sound like I'm comparing economics to bloodletting – plausible, widely applied, but wrong, and not just wrong, but dangerously wrong. And I'm not doing that. Well . . . maybe I'll do that a little bit, but a lot of economics is fantastic – fascinating, applicable, useful, and important. But some of it is complete garbage. Most of it is politically motivated. And yet you wouldn't know this from reading the average guide to economics.

I mean, here's an example: pretty much every introduction to economics will tell you that the word *economics* is simply the Greek for "household management", or something similarly prosaic, as if it was just an extension of discussing which shade of beige we should paint our bathrooms. But that is only the bland, uncontroversial explanation.

The word specifically comes from a book called *Oeconomicus*, written in 362 BCE by the Greek general Xenophon, and the book does, indeed, describe how best to manage your household (and your vast estate, should you happen to have one).

But Xenophon was a victorious general in Ancient Greece – he wasn't concerned with which direction the furniture should face or whose turn it was to put the bins out – the household that he was managing was a household of slavery. In an irony that is often missed, the original work on economics from which all others get their name is about how to manage *slaves*.

According to Professor Jane Whittle of Exeter University, when *Oeconomicus* was first published in English, in 1532, references to *slaves* were translated as *servants*, and "as a consequence of this translation, the form of management described by Xenophon fitted remarkably closely to the ideals of 16th-century English gentlemen, and it became a popular book".

Isn't there something odd there? An ancient Greek warlord explains how best to treat his slaves and the English upper classes went, "yup, makes sense, I'll try that", and then an entire academic discipline names itself after that book.

I'm not about to argue like some conspiracist crackpot that modern economics is all a secret ruse to keep us enslaved (at least, again, not *all* economics). But I am going to argue that this *that makes sense* attitude isn't just some 16th-century one-off.

The same pattern emerges repeatedly: a new economic theory is developed that supports the existing power structure, and the rich and powerful go, "yes, indeed, this sounds correct to me", then do their best to convince everyone else that it's the best idea going. Or alternatively, a new theory suggests the opposite – that economic power should be handed to the powerless, and the poor masses say, "that's the ticket, let's do it", and then they murder a lot of rich people in the process.

And, in hindsight, the theory is always obviously cobblers, but too many people wanted to believe it was true. Alarmingly, of course, this attitude never went away. It is very much still with us, often where we least suspect it. In fact, often in exactly the kind of popular economics book that this one is competing with.

There are some wonderful books out there about economics, and a lot of them are really interesting, but too often they're pushing one particular narrative or, worse, they're simply not, well, *fun*. Sometimes reading them is like reading a book on religion written by the Pope – they're missing the X-rated material and just possibly have a preferred set of beliefs.

Since 2022, I've been working with economists from across the spectrum, learning the ropes, as it were, from the inside. This book, as a result, tells two stories. One is a history of economics, but told in a way you might not have encountered before. The other is my story – how I came to be immersed in the world of economists, how I learned from them, and how I came to see the world in a different way (and that wasn't just because one of them offered me hallucinogens).

I wanted to write a book that was a page-turner, that was entertaining, and funny, that didn't shy away from all the absurdities and eccentrics, conspiracy theories, inconvenient facts, sex and violence, and this one weird professor who tried to get me to steal a boat.

We're going to see how free trade was championed by a millionaire who thought it was morally right for the poor to starve to death, hear a dangerously convincing conspiracy theory about the third most famous man in America, consider if there was a Soviet plot to put a tax on penguins, learn if an off-the-cuff remark in New Zealand is the reason mortgages are so expensive, and whether everything that has gone wrong with the world may be the fault of a political treaty signed in Germany in 1648.

By the end of this book, you should feel you have a new understanding of money, and appreciate just how much people lose their minds whenever there's money about.

And before I forget, my doctor told me to just "not sit down for a while."

Welcome to *Moneymania*.

1
WHY I NO LONGER TRUST LIVE TV...

"Economics is extremely useful as a form of employment for economists."
John Kenneth Galbraith, economist

It seems obvious now, but I should not have taken careers advice from someone who called herself a "Yoga Kitten".

"You'll be fine. It's easy," she had told me, sitting cross-legged in her kaftan on my living room floor, chewing pumpkin seeds and ignoring the screams of our kids upstairs as they played a game they'd invented called *battle fists*. "You could do this job in your sleep. All you have to do is talk about money."

Yet now, waiting for an assistant producer called Savannah-Rose to indicate that we had *gone live*, I realised that this was not easy.

For a start, if there's one thing you should never do as an anonymous author who has written a book about tax it's to talk about tax on an international news channel, without so much as a fake moustache to conceal your identity, and with your real name flashed in big letters across the bottom of the screen.

Savannah-Rose was listening to an earpiece. I hadn't been given an earpiece. I hadn't really been given anything, other than an instruction to look directly into the camera and, if I didn't mind, *tone down my British accent*.

Savannah-Rose seemed unsure how to respond when I suggested that "I could try an Irish accent, if that would help?"

My last book, *Taxtopia*, confessed to some possibly illegal behaviour and was a touch rude about a lot of rich and powerful people, so blowing my anonymity would mean, at best, losing my job and getting sued. I don't think it would mean prison time, but I didn't really want to test that theory. What the hell did I have to gain by going on television? Was I hoping that some half-forgotten girlfriend would call me up breathlessly, saying, "I just saw you on TV, you looked so handsome ..." or that the BBC would see my thirty seconds of mildly panicked flustering and immediately sign me up as the new David Attenborough? I wasn't even being paid.

I'd arrived at the studio in Manhattan early, hoping for something mildly glamorous like a quick tour or a chat with the presenters, but instead I'd been asked to wait in a windowless hallway with nothing more exciting to look at than a poster about evacuation procedures in the event of a fire. I stood there awkwardly for about twenty minutes as random members of what I guessed was the news team rushed back and forth avoiding eye contact with me. Eventually, Savannah-Rose appeared and introduced herself. She had a wonderful Texan drawl which she immediately used to apologise that I wouldn't be interviewed in the studio, as had been planned. Instead, they had decided it would be more *authentic* for viewers if I could be interviewed from England.

"Oh, right," I said, a little deflated, conscious that England was a good eight-hour flight away.

"Don't worry," she laughed and touched my arm, "that just means we'll put a British backdrop behind you." Then she led me down another unglamorous corridor to a small side room where I was plonked down between a wooden writing desk that looked like something my grandfather would have used and a wall-sized green screen that appeared to be attached to the low ceiling with string. There was a small camera, not much bigger than an iPhone, fixed to a tripod and an even smaller microphone clipped to the edge of the desk.

Savannah-Rose adjusted the tripod as I wondered if this was all, well, *normal.* She smiled reassuringly at me, I think sensing my unease. "We'll pretend you're on a Zoom call from London, it really emphasises the international nature of this issue."

Another young woman walked into the room, squinted at me like there was something wrong with my face, then perched on the desk next to me and asked me to close my eyes. It seemed rude not to, and when I closed them she dusted a powder onto my forehead. I couldn't help but think that this was all a bit odd.

"You good?" asked Savannah-Rose, perhaps sensing my nerves. "I'll be back in a short while. I think we're swapping leads."

So there I was, alone at a fake writing desk, forehead powdered, ready for a fake Zoom call, with no idea what "swapping leads" meant. Is live TV always like this? My phone vibrated. I realised I should turn it off, but checked the message first. It was from my boss, Ioannou, back in England.

> They r changing ur interviewer
> Now Rachel K not Rachel L
> U ok with that?

I didn't really know who Rachel K or Rachel L were. And why would it matter? Surely, they'd just ask the same questions I'd prepared for. *Is Trump right that foreigners will pay the tariffs rather than US consumers? Are tariffs a sensible economic policy? Will this bring manufacturing jobs back to America?*

So I typed back:

> Sure. No probs.

I hesitated before turning my phone off. After a couple of moments, I turned it back on, reopened WhatsApp, and added:

> Why would I not be okay with that?

Three dots appeared. Ioannou was typing. Then nothing. Then three dots again. Then nothing. And then, finally:

It may be a trap

What did that mean? I started replying along the lines of "huh?" when the door opened and Savannah-Rose reappeared with another smile.

"Two minutes," she said. "Have fun."

―

Once I'd mastered baking sourdough, hoarded all the toilet paper I could get my hands on and joined a very exclusive cocktail society (there were two members), I had spent the rest of the first Covid lockdown writing a book about my experience of tax evasion. Or rather (as explained in that book) not *evasion*, but frightfully clever and not at all morally questionable tax *avoidance* (which is the legal kind). I'd had the good fortune to get a book deal and that meant that Henrí (my wife, and only other member of my cocktail society) pretended not to mind that I'd come rather belatedly to the conclusion that I didn't really want to be a tax advisor any more.

Henrí indulged my authorial ambitions for a while. So, as the rest of the world recovered from coronavirus, I decided to carry on staying at home and write the obvious follow-up to a book on international tax avoidance – a children's novel that I pitched as a mix of Marvel's *Avengers* with the 1986 Christopher Lambert classic sci-fi movie *Highlander* (only with ten-year-olds). I then faced the disappointing reality that the publishing industry isn't ready for an ultra-violent super-powered tale of pre-teen angst and decapitation (though my ten-year-old loved it).

I'd toyed a little bit with consulting, and had done a few days' financial work for a theatrical props business (they'd had a *very* bad Covid), a couple of weeks at a company that cleaned sewage with robots (which were not called, in what I think was a missed marketing opportunity, R2Depoo), and I'd helped raise money from investors for a technology company that was trying to make underwater acoustic equipment for deterring fish. I say "helped", but I wasn't actually successful in persuading anyone to put cash into this fish disco.*

The only steady work I had managed to secure was delivering a lecture series on tax at a business school attached to what they described as a prestigious university. I rather liked the idea of this being my new career, but mostly because it meant that, consulting aside, I was only working one hour per week.

What I really wanted to do was write another book. I was toying with writing modern analogies of historical events and had started sketching out the plot for a satirical sci-fi saga in which the United States was colonised by aliens, loosely based on the East India Company's takeover of Bengal in the 18th century. My mortgage provider was less keen on this idea, and our declining bank balance had not gone unnoticed by Henrí.

So, one morning, while I was busy sketching out how the aliens' tax policies would lead to famine in Brooklyn, Henrí walked into our living room in her gym kit and announced that she had made a new friend at something called *kitten yoga*.

"She works for a think-tank and loves it," said Henrí. "And guess what? She says they're looking for someone with a tax background."

It wasn't exactly the most interesting gossip she'd ever shared with me – a few months earlier her Pilates instructor had been arrested for selling ketamine-infused kombucha. You're probably ahead of me here, but it took me a moment to realise that Henrí *wasn't*, in actual fact, gossiping – she was trying to get me back to work.

"*And* she says they spend half their time arranging finance. This job would be perfect for you."

---

* In fact, I think the only real contribution I made was when, on learning that they had a software program for identifying fish which they called "the fishbook", I'd suggested that they lose the "the". "Guys, how about just *Fishbook*?" I thought it was obvious that I was paraphrasing a line from the movie *The Social Network*, about the rise of Facebook (or, as it used to be, *The Facebook*), but they thought it was a fantastic idea and ended up paying me close to £16,000.

I gave a very non-committal *hmm*, so she added, "What I really mean is, *a* job would be perfect for you."

I didn't like the sound of this.

"I don't really know what a think-tank is," I protested, a little weakly.

"You'll love it. They analyse economic policy, have flexible hours and most of what they do is *writing*."

I clearly wasn't winning this one, so tried to change the subject, perhaps a little too snarkily. "Can I ask," I said, "are the kittens doing the yoga, or are they just in the room, avoiding all the mums and looking condescending?"

She frowned at me. "Don't be silly. You love thinking, and tanks. I've invited my friend round after school pick-up and told her all about you." And then she swept her hair back dramatically, "And *we're* the kittens, obviously."

—

The think-tank was called the Institute for Fair Economics, or IFFE. It was run by a man called Ioannou who had the excitable chattiness of a parakeet and a smile that looked like a wrinkle on a sock puppet. Henri's kitten-yoga friend was called Charlotte and she arranged for me to meet Ioannou over a coffee in a café overlooking the Serpentine lake in Hyde Park. He twitched when I greeted him like he'd already had too many coffees and indicated a seat at a table he'd saved for us, which still had the previous customers' empty cups on it. Or now I think about it, maybe had *his* empty cups on it.

He told me immediately that he'd heard from Charlotte about where I lectured and was super-impressed. I guessed that Charlotte hadn't told him about me only lecturing for one hour a week.

"We're also very well-respected," he said, enunciating each syllable of his words in clipped tones, like someone doing a bad impression of an unidentified foreign accent. It seemed like an odd thing to say. I mean, obviously I'd read up on his think-tank, and "respected" wasn't a description I'd come across. He kept asking me if I'd read various reports that IFFE had published and each time I replied with, "Sorry, no, actually", he looked a little hurt. So he changed tack, giving a funny little sort of shuffle-hop in his seat as he looked off into the distance. "Well, frankly, four-fifths of this job is really just trying to raise money, and the research and report writing is secondary."

Charlotte had pitched this coffee meeting to me as a chance to "have a chat" with Ioannou about "opportunities", and so it wasn't entirely clear which of us was meant to be convincing the other. If anything, it was more like a date. I had a horrible feeling that maybe I'd got the wrong end of the stick and it *was* a date.

"Well," I said, enthusiastically, flirtatiously, even, "I've just spent the best part of the last two years trying to raise money for start-ups." Which was true. Or at least, truth adjacent. I decided not to add, *unsuccessfully*. Or that by "best part" I meant *very occasionally, when I haven't been confessing to evading taxes.**

"Oh, really?" said Ioannou, matching my enthusiasm. "That's great to hear. If you can bring in the money, you'll go far. I should probably ask what you know about think-tanks?"

This bit, I'd now got my head around.

The first think-tank to be called a think-tank was the RAND corporation, whose former Chief Strategist Herman Kahn is said to have inspired the character of Dr Strangelove after writing a book about how to win a thermonuclear war. RAND still exists and calls itself a "nonprofit, nonpartisan research organization" (RAND is a contraction of *Research and Development*), though it's non-partisan in the sense of originally being an offshoot of the US Air Force and still being partially funded by the US government.

---

* I have a feeling that my date-chat may be awful. I should also confess that the think-tank wasn't really called IFFE. I mean, I've gone to enormous lengths to preserve my anonymity (largely because of all the tax evasion I confessed to in the last book), so it would be pretty daft for me to just say, "Oh, hey, I was one of the people who worked at this place and my photo is still on their website next to my real name, if you're interested." But IFFE is close enough to its real name to give you some idea of how they see themselves. And *iffy* is close enough to how I would come to see them, as may become apparent.

Nowadays, there are thousands of think-tanks, maybe even tens of thousands, in all sorts of different fields. Some specialise in healthcare or renewable energy, others in religion or theatrical arts, there are even think-tanks that specialise in the *future* and *deep time*. But most of them are concerned with, in one form or another, wealth and power.

Almost all of them claim to be independent. In practice, almost none of them are, for a simple reason – they all need *money*, and they get that money by telling their donors exactly what they want to hear.

Generally, the reason they exist is to influence the opinions of both politicians and the general public. Some think-tanks are tiny, single-issue outfits that research whatever their sole employee is interested in, others are huge; the Brookings Institute, based in Washington, DC, spends around $100 million per year on its operations. That sort of money buys a lot of influence.

In theory, think-tanks are not the same as lobby groups, which aim to directly change legislation in favour of a specific industry, usually not so much by using cool-headed academic research but more by taking politicians out for expensive lunches and, where the law allows (and sometimes where it doesn't), funding the politicians' political campaigns. There is a bewildering number of lobby groups, campaigning for everything from preserving the ivory trade, legalising python ownership, protecting dehydrated onions, and giving guns to schoolteachers.*

But, in practice, the line between think-tanks and lobby groups is a little blurry. Too often, the funding comes first, and the views follow. A 2014 investigation by *The New York Times* estimated that at least 64 foreign governments or state-controlled entities had donated to American think-tanks, seeking to influence US politics. Most of the 64 were dictatorships, but among them, oddly, was the Norwegian government, which transferred at least $24 million to American think-tanks which, shortly afterwards, duly advocated for Arctic oil drilling and expanding Norway's role in NATO.

---

* I'm obviously not accusing any of the lobby groups behind these campaigns of doing anything illegal, especially the ones that carry guns and/or pythons.

Indeed, in 2022, Brookings Institute president John Allen was moved to resign amid an FBI investigation into whether he had lobbied the US government on behalf of Qatar, an allegation he denied.

"I don't suppose you've been investigated by the FBI for arguing a foreign government's cause?" I asked Ioannou, with a slightly nervous chuckle that I hope demonstrated that I was joking.

"I should be so lucky," he replied.

We agreed that I would start off working two days a week, mostly on tax policy. This seemed ideal – two days at an economics think-tank, one hour (plus the commute) at a business school, which would leave two and a half days a week to write *The East America Company*.

I declined to tell Ioannou that I'd just written a book about tax, or indeed that the book was in the process of being adapted for a TV show, partly because I knew I'd then tell him that the opening scene of the show featured a Russian oligarch becoming trapped in an inflatable hippo's anus, and that was probably not the level of professional seriousness that Ioannou was looking for.

—

Savannah-Rose gave me a thumbs up. I guessed that meant we were now on air. There was no monitor for me to see who was talking, just a disembodied voice.

"I'm joined today live from London, England, by an economist at the Institute for Fair Economics."

Wait, how far through the show were we? What had already been said? How would I know if I was repeating a point that had just been made by someone else? Why did I need powder on my forehead?

There was no time to pause for answers. Rachel, the presenter, had continued talking without a moment for me to say *hello* and was now speaking rapidly and – perhaps this was my imagination – a little aggressively.

"In one recent poll of economists conducted by the Clark Center for Global Markets, seventy-five per cent of American respondents agreed that tariffs would reduce economic growth and only four per cent disagreed. Yet your institute seems to think that the majority of economists are wrong. That's pretty hubristic, wouldn't you say?"

I gave a nervous little smile. I think I understood what Ioannou had meant about this interview possibly being a trap.

2

... AND WHY I NO LONGER TRUST 19TH-CENTURY ECONOMISTS

> *"If the misery of our poor be caused not by the laws of nature, but by our institutions, great is our sin."*
> Charles Darwin, naturalist

In February 2025, US President Donald Trump declared a national emergency over undocumented migration and drug trafficking. To respond to this emergency, President Trump signed executive orders to introduce tariffs on all goods imported into the USA from Canada, Mexico and China.

A tariff is a tax. There's no getting around that. A lot has been written about Donald Trump's unconventional approach to engaging with the American electorate and hats off to him, he managed to sneak in some enormous tax rises largely by claiming that *someone else* will pay them. Voters love it when they think that *someone else* will pay more taxes. But whichever way you approach it, "raising tariffs" really means "raising taxes".

Indeed, tariffs may be the oldest type of tax there is. There are records from five thousand years ago from Assyrian trading colonies of local rulers charging caravan trains a fee based on the value of their imported goods. Ancient Athens levied a 2 per cent tariff on imported grain,

Ancient Rome charged import duties of up to 25 per cent on luxuries imported from Asia.

Even the word "tariff" itself is ancient. Trump called it "the most beautiful word", perhaps demonstrating his appreciation of the Arabic culture from where it originates. European merchants adopted the term as trade expanded at the dawn of the Renaissance, and by the 1590s the word had entered the English language, originally meaning any list of import duties but eventually coming to mean the tax itself.

One month after the undocumented migration emergency, Trump declared another national emergency, this time about the fact that America imports more than it exports (in the jargon, it had a constant *trade deficit*). It was a slightly odd thing to call an emergency, as America has imported more than it exports since the 1970s, but it gave him legal cover to sign further orders stating that tariffs would be introduced on *all* imports, not just those from Canada, Mexico and China. These new tariffs were country-specific and based on a seemingly sophisticated equation that looked like this:

$$\Delta \tau_i = \frac{x_i - m_i}{\varepsilon \times \varphi \times m_i}$$

As a general rule, if anyone tries to explain something to you using Greek letters in a mathematical equation, it's perfectly polite to ask them to explain what those letters stand for. In this case, all the equation means is that the new tariff rates would be based on the difference between America's exports and imports to and from a particular country, then divided by the value of imports. This *sounds* like quite a mouthful, but means the equation can also be written like this:

$$\text{Tariff rate} = \frac{\text{Exports less Imports}}{\text{Imports}}$$

... AND WHY I NO LONGER TRUST 19TH-CENTURY ECONOMISTS

Which doesn't look nearly so sophisticated. It also doesn't really make much economic sense, especially as the tariff rate is then divided by two, for no obviously good reason. Trump also ignored this equation for countries that *don't* export more to the USA than they import from it, and simply imposed a 10 per cent tariff rate, I guess just for the fun of it.*

The equation was a bit of a *guestimate*, but would mean a 46 per cent tax charge on goods imported from Vietnam (so a $100 pair of shoes would now cost $146), 34 per cent on goods imported from China, 20 per cent from the EU, 50 per cent on the tiny African country of Lesotho, and, most surprisingly, 10 per cent on anything imported from the Heard and McDonald Islands, a territory almost 2,500 miles off the west coast of Australia. These islands were specifically mentioned in Trump's list of new rates (unlike, say, Australia itself) despite the fact that the islands are entirely populated by penguins.

British Prime Minister Kier Starmer had rushed to the White House to try and negotiate a special deal to reduce tariffs on British goods. And that was why I, as a Brit with an occupational interest in taxes, had been invited onto American television to talk about the impact these tariffs would have on Anglo-American trade.

By the 1600s, tariffs were one of the major sources of most governments' revenue, and an entire economic theory developed to justify their use. The theory was called mercantilism, and for hundreds of years it was the dominant idea of how nations could increase their wealth.

The logic of mercantilism was that what made nations rich was owning gold – after all, the more gold you had, the richer you were. So it followed that the most sensible course of action for any nation's ruler was to encourage

---

* The two squiggly Greek letters ε and φ on the bottom half of the equation represent how much the quantity and price of imported goods would respond to the tariffs, but when multiplied together these two amounts cancel each other out (which also doesn't make sense), so don't really need to be in the equation at all, other than to make it look cool.

exports (so foreigners give you gold in exchange for your goods), discourage imports by putting tariffs on foreign goods (so gold doesn't leave your shores), and put the acquisition of precious metals (normally by violent conquest) at the top of the to-do list.

One major proponent was Jean-Baptise Colbert, background character in *The Three Musketeers* and Minister of State for 17th-century French king Louis XIV. Colbert aimed to transform the French economy by encouraging the formation of French industries to reduce France's reliance on imports, establishing (or seizing) foreign colonies to provide raw materials, and building up the French navy.*

Central to mercantilism's logic was pursuing a *trade surplus* – that exports should exceed imports. The main ways to achieve this were with subsidies for domestic industries, the occasional bit of violence, and tariffs. Effectively, mercantilism (and local variants like France's *Colbertism*) became economic orthodoxy from the late 1500s all the way through until the last decades of the 1700s.But then, in 1776, the modern "story" of economics begins, with the publication of Adam Smith's *The Wealth of Nations*.

Adam Smith was a deeply eccentric and absent-minded individual, famous for having loud conversations with himself, putting his bread in his tea pot, falling into a tar pit while distracted by his thoughts, forgetting to invite anyone to a dinner party and dying a virgin. He's also so celebrated by economists that in 2007 the Bank of England put a picture of him onto the back of a £20 note. This was somewhat controversial, because Adam Smith was Scottish, not English.†

Smith argued that a country's wealth comes not from gold and silver, but from its ability to make things. Money, he pointed out, is just a medium of exchange, not prosperity itself. And where the mercantilists saw trade as a

---

* The French construction company Saint-Gobain, which today employs around 160,000 people, was founded by Colbert; he was honoured as recently as 1956 by having a French missile cruiser named after him.

† The Bank of Scotland, which prints its own notes, chose at the time to feature a picture of a bridge.

zero-sum game, in that for one nation to get richer another must lose out, Smith argued that a free exchange of goods makes *everyone* richer, as both parties value what the other has more than what they themselves own (as otherwise, why would they trade?).

As part of his analysis of the importance of the free exchange of goods – of *free trade* – Smith highlighted an inherent problem with tariffs: that they enriched a few narrow interests, like domestic manufacturers (who were protected from foreign competition) at the expense of everyone else. In other words, a small number of producers benefited to the detriment of a huge number of consumers.

Adam Smith viewed himself as a moral philosopher, but he kickstarted the systematic study of how entire economies slot together, and consequently he is usually known as the "father" of economics. But the story of why Trump slapped a tariff on penguins actually begins a few years after the publication of *The Wealth of Nations*, with a different book, this one written by a young bond trader who would become the most influential economist that most people have never heard of.

In the early 1800s, Britain was in dire need of money. War was raging with Napoleon's France. The British government increased tax rates and introduced new types of taxes (like income tax), but it still wasn't enough. So, they did what governments always do when their expenditure exceeds their income, and borrowed. By 1815 (when Napoleon was finally defeated), the British government had borrowed around £600 million, which in comparative terms is more than Britain borrowed to fight either the First or Second World Wars.

When a government borrows money, it usually does so by creating and selling a *bond* – a promise to pay the money back later and to make interest payments in the meantime. Where bonds differ to the kind of loan you might make to your mates is that bond traders can buy and sell these debts with other bond traders. As Napoleon wouldn't have honoured the British government's bonds had he conquered Britain, when the war was going badly the price of the bonds would fall. When the war went well, the price would rise again. This gave shrewd bond traders an opportunity to make money.

One of the shrewdest of these traders was a mathematically gifted young man called David Ricardo.

At the age of 14, Ricardo had followed his father's (and uncle's and brothers') footsteps into a career in the London Stock Exchange, and by the outbreak of war he had already made a name for himself as a brilliant market analyst with an extraordinarily quick mind. He became so successful at selling bonds on rumours of military victories that by the end of the war he was one of the richest men in England, so wealthy that he bought not just vast estates scattered across the country, but also a stately home (inhabited today by Princess Anne, King Charles's younger sister) and a seat in parliament (because such things could be bought, back then – his was for a constituency in Ireland that he never visited). He then retired from bond trading and decided to become an economist, focusing mostly on why so many people (such as his staff) were poor.

For a bit of context, analysing why most people were poor was all the rage in the early 1800s. The leading theory of the day had been put forward in 1798 by the Reverend Thomas Malthus, who set out to prove mathematically the importance of "moral restraint": populations increase exponentially (that is, at an ever increasing speed), but food production doesn't, so inevitably there is not enough food to feed everyone. He concluded that poor people could have sex or bread, but not both. In other words, it's the poor's fault that they are poor – if only they didn't have so many babies they would all be a lot richer.

Reverend Malthus saw this as God's will – a divine example of the importance of virtuous living, but his mathematical "proof" eventually became known as the *Iron Law of Wages*: workers' wages would always tend towards subsistence levels, as anything more than subsistence allows the poor to breed like rabbits, at which point too many people will be chasing not enough bread.

With a couple of centuries of retrospection, of course, it's pretty obvious that the *Iron Law* wasn't true and Malthus got his calculations wrong, what with the world's population now being about nine times greater than it was in his day and there is such a surplus of food that some people in rich countries inject themselves with drugs every month just to suppress their appetites. But to Malthus's wealthy readership his "law" made complete sense. It wasn't that the rich were exploiting the poor, you see, it was that the filthy peasants couldn't stop shagging.

Indeed, when in 1817 David Ricardo published his major work on economics, called *On the Principles of Political Economy and Taxation*, it didn't occur to him to disagree with Malthus. Instead, he declared as fact that labour had a "natural price" that was just enough for the labourer to "subsist and perpetuate their race, without either increase or diminution", which nowadays is probably the sort of sentiment that would get you cancelled, but in his day led to his book becoming enormously influential and popular with the political elite.

There was more in this vein – he declared it "a truth which admits not a doubt, that the comforts and well-being of the poor cannot be permanently secured without some regards on their part, or some effort on the part of the legislature, to regulate the increase in their numbers, and to render less frequent among them early and improvident marriages."

So, again, the poor will remain poor unless they – or the government – restrict their numbers. Ricardo, incidentally, was one of 17 children, and had eight of his own, and his parents had disowned him when he improvidently married against their wishes at the age of 21. Not that I'm accusing him of being a massive hypocrite.

But what do an 18th-century reverend's abstinence-based economics or a bond trader's slightly suspect opinion that we need legislation to stop poor people getting married have to do with tariffs, let alone tariffs on penguins? Well, in the same book in which Ricardo complains about a "race" of poor people having too many kids, he outlined, over just ten pages, an idea that has become known as the *Law of Comparative Advantage*.

It is this "law" that underpins all arguments for abolishing tariffs and for allowing trade to be "free". It's a law that is in every economics textbook and is the starting point for all analysis of international trade deals. The University of Texas economist James Kenneth Galbraith[*] wrote in 2008 that due to the

---

[*] There are two J K Galbraiths in the world of economics – John and James. They are father and son.

Law of Comparative Advantage, free trade has attained in his profession "the status of a god".

University of Warwick professor Matt Watson has said that for the last two centuries "no training in the ways of the academic economist is considered complete if often wildly deferential tribute is not paid to Ricardo's "farsightedness" in having solved for all time the question of why free trade is to be preferred."

I figured that if I was going to work on tariff and trade policy at a think-tank, I should probably read Ricardo's book. As I read it, I started to wonder if Professor Watson's comment about Ricardo's farsightedness was actually a little sarcastic.

—

In the days following President Trump's announcement that new tariffs would be introduced on all imports, the value of American companies listed on stock exchanges fell by over $6 trillion – the biggest two-day loss in history. Stock markets everywhere from Japan to South Africa saw the worst crashes since Covid (which doesn't sound that dramatic, as Covid was only a few years ago, but the Covid crashes were *big*).*

Investors don't like tariffs because tariffs mean higher costs. For instance, a payment must be made to the government to, say, import a shoe made in Bangladesh before it can be sold to a customer in Michigan, or to import steel from Canada before it can be turned into a car in Wisconsin.

One of Trump's arguments was that these higher costs would encourage goods to be made in America, but that would *also* mean higher costs, due to wages in America being higher than wages in China. Share prices are based on expectations of future profits, and higher costs mean those profits will fall.

---

* To put this figure in context, if you divide $6 trillion by the population of the USA you get an average reduction in wealth of just under $18,000 *per person*. Obviously not all Americans own shares in American companies, but about two-thirds of American households have at least some exposure, and most pension funds invest in stock markets.

Due to the mere announcement of the tariffs, shoemaker Nike lost 13 per cent of its value, Apple lost 10 per cent and General Motors announced an expected billion-dollar hit to profits.

To escape the volatility in the stock markets, many investors sold shares and bought government bonds, causing an increase in bond prices. This was one small bit of good news for Trump, as higher bond prices mean lower borrowing costs.*

This good news wasn't to last. By the second week of April, investors started dumping American bonds (and buying gold and German bonds instead) on fears that tariffs would lead to inflation, recession and a lack of trust in the stability of the dollar. In other words, the markets' response to the new tariffs wasn't great. Though the price of coffee fell, so there was at least some silver lining.

—

Reading David Ricardo's *On the Principles of Political Economy and Taxation* was . . . surprising. He never actually refers to the Law of Comparative Advantage – other people coined that name decades later. He was merely trying to come up with an argument to oppose the big import tax of the day – tariffs known as the *Corn Laws*, which somewhat weirdly didn't apply to actual corn but rather to wheat and barley.

The Corn Laws protected British farmers from cheaper foreign competition by taxing imported food, which had the inevitable consequence that food prices were kept high, so much so that some people couldn't afford to buy bread.

The government tackled high food prices by enforcing *Poor Laws*, which required wealthier landowners (like Ricardo) to pay an annual tax based

---

* The interest paid on a bond is fixed for the duration of the bond, but remember that the price of the bond can change (for instance, if Napoleon invades). If you divide the annual interest payments by the price of a bond you get a *yield*, and this yield is the effective interest that a government must pay. This means that financially trustworthy countries have higher bond prices, so have lower yields, meaning they can borrow more cheaply.

on the size of their estates to subsidise food for the starving. Ricardo hated paying this tax, despite it only being about 1 per cent of his annual income. He saw it as an affront, but claimed that his antipathy was moral rather than selfish, writing of the Poor Laws that "every friend of the poor must ardently wish for their abolition".

To explain why giving bread to the starving was a bad thing, he asserted that "wages should be left to the fair and free competition of the market, and should never be controlled by the interference of the legislature". He didn't elaborate on what "free" or "fair" meant, but rather assumed this point to be self-evident. He certainly didn't seem to think it was unfair that, for instance, he got started in his own career because his father gave him a job.

Next, Ricardo took this assertion about free markets to its logical conclusion. At this stage, I had to re-read the same passages over and over, as it was astonishing, but not in a good way. "It is only after their privations have reduced their number," he wrote, that "the market price of labour will rise to its natural price".

Wait a minute – *privations have reduced their number*? That's a euphemism for *starved to death*, isn't it? It was possible that I was missing something, as his argument seemed monstrous – that his paying the equivalent of a 1 per cent income tax interfered with the free market, and the free market would naturally resolve the issue of labourers not being able to afford to eat by starving them to death, at which point the survivors' wages would rise. Surely this couldn't be the central argument of one of the foundational texts of modern economics?

Ricardo did acknowledge that labourers won't starve if demand for labour rises, and that sometimes the *market* rate for labour could exceed the natural rate, but to the millionaire Ricardo, his assertion that *every friend of the poor should just let the free market kill off the poor* wasn't him being callous, but a simple consequence of the mathematics that Thomas Malthus had already demonstrated, and you can't argue with mathematical laws (even the ones that turn out to be wrong).

I was so shocked by Ricardo's argument that I decided to check my interpretation with an expert, and got in touch with Nat Dyer, the author of the very brilliant book *Ricardo's Dream*. I asked him about my reading of Ricardo's argument.

"You're right," he said. "It was monstrous. For his maiden speech in the House of Commons, Ricardo argued that if 'parents felt assured that an asylum would be provided for their children, in which they would be treated with humanity and tenderness, there would then be no check to that increase of population which was so apt to take place among the labouring classes.'"

Nat Dyer points out in *Ricardo's Dream* that Ricardo "heaped misery on the poor and their children ... for what he considered to be the greater good", guided by what would turn out to be an incorrect theory (of population growth). It was also a viewpoint that *happened* to mean that rich people like Ricardo paid less tax. How fortunate for him, though as Dyer put it to me, "Ricardo would argue that his harsh position was just a result of the natural law of population, and he had no personal animosity towards the working classes."

Anyway, Ricardo wasn't content just to campaign to abolish the Poor Laws. He had the Corn Laws – the tariffs – in his sights, too, and this is where we see his arguments for free trade develop. He stated that the profits that capitalists could make were directly related to the wages they paid their labourers, writing that "every diminution in the wages of labour raises profits". In other words, his goal was to *reduce* wages, in order to make people like *him* richer.

Remember that he believed that wages tended towards subsistence levels, the so called "natural rate" – literally those wages that just about kept a labourer and their (small) family alive. Consequently, the only way to reduce wages without killing your staff would be to make the products they required for subsistence a little bit cheaper.

If the Corn Laws were abolished there would be no taxes on imported food, so wages could drop as food would be cheaper, and lower wages meant higher profits. In other words, it would be the rich who would benefit from scrapping import taxes, rather than the poor.

Supporters of the Corn Laws claimed that tariffs were necessary because foreign farmers would always be able to undercut Britain's farmers, since foreign climates were better for growing crops. Ricardo acknowledged that this was true, but argued that it would still benefit all countries to trade with each other, as they could mutually benefit from their *comparative* advantages.

He used the example of England's cloth and wine trade with Portugal. The brainwave he had was to measure the value of cloth and wine not in monetary amounts, but in how much cloth *won't* be made if wine is made instead (and vice versa).

For instance, if England is hopeless at wine but only mediocre at cloth-making, then England will not be sacrificing much wine to make cloth, so England would be better off producing cloth and then trading some of it for wine.*

Using this logic, Ricardo showed mathematically that *total* production will increase if each nation focuses on what it does least badly. This is almost the entirety of Ricardo's argument (he added a bit on the difficulties of migration, how exchange rates would shift and a few other assumptions).

In short, free trade and specialisation increase efficiency. This leads to more goods being made, so overall wealth increases. As a result, many economists treated (and still treat) his brief calculations with almost holy reverence, like a divine revelation handed down from on high.†

---

* He didn't have any actual data, so he made some up instead, exactly like this:
England takes 100 hours to make 1 unit of cloth and 120 hours to make 1 unit of wine.
Portugal takes 90 hours to make 1 unit of cloth and 80 hours to make 1 unit of wine.
So, making a unit of English cloth means not making 0.83 units of English wine, but making a unit of Portuguese cloth means not making 1.125 units of Portuguese wine.
And yes, all 19th-century economics books are this thrilling.

† The Austro-German economist Joseph Schumpeter coined the term "Ricardian Vice" to refer to Ricardo's tendency to oversimplify by using unrealistic assumptions. For the Law of Comparative Advantage to work perfectly, it has to be easy to retrain as a weaver and to convert wine presses into looms, and there must be full employment and no transport costs. Cue two hundred years of debate about whether it matters that none of these assumptions are true.

Yet Ricardo described the principal problem of economics as how the "produce of the earth" should be distributed between landowners, capitalists and labourers. In his analysis of the benefits of free trade, he explicitly stated that the extra wealth would flow to just one class – his own, the already rich capitalist. But nowhere in his book did he address whether this class structure is real, natural or fair. And at no point does he discuss the ethical or political ramifications if all the wealth from specialisation and free trade flows to only one class, despite "political" literally being in his book title.

It may be that reading a classic book on your phone is not the ideal way to experience it, but having always bought in to the logic of free trade, I'll confess that when I got round to actually reading Ricardo's argument, I was a little disappointed.

―

I wasn't actually in New York just to be interviewed about tariffs. I was visiting some family members, but while I was there my boss Ioannou got a call asking him if anyone from our institute would be willing to appear on TV to give a British perspective on the tariffs, and as I was staying just a couple of blocks from their studios he emailed me to suggest that I do it.

"What does a *British* perspective mean?" I asked him. Like all sixty-nine million Brits are going to feel the same way about something.

"Who cares?" he replied. "Publicity is half the battle. Be controversial. Talk up the threat of war with China."

I stared deeply into the small camera. A tiny, distorted reflection stared back at me. I pretended this reflection was my interviewer. She had just asked me whether my think-tank was *hubristic*. I was only 80 per cent sure I knew what that word meant.

"Yes," I acknowledged. "It's almost impossible to find an economist who thinks that tariffs are good for economic growth." And then I paused, and far from *toning down my British accent*, as the assistant producer Savannah-Rose had suggested, I uttered what I only realised later was a word not widely used in America: "But that's only because most economists base their arguments on assumptions that are, frankly, complete *tosh*."

There was a moment of silence. I'm not sure whether Savannah-Rose was actually listening to what I was saying, but she nodded encouragingly.

"Care to elaborate?" asked Rachel K or Rachel L or whichever one I was meant to be on a Zoom call with.

"Sure," I said. I knew I had, at most, thirty seconds to explain our think-tank's position. I'd been at the think-tank for about three years by this point, three years that had transformed my own understanding of economics, of wealth and power, and the *mania* that always swirls around money.

I'd practised my talking points the previous evening on a solitary, wind-swept walk around Central Park. I'd been interviewed a number of times by this point, sometimes live, but usually not, and never before on TV. There's meant to be a technique to media appearances – you acknowledge the question, then "bridge" to what you really want to talk about, then "control" the conversation. But in truth I've never been very good at that. I normally just want to reply with, "What?! What kind of crazy-ass question is that?"

In fact, in the first media interview I ever had, back when I was promoting *Taxtopia*, an American presenter told me, with a wink, that "in America we consider it our constitutional right to avoid paying taxes." Apart from not being an actual question, it was a statement that struck me as, well, *crazy*. She was too poor to avoid paying tax herself (tax avoidance is a rich person's game), so in whose interest was it that she *believed* in tax avoidance? Because it wasn't in hers.

I wondered, as I walked, if economics suffered from the same problem. People are so wedded to their beliefs, to their *politics*, that often they'll defend a theory even if it is plainly designed to protect the already powerful.

I paused by a fountain and took a selfie to send back to my family (Henrí liked it so much she printed it out and put it on our mantlepiece. It's looking at me as I write this). I had a particular phrase I wanted to use in my interview, one told to me by an economist I'd spoken to just a week into my time at the think-tank. And staring out across the lake beside the fountain, I found myself thinking of him – the first person who made me suspect that there might be a little madness at the heart of economics.

3

WHY THE TAX ON PENGUINS MIGHT MAKE SENSE, OR COULD BE THE CULMINATION OF A SOVIET PLOT

"The less we understand the economy, the better it does."
Paul Samuelson, economist

On my first day at the Institute for Fair Economics, I learned quite a useful skill: how to piss off a roomful of economists with just four words.

Ioannou had introduced me to what he called the "ideas team" (he liked to say "ideas" a lot) and I'd perhaps been lured into a false confidence by how many of them weren't economists. There was a former political speech writer who shook my hand enthusiastically, a plastic surgeon moonlighting from his day job in the NHS (who also shook my hand, then rotated it slightly to examine it), a retired advertising executive who greeted me with a "Yo!", a chap I assumed was some sort of IT whizz purely based on his wearing a T-shirt that said "computer nerd" and a woman in a multi-coloured dress who introduced herself as the "artist in residence" – though everyone else laughed when she said that, so I presume she was joking. Mostly, though, the team was made up of young graduate economists, fresh out of university. It was this last group that I found myself chatting to at lunch on my first day.

One of them was earnestly telling me about his analysis of *INSET* days – the mandatory teacher training days that shut all British schools for five days a year. "That's an entire term of lost schooling for children over their academic lives," he said, passionately, and while I didn't disagree with him (I *despise* INSET days), I was a little surprised that this was, for him, the most important economic issue he could find to analyse.

Perhaps disappointed by my lack of enthusiasm for his work, he rather sulkily asked what I had done before joining the think-tank. When I explained that I used to work for a firm of wealth managers in Mayfair, he looked incredulous.

"And then you moved *here*? For *real*?" Like most of the graduates, he was priced out of renting in London and still lived with his parents, so I guess what he was really asking was, *Why have you taken such a colossal pay cut?*

There were about eight or nine of us sitting at two tables alongside a kitchenette in the office, most of the young graduates eating from Tupperware containers they'd brought from home, the smell of microwaved tofu still lingering. Apparently, Ioannou encouraged the team to lunch together, *to let ideas blossom.*

"Well, Ioannou said that this institute is where great ideas come to life," I replied, and luckily they laughed. "But, no, seriously, I guess I just want to work out –" and this is where I probably should have held my tongue – "why economics has failed."

They stopped laughing. It was as if I'd just told them I'd voted for Brexit. One of them choked out their tofu.

"No offence," I added, perhaps a little late.

I honestly didn't think there was anything controversial about saying that economics had failed. I mean, every popular economics book outside of a small niche of extremist capitalism makes pretty much that exact point. Sometimes it's the misery of inequality, other times the failure to prevent market crashes, or the misappropriation of wealth by the financial sector or a looming environmental apocalypse.

Almost every textbook will tell you that economics is the study of how scarce resources can be managed to meet unlimited wants, but there are some lingering and awkward facts that suggest resources aren't being allocated so well. Like, surely there's something wrong in the system if, for every migrant who drowns each year, there are roughly two private jets in the world? I mean, if we've figured out how to allocate resources effectively, why didn't those migrants get a lift? Some of them even drown crossing from France to the UK, despite there being a fairly decent ferry service between the two countries, not to mention a tunnel. No one ever drowns in the tunnel (though the delays can be horrendous).

Or how is it that a third of global food production is wasted, as 700 million people go hungry? Or how can there both be 600,000 homeless people in the USA *and* 16 million vacant homes, unless somewhere along the line some economists have failed to do their job properly?

One of the graduates was called Michael. He was long-limbed and lank-haired and tessellated himself into my personal space. "That doesn't mean that *economics* has failed," he bristled. "Those are more *political* issues."

I found his response perplexing, but that perhaps showed my naivety. It would transpire that I'd stumbled across another theme that pops up throughout economics – that when it goes well, it's thanks to economists, but when it doesn't, it's a political issue.

I didn't know, back then, just how deliberate this separation between economics and politics was.

—

Ioannou asked me which aspects of tax I was most interested in. I knew my answer straight away.

In the closing pages of *Taxtopia*, I'd made the point that I'd never understood why in Europe we have a tax called *Value Added Tax*, in that surely the last thing we should tax is *adding value*? Instead, shouldn't we have a *No* Value Added Tax? i.e. one that encourages businesses to make things we like, and discourages them from making things we hate. Though, having read that the way to sound like an economist is to use unnecessarily complex words, I decided to express this idea slightly differently when relaying it to Ioannou.

"I'd like to do some research on negative externalities and Pigouvian taxes," I said, trying to sound, you know, *clever*.

A negative externality is simply something bad that isn't paid for (like crime, or pollution, or when someone else listens to music without their headphones), and Pigouvian taxes are things like sugar taxes or plastic bag taxes, designed to deal with these "negative externalities". You might think that the concept of taxing *bad* things would be as old as civilisation itself, but remember that people in power *love* doing bad things, so don't want to tax them, so the concept is actually named after Cambridge economist Arthur Pigou, who wrote about them in the early 20th century.

Ioannou's wrinkle of a smile folded itself across his face.

"We're doing a lot of work on the threat to the world economy posed by Chinese rearmament," he said. "Could you weave something into that?"

I looked at him a little blankly. "What do you have in mind?"

"There's a lot of anti-Chinese sentiment around at the moment, so we're developing a narrative that trading with China was a mistake. Could you find a tax angle?"

I told him I'd give it a go.

—

Something I struggled with when I first started analysing the effects of tariffs was why economists could be so fond of sales taxes (like VAT in Europe, GST in Australia, Canada and New Zealand, and, um, sales taxes in America) but be so vehemently opposed to tariffs. I mean, a sales tax makes a product more expensive by adding a tax onto it, and a tariff, err, makes a product more expensive by adding a tax onto it. Aren't they the same?

The answer, it turns out, is a bit nuanced. Sales taxes are (in theory at least) applied equally to all products, so don't distort the market. For instance, say there was a 10 per cent sales tax on spoons, that tax would then be chargeable whether you bought a locally made spoon or a spoon imported from

Azerbaijan. So, investors would put money into whichever location is simply *better* at making spoons.

But if only the Azeri spoon was taxed – because of a tariff – resources might be wasted investing in inefficient local spooning. Whereas if you tax every spoon maker the same way, you can sit back and let the best spoon win. In other words, it's all about the most efficient allocation of resources. You might recognise shades of David Ricardo's Law of Comparative Advantage here – if products are made with maximum efficiency, we all end up with more spoons.

What's curious about this, and why I assume I struggled with the concept at first, was that this is never how tariffs are criticised. No one ever brings up *efficiency*; criticism always takes on the tone of a paranoid mania: "Here's what could get more expensive" was NBC's response to Trump's tariff hike. *The Independent* warned that "Toyotas are about to cost a whole lot more". Fox News dangled a list: "10 things that could cost more under new tariffs." Where was the headline that shouted out, "Tariffs likely to adversely distort resource allocation over the next decade"? Weird that they didn't go with that one.

Economists are often no better. There's always a focus on *money*. The most cited paper on the effect of tariffs was a report published in 2019 by an American think-tank called the National Bureau of Economic Research, which demonstrated that tariffs that had been imposed on Chinese washing machines in 2018 had led to price increases of 12 per cent, costing American consumers an extra $1.5 billion. It's a wonderful piece of statistical analysis, but tells us little about whether resources are being used more or less efficiently. When David Ricardo wrote about trade between England and Portugal, he proved his argument by looking at the labour hours needed to make cloth or wine, not how many shillings an English seamstress was being paid or what a bottle of Touriga Nacional would set you back.

Politicians are at it too. When Trump claimed that his tariffs would encourage businesses to make things in America, rather than rely on imports, Democratic congresswoman Madeleine Dean brandished a banana at Trump's Commerce Secretary Howard Lutnick and reminded him that "we cannot build bananas in America". Trump's tariffs would make bananas more expensive, she pointed out, and "Americans love bananas."

But an everyday sales tax on Toyotas, washing machines or bananas would also make those things more expensive. Indeed, there are very few countries that *don't* tax cars and washing machines (though only a few tax bananas). We shouldn't lose sight of the fact that we're meant to oppose tariffs not because they raise costs, but because they lead to a reallocation of resources away from the most efficient producer, and towards the less efficient.

Indeed, from a purely Ricardian perspective, there's nothing wrong with America putting a tariff on bananas – since as bananas aren't "built" in America there's no efficiency loss in taxing "foreign" bananas.*

As for a tariff on penguin exports, there are two possible interpretations.

One is that the Heard and MacDonald Islands were included in the tariff list to prevent what's known as *transshipping* – where goods pass through a third territory en route to their final destination. Indeed, they don't even need to *physically* pass through a third territory, which is lucky in the case of the Heard and MacDonald Islands as there are no ports there to handle the goods. You could just fudge the paperwork to make it *appear* that your goods originated from, say, an island with a human population of zero, rather than, say, Australia. So, if that penguin island's exports weren't taxed, then tariffs could be evaded entirely.

The other interpretation is that the islands were included in the list of tariffs by mistake, due to coding errors in shipping data.

I'll let you decide which interpretation you prefer.†

—

I don't know whether Ioannou picked up on the fact that I'd alienated myself from the young graduates by insulting their chosen profession, but he told me

---

* Or, more technically, a tariff on bananas is no worse than a sales tax on bananas, in that they'll both have the exact same effect – the government will collect taxes and fewer bananas will be sold.

† I suppose there's a third option – that Trump just really hates penguins.

that he and one of the other "older" employees at the think-tank were going to have a "wild night out" on Thursday evening, and would I like to join them? He didn't mention, until after I'd said that I'd love to join them, that the wild night out was attending an evening debate at one of London's universities on the subject of "Twenty Years of China's membership of the WTO".

I felt an instant sense of dread, much as I had as a junior accountant when I was told I had to take notes at a day-long discussion about possible construction industry exclusions from a proposed revision to the aggregates levy. That had been one of the most boring days of my life, but at least it hadn't stolen an evening from me.

What I couldn't have predicted, when I accepted Ioannou's invitation, was that by the end of Thursday evening I would be hiding in a bush, dripping wet, trying not to throw up on one of Britain's most distinguished academics.

—

President Bill Clinton welcomed China into the "WTO" – the World Trade Organization, in 2001.

The World Trade Organization is the international body that sets and enforces the rules of global trade. Before their membership of the WTO, trade with China was possible but extremely difficult. Tariffs were high, making Western imports too expensive for Chinese consumers to buy (not that the Chinese consumers had much money); a byzantine web of laws, licences and quotas restricted foreign firms from operating, and even those that were licensed had to go through state intermediaries. Rules were opaque and applied inconsistently, many sectors (from banking to high street retail) were entirely off-limits and the piracy and theft of Western intellectual property and technology was rampant.

Clinton believed that welcoming China as a trading partner would be mutually beneficial. Western businesses could export their goods to China, but more than that, the West could export their *ideas* to China, too. Trade would create not just peace and prosperity, it would also spread democracy.

To be allowed to join, China had to agree to lower tariffs on imports, promise that state-owned enterprises would act on commercial considerations rather than government orders, and set about opening up those previously restricted industries to foreign competition. Trade disputes would be settled by the World Trade Organization's headquarters in Switzerland. No promises were made on political reform.

The Chinese government had already spent years investing in infrastructure (such as ports able to process vast quantities of goods), and had hundreds of millions of ultra-cheap and well-educated workers (a Chinese factory worker in 2002 would earn the equivalent of $5–7 per day). It didn't take long for Western multinationals to set up factories in China, or for local industries to expand. In just over ten years, China went from exporting around 4 per cent of the world's goods, to overtaking the USA as the world's largest trading nation.*

However, over the next couple of decades, trade between China and the rest of the world didn't develop as expected. Western firms continued to complain about technology theft, few Western financial or telecoms firms were able to gain much access to Chinese markets, and the Chinese government, despite assurances, continued to subsidise strategically important industries, from steel and semiconductors to solar panels, electric vehicles and artificial intelligence.

More significantly, and controversially, the Chinese government imposed an official exchange rate of just over 8 yuan to the dollar, which was far less than the yuan was worth. This made Chinese exports (and wages) seem even cheaper than they should be, further fuelling China's manufacturing boom. As dollars were now flooding in, there should have been huge market pressure to strengthen the yuan, and in any other country that's what would have happened. But China isn't any other country.

The People's Bank of China simply bought these dollars and stashed them away – building up a reserve that peaked at almost $4 trillion in 2014.

---

* It wasn't just cheap workers that attracted Western companies. China also has strict laws against trade unions – there's only one labour union and it's run by the Communist Party. All other unions are illegal, because what self-respecting Communist regime would allow their workers to unite?

At the same time, China restricted the amount of money that Chinese citizens and businesses could move abroad and, to contain inflation, restricted local lending. The United States and other Western nations complained about this currency manipulation, as it ensured that China could forever undercut the rest of the world.

This was hardly the "free trade" that David Ricardo (or Bill Clinton) had imagined. Ricardo believed that if a country exported more than they imported their currency would strengthen, leading to lower exports and more imports. But by artificially suppressing the value of the yuan, that rebalance of trade never happened.*

But Ricardo was certainly right that lower production costs increased profits at Western firms while keeping prices of consumer goods low, and meanwhile hundreds of millions of Chinese people were lifted out of poverty.

—

The evening's debate about Chinese membership of the WTO had been delayed a couple of years due to coronavirus, and the debate's host, a thin man in his fifties who was clearly delighted to be holding a microphone, made a rather weak joke about how the panel had all changed their minds over those two years. There were four people due to speak, one of whom, Ioannou told me, had been his tutor at university. We were in a smallish lecture theatre and I sat near the front with Ioannou and a guy in a woolly jumper who was introduced to me as Phil, whom apparently I now worked with but don't think I ever saw again. I'd smuggled some wine in.

I thought I knew what everyone was going to say – that *sure, manufacturing jobs had been lost in the West, but more valuable, higher paid jobs had replaced*

---

* The Chinese currency can be referred to as both renminbi or the yuan, much as how Britain's currency can be pound sterling or just pounds. The yuan is no longer pegged at 8 yuan to the dollar, but has been kept deliberately undervalued by the Chinese leadership for most of the last 25 years, meaning that Chinese goods (and labour) have for years seemed cheaper than they really should be. The World Trade Organization, incidentally, has no powers to deal with currency manipulators, leaving it to individual countries to slug it out.

them. I assumed this debate would just be a dispute over the methodologies used to quantify the job numbers.

So I was a little surprised when the host started talking about black market tagliatelle. It took me a moment to work out what he was referring to, but the gist seemed to be the unintended consequences of restricting free trade. Apparently, in the 1960s, the Italian government passed a law requiring all pasta sold in Italy to be made exclusively from durum wheat, which effectively restricted the import of a lot of foreign pasta.

The justification at the time, apparently, was that it would protect Italy's durum wheat farmers, but instead it devastated artisanal pasta makers in Italy who used different wheat types, as well as enticing organised crime into smuggling specialist spaghetti. Our compere referred to it as the Pasta Wars, which Ioannou thought was the very height of comedy.

"Eventually the Italian government backed down," said the host, at last, "but will any of our panellists back down this evening?"

Ioannou used his elbow to give me a nudge. "This is so exciting!" he whispered.

I thought he could just as easily have mentioned what happened when Australia called for a public enquiry into the origins of Covid-19 (specifically whether it had leaked from a Chinese lab). The Chinese responded by hiking tariffs on Australian wine, but all that happened was that Australia diverted their wine to other Asian countries and to Europe while French exporters added a fat mark-up and sold more French wine to rich people in China, meaning Australia was pretty much unaffected, China lost out and the French won.

The first panellist to talk was a journalist from a well-known business paper who described her experiences of touring Chinese factories and her dismay when her husband had asked her if his beard trimmer had broken because it was "made in China".

"I don't think many people realise how high-tech Chinese manufacturing has become," she said. "Which is itself an irony, that just as people in the West lament the loss of their manufacturing jobs to China, so too are Chinese factories laying off their employees and replacing them with robots. Manufacturing is simply not a twenty-first-century career, *anywhere* in the world."

All right, that was quite interesting, I thought. But not *spending an evening in an uncomfortable chair with work colleagues* interesting.

There was then a speech about trade deficits (that issue of importing more than you export) from a very serious-looking head of *something* at an American bank. He had a wonderfully gravelly voice that reminded me of Henry Kissinger, and practically growled as he spoke. His main point was that he never understood why anyone ever became upset about America's trade deficit with China: "If Americans buy a Chinese product the Chinese get some dollars. The only place they can spend these dollars is in America. We get the product, and keep our dollars. It's the same here in Britain, any pounds you give to China will come back to you."

Ioannou nudged me again and rolled his eyes. I wasn't entirely sure why. But it was at this moment that Ioannou's old tutor, who was now a well-known professor at a famous university (Ioannou called him "Berry", apparently after a Shakespearean character called "Dogberry"), decided to interject. This was, after all, meant to be a debate.

"Every time you buy a Chinese beard trimmer you may as well sign over the deeds to your house," he began. He had wonderfully unkempt white hair and holes in the elbows of his blazer but had a very commanding presence and the Henry Kissinger clone was clearly furious at being interrupted (though the journalist who'd talked about her husband's beard trimmer burst out laughing).

"It's true." He was waving a finger at the banker like an orchestral baton. "It's no use saying, 'Oh, don't worry, the dollars will end up back in America', because the Chinese aren't buying American goods. They're buying America itself. Ports, telecoms, farmland, apartment blocks – even the Waldorf Astoria is now owned by the Chinese."*

---

* I checked this afterwards. He could have also added the car makers Volvo and MG Rover, French holiday firm Club Med, fashion brand Cerruti, hoover maker Hoover, GE Appliances, Motorola, Skyscanner, Tommee Tippee, London's Walkie-Talkie skyscraper and many others. Even Inter Milan football club was Chinese owned until 2024.

The banker first sighed and then sneered, "So what? Why does that matter?"

Berry gave him an angry stare. "Why does it matter that you are selling your country? Think of the influence that gives China. Think of the power. And it will only get worse. The dollar is kept artificially strong because it's the currency of international trade, so there's always demand for it."

I was intrigued by this point. I'd heard about Chinese currency manipulation before – the point I made a few paragraphs back about the yuan being kept artificially weak, but I hadn't heard the argument that the dollar was kept artificially strong.

The banker looked like he wanted to eat his microphone. (Maybe that's why his voice was so gravelly?) "So what are you saying?" he asked. "That this is all the fault of Bretton Woods?"

Berry gave him a devilishly sly smile, as I desperately tried to remember who or what Bretton Woods was.

"That's where the trouble began," Berry said, with the sudden air of an old man reminiscing about his youth, "but we can be more specific. Everything that has gone wrong with not just our dealings with China but the entirety of international trade is the fault of just one man..." He turned to the audience, keeping a moment of suspense. "Harry Dexter White."

The banker folded his arms defensively, as if conceding the floor to his opponent, though someone behind me muttered, "Preposterous."

—

This bit I had to fill in later: it all started, it seems, with the rise of the automobile and the response to this new technology by a man with the wonderful name of Reed Smoot.

By the late 19th century, up to a quarter of all US farmland was used to grow horse feed, but then when cars began to replace horses in the 20th century, many farmers began to struggle. So, in 1930, Republican Senator Reed Smoot, together with Congressman Willis Hawley, proposed an idea: they would save US farmers by protecting them from foreign competition. After all, if tariffs made *foreign* food more expensive, domestic consumers would buy American. It was like the Corn Laws all over again.

As the bill passed through the legislative process, other congressmen added amendments to ensure that their local businesses were protected by tariffs too, until eventually tariffs were raised on over 20,000 imported goods. Industrialist Henry Ford called it "economic stupidity", but failed to convince President Hoover to veto the bill.

America's allies were outraged that their exports were targeted with taxes. Canada imposed retaliatory tariffs on a third of US exports, and France, Italy, Spain and Mexico enacted similar measures. The British threw a tariff wall around their empire. European consumers boycotted American cars. The Smoot–Hawley tariffs hit Cuba especially hard, as they had been exporting 80 per cent of their sugar to the US, and the resulting recession in Cuba led to a surge of anti-American feeling that then led to an anti-American revolution in 1933. American–Cuban relations never recovered.

The effect of all these reciprocal tariffs was to dramatically and drastically reduce international trade, which was already suffering after the Wall Street Crash of 1929. Historians debate how much of the collapse in world trade that followed the Smoot–Hawley Tariff Act was due to or was merely exacerbated by these tariffs, but the combination of recession and tariffs resulted in US imports falling by 66 per cent, US exports falling by 61 per cent and unemployment rising from 8 per cent in 1930 to 25 per cent by 1933. Many of those unemployed were the farmers that the Act was meant to protect, who had both lost their export market due to foreign reciprocal tariffs and now had fewer American consumers who were able to afford their produce.

So, in 1944, representatives from all the allied nations met in the Mount Washington Hotel in Bretton Woods, New Hampshire, to discuss how trade – and tariffs – should work in the post-war era.

The United Kingdom was represented by John Maynard Keynes, an economist who had by then acquired a celebrity status – he had successfully predicted that the reparations imposed on Germany at the end of the First World War would end up destabilising Europe and was a prominent member of the fashionable, intellectual and sometimes promiscuous Bloomsbury Group of artists and writers.

Keynes had written a groundbreaking book during the recession of the

1930s in which he argued that governments need to step in when private enterprise fails. In essence, if there were insufficient job opportunities provided by companies, which resulted in insufficient *demand* for goods, then the government should create those jobs, to create that demand. This might seem obvious now, but the prevailing economic view at the time was that free markets naturally self-correct so unemployment is only ever temporary. Keynes disagreed. Unemployment led to low spending, he said, which meant failing businesses, which meant more unemployment. This vicious cycle could only be broken by a government cutting taxes and boosting its own spending.

As he put it, blind faith in free markets alone was absurd: "the extraordinary belief that the nastiest of men for the nastiest of motives will somehow work together for the benefit of all."

Keynes also introduced the concept of the *multiplier* effect – that economies grow by far more than any initial investment. For instance, say the government pays an engineer to build a bridge, that engineer could then afford to buy themselves lunch at a café every day, so the café owner would be able to buy some bacon from a farmer, who would now have cash to buy gasoline, and so on.

Keynes joked that he sometimes had difficulty following his own reasoning, and mainstream economists initially described his work as heretical, though within twenty years *Keynesianism* became very much economic orthodoxy.*

At Bretton Woods, Keynes suggested that the goal of the assembled representatives should be establishing a system that avoided any country running up persistent trade deficits or trade surpluses.

This was a practical acknowledgement of the weakness of trade theory,

---

* Keynes was not just an economist but also a wildly successful lover who ended up marrying a ballerina. He kept a meticulous list of all his sexual conquests, of which there were an enormous number. He was also friends with one of my great-uncles – my family still have some of their correspondence, and I read through it wondering if I'd find evidence that they were, you know, more than just *friends*. Something like "how I long to stimulate your demand curves with my massive intervention". But no, nothing. What a shame.

as *in theory* if countries trade freely with each other any persistent trade deficits should be wiped out by a weakening currency, but in practice *capital flows* (like China buying up Western real estate), or currency "management" (like pegging eight yuan to the dollar) and other political interferences can allow trade deficits and surpluses to persist.

Keynes proposed a novel solution: the introduction of a new, supranational currency called the *Bancor*, in which all international trade would be recorded in accounts held at a new International Clearing Union. Countries that ran up either constant trade surpluses or constant deficits would have to pay money to the International Clearing Union, to be distributed to countries that weren't so naughty.*

The idea was that no one country would have a long-term advantage over another, as countries would be under heightened pressure to strengthen or weaken their currencies to adapt to persistent trade imbalances.

The national representatives at Bretton Woods had already agreed on the formation of a new International Monetary Fund (IMF) and what later became known as the World Bank, so one more international organisation like the International Clearing Union didn't seem so far-fetched. For a while, it looked like John Maynard Keynes's idea – the Bancor – would be adopted.†

---

* Nowadays, countries like China and Australia consistently export more than import, so have trade *surpluses*, while places like the USA or UK import more than they export, so have consistent trade deficits. This was largely the other way round before the Second World War.

† The IMF and the World Bank are pretty similar, in that they both lend money to countries in need. The IMF acts a bit like a parent should – if you find yourself in trouble they'll lend you some money, but with strings attached: raise taxes, sell your motorbike and get a haircut.

Whereas the World Bank is more like your half-crazed rich friend who suggests you go in large on a wild new scheme. "What you need is your own airport! I'll lend you the money and you pay me back out of the profits." The World Bank also does great work reducing poverty and fighting diseases.

The IMF is currently the larger of the two, with about $900 billion available to lend vs the World Bank's measly $100 billion (though both these numbers fluctuate a lot).

But after Keynes had laid out his plans for the Bancor, the American representative took his turn to speak. He was a former lieutenant in the US infantry who had taught soldiers how to bayonet the enemy in the First World War before switching to teaching economics at Harvard University, followed by a post at the US Treasury. His name was Harry Dexter White, and he had a different idea for how to manage trading relationships.

What if, he said, instead of using some newfangled currency like the Bancor, international trade was denominated in good old American dollars? Other currencies could be convertible to dollars at a fixed exchange rate, and dollars themselves would be convertible to gold. Wouldn't this ensure an era of stable, predictable trade, just like in the old days, with the world's most powerful central bank in charge? It would also, in what I suppose was just a happy coincidence, mean a huge amount of lucrative work for the American bankers and brokers who managed all those dollars.

Harry Dexter White's idea would give America an enormous international advantage. The United States would have the power to sanction other countries by refusing to process their dollars – effectively cutting them off from a lot of international trade, and America would also have a constant source of cheap credit (as everyone would need dollars).*

Had the Bretton Woods conference taken place at any earlier time, the European nations would almost certainly have vetoed Harry Dexter White's idea, as it shifted enormous economic power to America, but in the closing chapters of the Second World War they were in no position to do so. The Bancor was abandoned.

The American dollar quickly became essential to world trade. Commodities like oil and gas, wheat, coffee, soybeans, aluminium, copper and gold would all be routinely denominated in dollars, as would international

---

* This is a slightly technical point – if trade is in US dollars, then countries (and companies) need to keep reserves of US dollars, and the safest way to do that is to buy US government bonds, meaning there's always demand for US debt, which allows the US government to pay low interest rates. Similarly, if your exports are priced in US dollars you will end up with dollars in your pocket, and the easiest way to save them is to buy US bonds.

shipping, insurance contracts, the loans made by the IMF and World Bank, global arms sales, and the vast majority of other trades.*

Even today, almost a century after Bretton Woods, around 90 per cent of all currency exchanges involve the dollar and the majority of all worldwide trade is denominated in dollars. If a Vietnamese restaurant wants to buy Peruvian alpaca meat, it's far more likely that the invoice will be in US dollars rather than dongs or sols. As of 2024, half of all goods imported into the EU are paid for with American dollars, as are over 85 per cent of Australian exports (despite Australia having a perfectly good dollar of their own).

This has resulted in an almost insatiable demand for US dollars, and consequently a consistently powerful – and arguably overpriced – American dollar.

"My favourite conspiracy theory," said Berry, with a smile that I'm pretty sure indicated that he didn't really believe it, "is that Harry Dexter White was a spy for the Soviet Union. There's some evidence for it . . . Allegations were made during the Cold War that he passed secrets to the communists. Just imagine it – if the man who instigated decades of American industrial decline due to an over-valued dollar was secretly a Russian spy!"

—

President Truman is said to have once requested an economist with only one hand, as every economist's arguments always ends with *on the other hand* . . . and on global trade I can certainly see his point. At this stage, I had no idea what I was meant to believe. Was the yuan deliberately undervalued to ensure that China remained the production centre of choice? Or was the dollar overvalued due to its central role in international trade, which has led to persistent American trade deficits and a decline in American industry (as American goods will seem more expensive to non-Americans)?

---

* It wasn't that this was a law – it just became standard practice. There are exceptions where other currencies are used for these trades, but they're rare. Visitors to Antarctica occasionally use Antarctic Dollars (though Antarctica's sole ATM doesn't stock them, apparently).

I felt my personal prejudices seeping in. I'm part American and I'd rather side with a democracy over a dictatorship . . . but should that be how cool-headed economic analysis works? I wondered if other economists were affected by their prejudices, too.

—

At one point, Berry and the banker just talked over each other, with the professor jabbing his finger in the banker's direction and insisting that everything the banker was saying was *moronic* and *superficial*. I started to enjoy myself.

The beard-trimming journalist delivered a few other punchy lines, though the fourth panellist barely got a word in, other than slightly unnecessarily (and I thought, suspiciously) mentioning his au pair. Ioannou looked like he couldn't have been happier, and when the debate ended, he clapped for far too long. My colleague in the woolly jumper made his excuses and slipped out, and I probably should have done the same.

Instead, I latched on to Ioannou as he went to congratulate his old tutor. Ioannou then introduced me, at which point Berry said something that would lead to me fundamentally rethinking what I understood about economics. It wasn't anything especially novel or complex. He simply gave us both a big grin, and said, "Shall we go for a drink?"

I probably should have said, "No."

4
WHY FREE TRADE MIGHT NOT BE FREE (AND WE TEST THE DEPTH OF A LAKE)

"The First Law of Economists: For every economist, there exists an equal and opposite economist. The Second Law of Economists: They're both wrong."
David Wildasin, economist

After I had accepted the offer from Ioannou to join the Institute for Fair Economics, I had invited one of Henrí and my friends round for dinner. As he was a senior professor of economics at one of the London universities, I thought he'd be the ideal person to grill about what I was getting in for.

"Well, my job is explaining the past," he'd told me, "and your job will be explaining the future."

I nodded, then I asked what I thought was a sensible follow-up: "So... how does this all connect to the real world?"

"The real world?" he said, in mock disgust, laughing as he replied. "I'm an academic economist. How dare you! I have no idea about the real world."

I mean, he was joking about academic economists, of course. Or at least, so I thought.

—

It quickly became clear that Professor Berry had no intention of engaging with the traditions of the real world. Like, you know, "going for a drink" meaning "having a beer", and not "having a four-course meal" or "getting so drunk you try to steal a boat".

As we left the lecture theatre where the debate had been held, he claimed that he "knew a place". Ioannou, Berry and I must have walked past a dozen pubs before Berry darted into a restaurant to see if they had a spare table. For someone so old, he sure moved fast. We were not in a particularly cheap part of London and the restaurant was the sort where every dish contained at least one ingredient I'd never heard of. Ioannou gripped my elbow and pulled me back.

"I told him this was my treat," he whispered, as Berry haggled with the maître d', who seemed unimpressed by Berry's tatty attire. "Do me a favour and don't let him get too carried away."

"They do a sashimi starter that's sublime," said Berry once we were seated. "Oh, and Sake. *Christ*, I should have mentioned Japan."

"We could just get a dessert?" suggested Ioannou.

Berry ignored him. Actually, come to think of it, so did I. "Why should you have mentioned Japan?" I asked. I'd tried to impress Berry on the walk to the restaurant by name-dropping David Ricardo, and I worried that I'd done so more in the manner of an enthusiastic undergraduate rather than a serious professional economist. Though, as the evening progressed, I realised that Berry just loved enthusiastic undergraduates, especially when their boss was paying for dinner.

"Because they're *the* case study in the problem with Ricardo's Law. When the Second World War ended in 1945, Japan was desperately poor, but there was one thing it did better than anyone else – produce silk. According to the "Law" of Comparative Advantage, they should have stuck to that – silk, silk, silk, all the way. The profits they made from silk could be used to buy whatever else they needed, like cars, from other countries, like America. Are we ordering wine?"

"OK, sure," said Ioannou. "I think they do it by the glass…"

Berry pulled a face, then looked at me like a co-conspirator. "But the

Japanese government thought otherwise. In the 1950s, they put enormous tariffs on imported goods like cars and electronics while propping up their own domestic car and electronics companies, mostly with soft loans and supportive legislation. To free-trade advocates, which is to say, most of my colleagues, this was madness. Japanese consumers would now have to either spend much more on foreign cars or buy expensive, unreliable Japanese ones. I love an English sparkling wine. How about a bottle of the Prestige Cuvée?"

Ioannou looked a little white, and muttered, "Er, *Cuvée* doesn't sound very English…"

"And of course, the economists were right – for all of the 1950s and most of the 1960s Japanese industry was inferior and consumers suffered. You're too young to remember this, but when I was a kid, if something broke unexpectedly there was an easy laugh for asking, *Was it made in Japan?*"

He took a moment to enjoy recalling such a joke, his cheeks getting redder, then continued, "But slowly and surely, Japanese car companies improved, their electronics industry became world-leading, and they also became experts in other fields like shipping and steelmaking, rather than just silk. It took a couple of decades, but who would mock Japanese manufacturing today?"

I thought about this, and desperately wanted to sound clever. I'd just read an article about the problems several South American countries had in the 1980s with protectionist measures – they had kept out foreign goods, including computers, but their domestic infant industries never matured (there is no South American computer manufacturer), so South American citizens got the worst of both worlds: higher prices and trashier products.

"But couldn't it be argued that these countries succeeded despite their protectionism, not because of it?" I tried.

"Pah! That would be some coincidence. The same *protectionist* measures were also used in Taiwan and South Korea and, you know what, if you go back far enough, in the USA and the UK too. You know what Hamilton said?"

"In the musical?" I asked.

"What? No. Alexander Hamilton. The first Treasury Secretary of America.

He argued that infant industries didn't have the same economies of scale of mature foreign businesses, so needed to be protected and nurtured until they were big enough to compete internationally, and do you know where he borrowed that idea from? British Prime Minister Robert Walpole. America maintained some of the highest import tariffs in the world until the end of the Second World War. And look how rich they were."

"But didn't they get richer after they scrapped the tariffs?"

"Oh sure – once they were richer than anyone else they were ready to trade. Look how beneficial 'free' trade is to rich countries. I mean, where does the best chocolate come from? Maybe Belgium, or Switzerland? Yet where does cocoa, the key ingredient of chocolate, come from? Also Belgium and Switzerland? No, it's some impoverished African country that captures very little of the value of the finished product because, remember, they should stick to doing what they do best, which is growing cheap unprocessed foodstuffs for export. Do you know who I mean by J K Galbraith?"

I figured a guess was better than nothing. "Um, he wrote the Father Brown mysteries?"

"What? No, the economist. Look him up – he's a great one to quote. Galbraith said that nations trapped into specialising in agricultural products would be 'condemned to perpetual poverty'. That's bad for them, but means we won't have to compete with their chocolate brands. Lucky us."

"So, what you're saying is, um, David Ricardo was wrong?"

He paused as a waiter took his wine order. I'm not quite sure how, but Berry and the waiter seemed already to be on first name terms, and Berry gave him a friendly pat on his hand, in the way you probably can if you look like someone's grandfather. "Not *wrong*, no, but the law of comparative advantage only makes sense *today*, in much the same way that it's true that the oak sapling in my garden is very small... today. But one day it will be a hundred feet tall and it will undermine my brickwork. Telling countries to focus only on what they're best at *today* is like looking at your toddler scribbling on a wall and saying, 'Well, let's not bother with school for the next twenty years, clearly his talents lie in art.' Ricardo himself said that Britain's specialism was in manufactured goods, which is now hopelessly outdated."

I could concede that Berry had a point, but I still felt wary about agreeing with him. I felt like he was arguing against *freedom*. I mean, it's called "free" trade. I said this to him.

"I'll tell you the big problem with economics, and Ioannou will agree with me here, though he'll pretend not to." Berry eyed a peach dessert that had just been set alight at a neighbouring table. "Too many economists pretend that they're not playing politics – that they're just number crunchers, *scientists*, even. But if you crunch numbers then your solution to everything will be measured in numbers. In *money*. You may have noticed economists pretending that the *costs* of labour are the same as the *efficiencies* of labour.

"But we don't need to play that game. The truth is far more straightforward: if there's some bully down your street who beats his wife, would you sell him a pair of knuckledusters and call it a free trade? Yet that's exactly what the free trade economists advocate! A genocidal dictator says, 'Can I swap you these diamonds for your guns, so that I can kill my own citizens?' *Whoop-de-do, cheap diamonds.*

"But come on! That's hardly a beneficial free trade for those citizens, even if David Ricardo says that it would be less efficient for the dictatorship to make their own guns, so their people would be poorer. They'll be poorer and *alive*, Ricardo!"

The waiter had returned with a bottle of something that I'm guessing was hurtfully expensive, but hesitated to pour it as Berry wagged his index finger at an imaginary Ricardo. I had a brief panic that our waiter may have told us that *his* name was Ricardo. Anyway, once our glasses were filled, Berry downed his like a student taking a shot of cheap vodka, then carried on, growing even more animated.

"But what do we really want out of free trade? Is it just cheaper goods, or is it peace, or spreading democracy, or resilience to sudden changes, or development, or helping the world's poor? Ideally it would be all these things, but we need to *consider* the trade-offs. And unfettered free trade does not *consider* these things. It is *inconsiderate* trade."

I liked this phrase, *inconsiderate trade*, and later when I went to the loo

I emailed myself with the phrase in the email's subject header. It seemed like the sort of thing that would look good in a report.

—

I don't want to give you the impression that all economists talk about is economics. We also talked about the ethics of octopus farming and why the fourth panellist at the debate had repeatedly mentioned his au pair, about which some of Berry's speculations were definitely not *economic* ones. I found myself defending his fellow panellist, especially as I also had an au pair.

"What's weird about having an au pair?"

Berry laughed so loudly that other diners turned to look at us. Apparently, it was my use of the word "having" that set him off. I began to wonder if he was perhaps a tad less sophisticated than his reputation suggested. It didn't help when I added, perfectly truthfully, that mine was "a nice nineteen-year-old French girl".

Berry folded his arms and shook uncontrollably. His cheeks flushed, which under his white hair made his face look like the flag of Poland. Ioannou looked understandably uncomfortable. Berry had ordered a third bottle of wine by this point, yet I think Ioannou had only had a glass at most. But then suddenly Berry stopped laughing, visibly struck by a thought. He leaned in towards me, and a little oddly, and tipsily, said, "Tell me something, have you ever heard the phrase '*usine à gaz*'?"

I didn't recognise the phrase, though in truth that's probably true of all French phrases except *je voudrais un croissant*. I assumed that this would be another example of his schoolboy humour. But Berry explained that it wasn't rude, or at least he didn't think so. He'd heard recently that the French describe any complicated, bureaucratic mess as a "gas works" – an "usine à gaz". Supposedly, said Berry, this dated from a time when the gas used in French homes for heating or lighting was coke-gas, a by-product of making steel. Many French towns would have their own coke-gas plant, which were a jumble of pipes surrounded by mounds of coal, belching out pollution. A messy, complicated *gas works*.

"Err...?" I said, not entirely sure what the point of this was.

"Here's the point. The phrase has outlasted the gas works. The French don't heat their homes with locally made coke-gas. Like the rest of Europe, they use *natural* gas. They don't produce much natural gas themselves, so they have to trade for it. And where do you think most of it comes from?"

I'm not going to pretend that I can remember this section of the evening word for word, and some of it I've had to fill in from other sources, but Berry then told me a story I'd never heard before. He described it as an example of what he meant by *inconsiderate trade*.

It was a deal known as *pipes for gas*, and began, according to Berry, with a secret meeting between the West Germans and the Soviets in an old castle in Austria in 1967. The Russians had discovered enormous gas fields in Siberia but didn't have the technology to extract it – but the Germans did. So, in the middle of the Cold War, an unlikely deal was made. The Germans would build the pipelines, the Russians would sell the gas to the Germans, from where it could be re-exported to the rest of Europe.

Practically, of course, the West Germans and the Soviets were enemies, but German Foreign Minister Willy Brandt (who later became chancellor) argued that trade would bring peace. Germany would not become dependent on Russia, you see, rather both countries would depend on each other.

A succession of American Presidents warned of the political risks. Nixon, Carter and Reagan all took their turn to criticise the deals, even embargoing the export of certain pipeline technologies to Germany.

"You see," said Berry, "this is where free trade really breaks down. The economic arguments assume that we also have free markets – that people can choose where they work or what they spend their money on, and so capital, *wealth*, follows those desires. But really the trade was only *free* on one side. Had the Soviet Union been a capitalist, free-market economy, the payments for gas would have been used to purchase goods that the Russian people needed or wanted from international markets. But the Soviet Politburo had other ideas. The income from the sale of gas was instead used to prop up the Red Army, fund terrorists and extremist organisations in the West, and promote propaganda that would subvert democracy. But hey, the Germans had cheap gas, and did I mention that trade creates peace?

"At the time of Russia's invasion of Ukraine in 2014, when Crimea was seized and illegally annexed, about a third of Germany's gas came from Russia.

"And what was the German response to their old enemy invading a European country?" asked Berry, waving a glass of brandy around. "It was not only muted, they actually *increased* their gas imports from Russia. So much so that Germany was buying fully *half* their gas from Russia when Putin launched his all-out war against Ukraine."

"So trade didn't create peace?"

He shook his head. "The gas was cheap, but that doesn't mean it wasn't expensive. If you want to see just how expensive 'free' trade can be, look up how much the war in Ukraine has cost."

We weren't to know when we had that meal that the war in Ukraine would drag on for years. Since Putin's February 2022 invasion, the West has responded with (as of 2025) some $500 billion of financial and military aid. Non-American members of NATO have committed to increasing their spending on defence, and every extra 1 per cent of GDP spent on rearming is about $200 billion per year not spent on other things. At least another $500 billion will be needed for reconstruction in Ukraine. Meanwhile, Russia has spent up to a billion dollars *per day* fighting the war. And this is not even to mention the hundreds of thousands of people who have died a violent death.

Put these figures together and the war in Ukraine has cost around $1.5 *trillion* so far, without even counting the increased cost on defence spending throughout the Western world in response to the conflict – which *The Economist* magazine estimates at $800 billion *per year*.*

"Of course," added Berry, as Ioannou stared in horror at our bill, "it's too simplistic to say that the war in Ukraine wouldn't have happened if the

---

* For comparison, $800 billion is similar to the entire annual turnover of Apple, Google and Ford combined, or the annual output of a country like Switzerland or Poland.

West Germans had sourced their natural gas from elsewhere, but it's not unreasonable to ask whether trade really does create peace."

I nodded. It did sound a bit simplistic, but also plausible.

—

One of my favourite "simplistic but plausible" theories is that the Arab Spring of 2010 was triggered by, of all things, a drought in Russia.

That year, Russia's wheat harvest failed catastrophically due to severe heatwaves and wildfires. The Russian government responded by banning wheat exports to protect domestic supply. Unfortunately for everyone else, Russia was one of the world's biggest wheat exporters – especially to countries like Egypt, Tunisia, Libya and Syria.

As global wheat prices surged, the cost of bread and other staples shot up in exactly the places where large parts of the population were already struggling. Protests over food prices quickly morphed into broader anti-government demonstrations, which in some cases spiralled into outright uprisings.

Obviously, there were an enormous number of other issues that created the tinder-box, not least many decades of economic frustration and political repression, but, just to mix metaphors, that drought may have been the spark that lit the fuse of revolution.

—

We were the last ones to leave the restaurant. Ioannou said he was going to get the last tube home. Berry was staying the night at a friend's house, which was a walk away. I offered to accompany him.

"Great," he said. "Let's go through the park. I'll just get something for the journey." He disappeared into a brightly lit store, only to re-emerge clutching a bottle of whisky triumphantly, like a trophy. My recollection starts to seriously break down at this point, though I remember there was a moment when Berry claimed that the cotton in my shirt had been picked by slaves. And the garlic in our dinner. In fact, as we staggered towards the park, he mostly just pointed at things and said *slaves* a lot.

"And solar panels! Most solar panels are made by slaves. It's hardly a free trade if the products are made with forced labour."

"You mean China?" I asked, finally clocking on.

"Of course! China has interned something like a million Uighurs in camps with shoot-to-kill policies for anyone who tries to escape, with millions more forced to work in cotton fields or food processing plants or in mines. And what do we do? Exactly the same thing that our forebears did when slaves were being shipped across the Atlantic. We ignore it. Then we buy the cotton, and marvel at how cheaply China produces it."

I emailed myself a slightly incoherent message along the lines of *China -> slaves?* as Berry went to relieve himself behind a tree.

According to the international human rights group Walk Free, who compile the world's most comprehensive data set of modern slavery, there are around 5 million slaves in China. Almost $500 billion worth of goods imported by the G20 group of rich countries are at risk of being made by slaves.

In 2021, the USA imposed import bans relating to solar panels on five Chinese entities, including a paramilitary outfit, due to allegations that they used forced labour in their production process.

Berry stopped suddenly when we were about halfway through the park. "Look, that gate's unlocked. Let's see where it goes."

I don't know why I followed him. Or rather, of course I know why I followed him. I was drunk. And besides, *Rebel* is my middle name. Berry had staggered ahead of me and turned round ecstatically.

"Pedalos!" he shrieked. "I've not been on a pedalo in years..."

Look. I was drunk. Get off my back.

Pedalos are harder work than they look, especially in the dark, especially with a sozzled septuagenarian, but most especially when they're locked up with a giant chain. We didn't actually go anywhere, though I don't think we realised that for about a minute. Then we gave up and lay back to stare at the sky. It was a peaceful, contemplative moment, if you ignore the attempted Grand Theft Boato.

"I did the debate because I worry that our trade with China is just history repeating itself," said Berry, sounding a little morose. "The Germans claimed that buying Russian gas would bring peace. So did Clinton when China was admitted to the World Trade Organization. 'Reform in China and peace on Earth.' They all imagined that with wealth came democracy. Clinton laughed at the notion that the Chinese government could somehow police the internet or keep Western ideas out.

"They were wrong, there was no democratic reform in China. The Chinese government oversees a surveillance state in which free speech is banned, the internet is censored, elections are outlawed…"

"They ban TikTok," I added.

"… and human rights activists are imprisoned or executed. Both the UK and US have accused them of genocide. But who cares if they can churn out cheap washing machines?"

I may have closed my eyes at this point, I don't know if the pedalo was gently rocking or my head was spinning.

"Everyone keeps focusing on jobs being lost in the West to cheap competition. But that's a bullshit distraction. China now has more warships than the United States, it's tripling its nuclear weapons capacity. China's dictator, Xi Jinping, has warned that 'no one can stop' China taking over Taiwan – which remember is a peaceful, democratic and more prosperous place."

"That's scary," I said.

"Isn't it? If anything, Taiwan should be taking over China. There's your inconsiderate trade. In the short term we've all got cheaper goods, and Ricardo's right that that means we're richer, but I wouldn't even want to guess the economic damage that future Chinese wars will cause. Did you know that China is stockpiling raw materials, like oil and gas, and nickel and copper, giving them months of supplies if a war broke out?"

I shook my head.

"But they're not the only ones who are stockpiling in case of war. The EU stockpiles wine."

I laughed, then Berry suddenly grabbed my arm and whispered, "*Christ*, is that for us?"

I opened my eyes. In the distance, in the park, there was a revolving flash of blue lights.

"Quick, help me up," he said.

One of the biggest problems in economics is when a theory rests on a mistaken assumption. Malthus thought populations would grow for ever. Ricardo thought wages tended to subsistence levels.

I lost my balance trying to follow Berry off the boat, and rather than fall sideways into the boat I made a split-second decision to put one foot into the water, assuming that the lake would be less than half a metre deep.

It wasn't.

—

My lecture on taxation at the business school the next morning was not the best performance I've ever put in. But I did look up some of the claims Berry had made.

Here are four issues that I was startled by:

1. The research organisation Bloomberg Economics estimates that a war between China and Taiwan would cost $10 trillion, dwarfing the cost of the Ukraine War – and that's if it doesn't escalate to all-out war between China and the USA, which it could, as the Taiwan Relations Act, signed by President Carter, commits the US to "resist any resort to force [against] Taiwan".
2. Before China joined the World Trade Organization, just 3 per cent of Chinese people had any disposable income left after spending on food, shelter and clothing. Now more than 700 million Chinese people do (though that means that about half China's population are still desperately poor. Indeed, on some estimates the *average* Chinese person is still poorer than the average Cuban).
3. China spends around $10 billion per year on an anti-Western global propaganda campaign, for instance, running Swahili-language news channels in East Africa that push the narrative that the West is in moral decay, that strong leadership is more

important than democracy, and that Putin had no choice but to invade Ukraine.
4. China has over two hundred times the shipbuilding capacity of the US. That may be problematic if war does break out between China and the USA.

—

I wasn't quite sure what to make of all of this, or how to squeeze the threat of war with China into a policy paper about tariffs. Berry's comments seemed to be *political* ones: that if the motivation for trading with China had been to spread democracy, shouldn't we have attached more humanitarian strings to our trade deals? And shouldn't we now be focusing more on promoting trade with liberal democracies and be more cautious about empowering oppressive regimes?

But was this economics? Did it have any place in an analysis of the impact of tariffs? To be frank, I didn't know. I mean, the young graduates I'd met earlier that week had sneered at letting politics interfere with economics, but isn't that exactly what Berry was proposing?

And another question bugged me. Was there CCTV at the pedalo pier?

5
X-RATED ECONOMICS (IN WHICH WE STRUGGLE WITH PAGE ONE OF THE TEXTBOOK)

> *"Study economics, but study it with scepticism."*
> Joseph Stiglitz, economist

My relationship with economics started with an **X**.

It may have been the hormones, but I found this **X** pretty exciting. When I was at school, I had an economics teacher I had a slight crush on called Mrs Fench, and in her first lesson with us she took out a marker pen, turned to the whiteboard, and drew two gently curved lines, one starting at the bottom left of the board, and sloping up, the other from the top left, sloping down. And where these lines met, where they crossed, Mrs Fench drew a circle and turned back to face us – actually not *us,* I swear she was looking just at me.

"And this," she said, tapping the circle in that **X** with her knowing fingers, "is where the magic happens."

That, I now realise, was a lie.

I fell in love with the ideas Mrs Fench explained to me, with mature, suggestive themes like the *Invisible Hand* and *Supply Side Constraints*. It was exotic and adult and seemed to explain the world in a way that my

English Literature teacher had never managed. What was Shakespeare's *The Merchant of Venice* to *The Law of Supply and Demand*? Could Wordsworth's daffodils explain the problem with rent controls? Sylvia Plath was just depressing, and not once did she suggest a theory on government stimulus.

I was a convert to the ideas. A believer. I became a card-carrying teenage capitalist. Here was a subject that not only could I fall in love with, but unlike, say, *geography*, could also make me rich.

The **X** was this one:

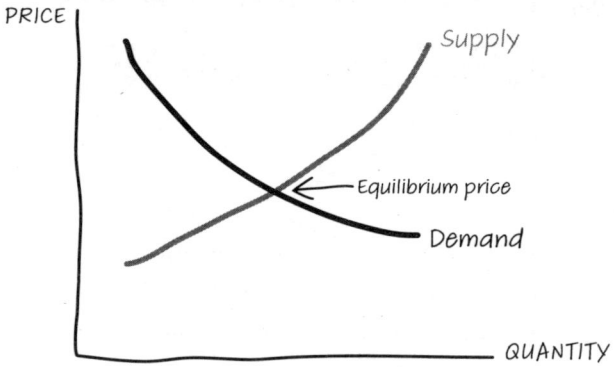

It's more or less the most fundamental idea of modern economic theory. It is taught to schoolchildren who are just dipping their toes into economics for the first time and retaught to postgraduates with dozens of adjustments and special situations thrown in. Whenever someone complains about the high cost of something, there's usually an easy rebuttal: "Don't you get it? It's simple *supply* and *demand*."

The graph shows how if the price of something rises, fewer people will want that thing (that's the line labelled "demand"), but more people will want to sell it (that's the "supply" line). The two lines slope in opposite directions so there's a magical moment – the one Mrs Fench seemed so excited about – where the two lines cross, and this is where we find an equilibrium price.

The supposed magic of the equilibrium is that there is neither a shortage nor a surplus of goods made, and there is both a large number of buyers who feel like they've got a bargain (as they would have paid more than the *equilibrium* price, but didn't have to) and a similar number of sellers who would've sold the product for less (but didn't have to) so feel like they've won, too.

Both these lines can move to the left or right. For instance, when politicians cut taxes or slash regulations, what they're trying to do is shift their entire nation's supply line to the right, to keep prices low while boosting production, like this:

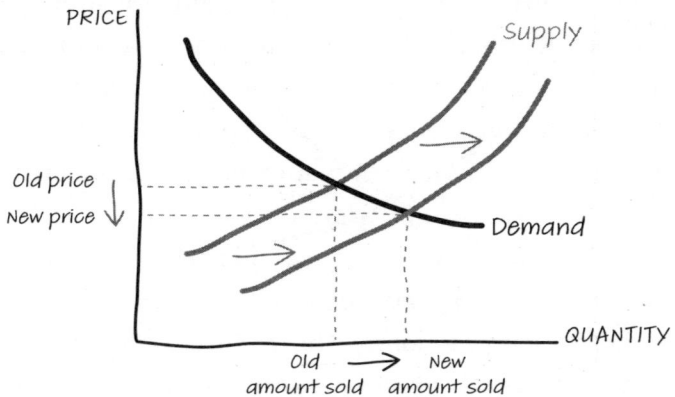

The shape of the lines can also change – becoming steeper or flatter in a phenomenon called *elasticity*. Demand for cigarettes, for instance, is *inelastic*, meaning smokers still buy them even if the cigarettes become a lot more expensive. (A kid in my class asked Mrs Fench for an example of something that was *elastic*, and she deadpanned "bungee jumping". I made a note and later wrote that down in my exams.)

Pretty much every economics textbook published since 1890 has included this diagram, and this explanation. It seems so obvious, and so plausible – do you remember the price of hand sanitiser during the Covid pandemic? Demand shot up, supply didn't rise as much, so the price skyrocketed. Sanitiser got so expensive that I had a bottle of it nicked from my car (they left my Metallica CDs behind).

To true believers in free market economics, this **X** is central to all of our lives. For me, this **X** was the next stepping stone in the collapse of my faith in the system.

—

In 2013, students studying economics at Manchester University in the UK staged protests about the content of their courses and formed a "Post-Crash Economics Society" to help expose students to alternative economic ideas. Many academic economists supported them – in a letter to *The Guardian*, professors from half a dozen British universities lamented that "The shortcomings in the way economics is taught are directly related to an intellectual monoculture", which, they argued, was a result of a funding model "heavily biased in favour of orthodoxy and against intellectual diversity". The professors ended with a call for economics to have a "renewal of its core historical concerns with the nature of growth, underemployment and financial instability and the distribution of income and wealth".

Quite a lot of universities shrugged off these concerns as typical leftie-student whining – *they'll change their tune when they start paying taxes* – but some took it very seriously. The reason I'd been brought in to teach postgraduates about tax was precisely because I wasn't an academic. I had been interviewed by a woman called Professor Wilding, who told me a joke about academic economists – that they would look at a real-world solution to a problem and say, "Ah, yes, but does it work in *theory*?"

I had assumed at the time that Professor Wilding was being self-deprecating, but it transpired that she was not an academic, despite having the title professor. I had not known that this was possible. She was an administrator, a *manager*, who happened to deliver the occasional lecture. Another professor eventually explained to me that universities have it in their power to confer *professor* status on any one they want, and senior managers routinely nominate themselves for professorships.

"Bring in lots of real-world examples," Professor Wilding told me, which seemed like carte blanche to explain how tax avoidance schemes work to impressionable young minds.

I'm proud to say that my tax lectures were popular. I told my students that

I got all my best anecdotes from a great new book called *Taxtopia* and that they should definitely go out and buy it. I began to feel ready to teach for more than one hour per week, so I casually mentioned to Professor Wilding that if they ever needed help on any other courses, I'd be happy to step up to it – though except on Mondays and Tuesdays, when I would be working at the Institute for Fair Economics. Her eyes lit up and she took me to one side.

"Our students are desperate to hear from *real world* economists. Why don't you teach a course on economics?"

"I've only been there a few weeks," I told her.

"But they won't know that," she said.

Unfortunately, it wasn't as straightforward as just being given a course to teach, I had to actually apply for a lecturing job at the economics department, and that meant that I would have to demonstrate my mastery of the subject to a roomful of experts. How hard could that be?

—

In 2023, I was invited back to my old school for a reunion event. Wine was served in the main hall and for the first hour I chatted to people I hadn't seen for a couple of decades. They were mostly lawyers, which was a bit uninspiring, though one of my old geography classmates now ran an international mining company. My old English teacher didn't recognise me, so I told him he'd taken us to an appalling production of *The Merchant of Venice*. That seemed to trigger something, he nudged me with his elbow like I was still thirteen and quoted, "Ah, yes, *'my ventures are not in one bottom trusted'* – that line was always a hit."

"Who said that?" I asked, vaguely remembering.

"Antonio . . ." and then when I looked blank, "*the* Merchant of Venice."

"Ah, right," I said, slightly unsure where this was going. He asked me politely what I was doing with my life, and I explained that I was working at the Institute for Fair Economics.

He gave me the same frown as he had two decades ago. "That 'bottom' line is *pure* economics. It's not a theory of *bottoms*, though with Shakespeare you can never quite be sure. It's portfolio theory, isn't it? A 'bottom' is a boat, Antonio is spreading out his risk." He shook his head, disappointed in me.

I felt briefly embarrassed, and unsure what to say next. But then over my English teacher's shoulder I saw something wonderful. An old crush.

"Hello, do you remember me?" I asked Mrs Fench. Two thousand pupils must have passed through her classroom since last I'd seen her.

"Of course," she replied, "but do you remember me?" And I swear to God she gave a slight wink.

"You made me fall in love," I told her. There was an awkward moment. "Um, with *economics*."

"Economics?" She looked surprised. "Oh, yes, I'd forgotten I taught economics, how funny. Your class must have been the only time I taught that."

I was gobsmacked. "Really? But you were so passionate about it . . ."

She laughed. "I was a PE teacher. The school asked me to cover other subjects sometimes if they were short-staffed." She leaned forwards and jokingly half-whispered, as if a secret was being shared, "The truth is, you only ever have to be one page ahead of the class. I probably read the day's course notes on the bus ride in."

She laughed some more, enjoying the reminiscence more than I was – for me, this was like a priest saying that far from reading from the holy book every Sunday, he'd just been making it up. Her classes had been so convincing. I told her so.

"I never studied economics myself," she confessed, with a smile. "In fact, when I applied to the school I had to give a demonstration of my teaching skills – I didn't know any of the academic subjects, so I taught the headmaster to juggle. He thought it was hilarious. I remember he said –" and she put on the old headmaster's upmarket Yorkshire accent – "'Anyone can learn anything, but not everyone can teach.' I think it was the nicest thing he ever said to me."

This stayed with me. The person who had convinced me of the beauty of economics had just been winging it. What if others had, too?

—

I told myself that it didn't matter if I got rejected for the economics lecturing post, as I was enjoying my work at the Institute for Fair Economics (though I didn't like the actual building. Their offices were an odd assortment of rooms in a pile of concrete near the Houses of Parliament that had clearly been designed by an architect who hated humanity – it was modern in a way that was not so much *Brutalist* as *Thuggish*).

Ioannou explained that our office had been donated to us by a wealthy benefactor who had at one point wanted to fund a "radical centrist" political party, but had long since lost enthusiasm for the project. Most of the other rooms in the building were rented out to lobbyists.

At the back of my mind, though, I worried that while I was happy writing reports about the economic impact of taxes and tariffs and trade, I still wasn't a "real" economist, particularly as most of the young graduate economists I was surrounded by spent their days utilising a skill I didn't have: writing computer code that allowed them to trawl through data sets for correlations.

This has, apparently, become the grunt work of modern economics. To the graduates, this data crawling was "real" economics. It was *science*. They viewed my lack of technical savvy with disdain, and laughed that I called it *computer* code, as if I needed to distinguish it from Morse code. They all also wore giant headphones as they did so. I remarked on this to Ioannou.

"I don't think it's a neurodiversity thing," he said. "I think they're just a bit hostile."

—

In most countries, the politician in charge of taxation policy and government spending would just be called a finance minister or treasury secretary, but Britain has stuck with the title "Chancellor of the Exchequer" since at least the 1200s. Chancellor is just an anglicised version of *cancelier,* an old French term for an administrator who sat behind iron crossbars ("cancelli") – a bit like shopkeepers in rough neighbourhoods these days sitting behind armoured glass. The exchequer bit comes from a chequered tablecloth (*échiquier* in French) that was used to visualise payments.*

---

* There's even still a tradition that Chancellors of the Exchequer are allowed to drink anything they want while announcing their budgets – and some of them have really hit the booze; the worst offender was 19th-century chancellor (and sometime prime minister) William Gladstone, who opted for a mixture of sherry and egg.

The current (as of 2025) UK Chancellor of the Exchequer is Rachel Reeves, who once told *Stylist* magazine that she "spent a decade working as an economist at the Bank of England". She repeated the claim at a Labour business conference in February 2024, though this time it was for "the best part of a decade", and for good measure her LinkedIn profile described her former job title at Halifax Bank of Scotland (where she moved after the Bank of England) as *Economist*.

The political website Guido Fawkes alleged that this simply wasn't true. Reeves had worked "in a mundane support role" in a team of three that was "far from the Economics Department". Reeves quickly amended her LinkedIn profile, removing the reference to being an economist. Her spokesperson said she simply meant that she was "using her economist background".

I suspect most British people who heard this revelation were a little alarmed. I found it extremely reassuring. If the British Chancellor of the Exchequer could pass herself off as an economist on the basis that she'd studied economics many years before, then given I'd applied for an actual economics job in an actual university, surely I could, too?

—

The assessment for the teaching job mostly took place in a lecture theatre at the university, where one by one all the candidates took turns giving a demonstration of their teaching skills. As I waited for my turn, I felt weirdly anxious about being in a lecture theatre and *not* being at the front. One of the other candidates ran through a presentation about a statistical concept called *Heteroskedasticity*. I wasn't really listening, I was rechecking the contents of my bag to make sure that nothing was leaking, and sweating a little. The woman in charge of the room thanked the presenter, and then asked another young man to take his place. This man was to speak for ten minutes, and had chosen to talk about a mathematical system to price derivative contracts correctly. *Derivatives?* I thought. *I may have made a mistake.*

The instructions I'd received from the economics department didn't stipulate what sort of presentation I was meant to deliver. It just said, "on a subject of your choice".

The applicant before me had prepared slides titled something like "The Avoidability of Liquidity Traps".

When I was called up for my go at the lectern, the professor in charge looked at the plastic bag I was holding and asked what was in it.

"Um, I've brought some fruit," I said. I think they all expected some sort of financial metaphor. But no. I'd taken Mrs Fench's words to heart. "I'm ... going to teach you all how to juggle."

At any one time there are around 250,000 people studying somewhere in the world for an MBA – a Master of Business Administration (and the main thing that most business schools offer). The cheapest MBA in the UK will cost about £20,000, whereas an MBA from Harvard Business School will cost over $170,000 (not including the mandatory health insurance). A more straightforward degree in economics is not much cheaper, and can even cost more, as the courses last longer.

To justify their tuition fees, top business schools and economics departments have to offer a higher calibre of lecturer.

The dozen or so other people in my lecture theatre, half of them assessing me, half of them rivals, watched as I tossed a satsuma in the air.

"The trick is to start with one. Anyone can catch one ball – or piece of fruit. Don't look at your hands. Once you're happy with that, try two."

I passed the extra satsumas round.

"And then juggling with three is really the same as juggling with two, you just throw the third satsuma before you catch the second one."

A few people laughed, nervously.

I told Henrí that I didn't think it had gone very well.

"Oh, what a shame," she said. "You could always go back to getting a high-paid job in the City."

But then my phone rang. It was Professor Wilding – the administrator who'd encouraged me to apply – with the good news.

Thanks to my real-world experience as a *sort of* economist, plus my decent teaching (or juggling) skills, I would now be teaching economics.

I had some brushing up to do.

—

The first course I had to teach was called "An Introduction to Business Economics" and there, on the first page of the textbook, was that **X**.

I didn't want my course to be dry. I didn't just want to draw the graph and say to my students, "This is the equilibrium point." I wanted to show them the magic, inspire them, like Mrs Fench had done to me, though with maybe less flirting.

Despite Professor Wilding suggesting this job to me because the students supposedly wanted a more varied exposure to economic ideas, the Head of Economics told me that students would complain if they didn't feel they're being taught the syllabus, because that's what they're tested on.

"But don't we write the tests?" I asked.

He frowned at me.

All the same, I went hunting for some real-life examples of supply and demand that I could juggle with. And that's where I found a problem.

At first, it just seemed strange. The theory of supply and demand is quite simple: as prices rise more people will want to sell something, but fewer people will want to buy that thing, so the market will find an equilibrium price.

I found loads of literature about markets that didn't reach an equilibrium. One of these exceptions was even on the course I had to teach. It was called the "hog cycle", which is the fact that livestock prices never reach an equilibrium because of the time it takes to raise new animals (if bacon prices rise, pig farmers breed more pigs, but that leads to an oversupply of pigs, so prices crash, so farmers stop breeding them, which leads to an undersupply and higher prices, and round and round it goes). There was also a hog cycle of sorts in oil markets, and mining and grain and bitcoin and share prices – anything with a feedback loop got knocked out of equilibrium immediately.

In fact, these markets never got into one – every sale creates a new piece of information that affects both supply and demand.

I had an idea. Why didn't I demonstrate supply and demand by talking about how much my trainee economists could expect to earn, once they qualified? Given that the supply and demand graph is very simple – it literally only records a price and a corresponding quantity – I figured I'd put some numeric figures on screen of, say, the number of economists graduating each year compared to the number of annual job listings for newly qualified economists, to show how changing quantities of supply and demand affected graduate incomes.

My plan hit a snag almost immediately. There appeared to be about fifty times as many people graduating with a degree in economics each year than there were job listings with "economist" in the title. That probably wasn't a great statistic to wave in front of trainee economists. I thought about expanding my economist job definition for anything that included *finance* or *consulting* or *analyst* in the description, but that felt a little too broad.

So I tried another angle of approach. Rather than talk about graduate wages, I would talk about minimum wages. I was quite pleased with this idea, as supply and demand graphs are often used to make a simple and powerful argument *against* minimum wages – and it was an argument I was meant to make in the course I was about to teach. Though really "argument" is the wrong word, my textbook just presented this as a fact:

If the government sets a "floor" price for labour (i.e. a minimum wage) *above* the equilibrium point there will be more people trying to get jobs, but fewer employers wanting to employ them, so the simple, inevitable, mathematical consequence of minimum wages is unemployment.

Presented graphically, this argument looks like this:

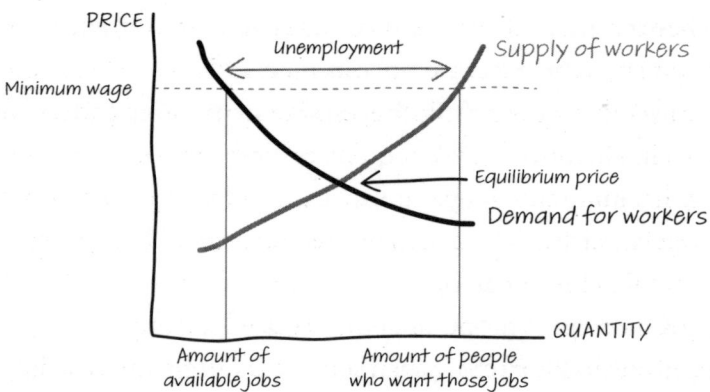

This is, in effect, a mathematical, scientific proof that governments should not interfere with free markets – or at least the free market for jobs. And sure, this is bad news for poorer people, but what kind of fool would argue against maths?

I assumed, naively, that what with this being *literally in the textbook* it must have been widely observed in the real world, but then I went looking for the case studies to impress my students with. I appreciate that this is a spoiler, but my assumption was wrong.

In 1966, the hugely influential economist Milton Friedman lamented that, in the US, Congress had just agreed to increase the minimum wage to $1.60 per hour from 1968. "The effect will be and must be to add to the ranks of the unemployed," he wrote, in an article for *Newsweek*. Like David Ricardo before him, Friedman explained both that this was a mathematical certainty and that his opposition to minimum wages made him a friend of the poor: "the groups that will be hurt the most are the low paid and unskilled," he added.

In actual fact, unemployment in America fell after the minimum wage was increased. So much for "the effect *will be* and *must be* to add to the ranks of the unemployed."

In 1995, two prominent economists, Alan Krueger and David Card, published a book called *Myth and Measurement* in which they analysed the effect on unemployment of various changes to minimum wages in America (where they're set at both national and state levels) and found that, put simply, unemployment *didn't* increase when minimum wages were raised.*

This ran counter to prevailing economic orthodoxy. Indeed, for anyone with faith in the power of deregulation and market efficiency, a book claiming that minimum wages did not cause unemployment was practically heresy. David Card said that many of his colleagues "became very angry or disappointed" at his research.

The UK didn't get a proper minimum wage until the Labour government introduced one in 1999 (more than sixty years after America did, and more than a hundred years after New Zealand first introduced the concept). I remember it well because I felt quite smug at the time – the minimum wage was £3.60 per hour, yet I was getting £4 per hour, working in a pub.†

The rival Conservative party argued exactly along Milton Friedman's lines – along the supply and demand lines – that the minimum wage was a mistake. Unemployment would ensue, the economics was clear about that. They decided to ignore Krueger and Card's research.

But once again, unemployment didn't follow in the footsteps of the new minimum wage.

In 2016, the UK's Low Pay Commission extensively reviewed research into the impact of the introduction of minimum wages, and the UK government commissioned further comprehensive research in 2019, and on both occasions little evidence was found that raising minimum wages had a detrimental effect on employment, though it had a huge positive impact on the lowest paid.

What the hell was I meant to do with this research? I was tempted to put up the minimum wage graph that I just showed you and say, "This will be on your test, but I can't find any evidence that it's true, though I'm not sure why

---

* Despite this, the national minimum wage in America hasn't increased since 2009, and as of 2025 is still just $7.25 per hour. Measured by spending power, minimum wages in America actually peaked in 1968, when that $1.60 per hour that Milton Friedman opposed was the equivalent of about $15 per hour.

† £4 was enough to buy two pints of beer. I never once got a tip.

not. Sorry." There didn't even appear to be any decent research on how high minimum wages could go before they would have a detrimental effect, other than some wildly hypothetical models, for the simple reason that no country has ever raised them to that level.

A creeping doubt started to come over me. I'd always thought of economics as a mathematical science, yet this simple application of supply and demand to, well, *anything*, was seemingly beyond the wit of anyone. I mentioned my despair to Ioannou, in a WhatsApp.

He replied with a link to a research paper called "The Case for Uber".

In 2016, five economists (including Steven Levitt, the author of *Freakonomics*) attempted what is probably the largest ever analysis of an actual, real-world, "demand curve" (i.e. the downwards sloping line in the supply and demand diagram).

They used data from 50 million Uber trips to try to understand how Uber's customers responded to "surge" pricing, which is when Uber ramps up their prices to deal with spikes in demand and/or drops in supply.

But the authors of "The Case for Uber" had an immediate barrier to their analysis: people respond differently to price changes at different times of the week – obviously we feel the urge to splash on a cab more on a rainy Saturday night than we do on a lazy Tuesday afternoon (and the authors acknowledged that they didn't have any good data on weather).

To deal with this, the economists had to split their analysis up into different slices of time and location. Immediately, that shows that *time* affects demand, not just price. Taxi trips are also a slightly odd thing to analyse, as you don't arrive at the restaurant by taxi and say, "That was fun, let's go round again", but rather you might get another Uber next week if the last one was cheap, so one of the variables the authors had to look at was the number of *previous* Uber trips a customer had taken, which suggests that there's a feedback loop in demand.

What the authors were trying to do is find a "line of best fit" – a straight or curved line that passes through the mid-point of all the available data. They couldn't. Even with 50 million data points the conclusions are necessarily caveated as estimates and approximations, with mathematical adjustments for other variables, and even still some of the demand curves look more like lightning bolts than neat mathematical lines.

Two of the economists conducting the study worked for Uber and the paper, as I've mentioned, was called "The Case for Uber", but amazingly the authors of the report found that Uber was sucking money out of the economy. Oh, no, wait – sorry, I read their results the wrong way round. The main takeaway of Uber's economists' analysis of Uber's data was that Uber's customers were gaining billions of dollars in *consumer surplus* from using Uber. Uber must have been so relieved.

A consumer surplus is a consequence of the **X** of supply and demand: there should always be people who would have paid more for a product but instead only paid the equilibrium price, so feel they've got great value for money. In theory, this should be measurable – just add up all the people who bought something and find out how much they would have paid, then deduct what they actually paid. The consumer surplus is this bit on the graph of supply and demand:

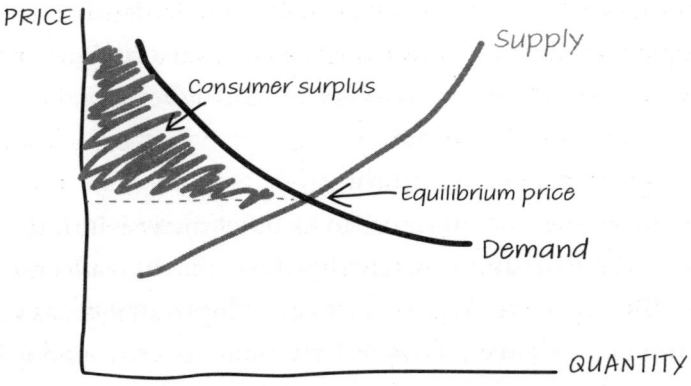

This is what Steven Levitt and his colleagues were trying to do when they crunched the Uber numbers. To find the consumer surplus, they needed to draw the *demand* curve. And by their own admission, the best they managed, even with 50 million data points, was a "back of the envelope calculation".

Reading "The Case for Uber" didn't do much to dispel my sudden distrust for supply and demand diagrams. It was like learning that chemistry teachers have been teaching us about atoms for the last century but no one had ever confirmed they existed – or the one time they really tried to find some atoms using 50 million data points the conclusion was "yeah, back of the envelope... we *think* they exist, especially on Saturday nights".

Though maybe that's unfair. Maybe it's more like astronomers talking about *dark matter* – which astronomers are pretty sure exists but don't know what or where it is, and can only ever infer its presence indirectly. But then, dark matter isn't on page one of the physics textbook, and Uber isn't using it to justify their expansion or their pricing strategy.

Eventually, I think I got to the bottom of why raising minimum wages didn't follow the pattern suggested by supply and demand diagrams.

There was one slightly technical argument that reminded me of David Ricardo – that raising wages lowered profits, so what was really going on was a redistribution of wealth from business owners to employees. In theory this should slow the growth of businesses, but it transpired that the employees were more likely to *spend* their new wealth than the business owners had been, and that extra spending was more beneficial to business than paying higher wages was detrimental. In other words, higher wages meant richer *customers*, which is good for business.*

The other argument was less technical, but far more fun. It had been put forward in 1933 by an economist called Joan Robinson, who suggested that wages are not so much based on supply and demand, they're based on power.

Joan Robinson was perhaps more aware of how messed-up and unfair labour markets are than many of her contemporaries, as she had finished

---

* This theory hinges on what economists call the "Marginal Propensity to Consume", which is a fancy-pants way of saying that for every $100 someone receives, how much will they spend on buying things, versus how much will they stash away for a rainy day. Generally, poorer people (like those on minimum wage) have a higher marginal propensity to consume than richer people do, so making poor people richer at the rich's expense can be good for the economy (though this is a much-debated point).

her studies at Cambridge in 1925 but had not been awarded her degree. This wasn't because she had done something wrong, but rather because Cambridge University refused to give degrees to women until 1948, on the grounds that doing so would diminish the importance of the men's degrees.

Other British universities had been awarding degrees to women since the 1890s (Oxford did so from 1920), but one of the most prominent opponents to Cambridge doing the same was an economist called Alfred Marshall, who ironically, despite being one of the world's biggest promoters of free competition, couldn't countenance competing with *women*. His students even put an effigy of a woman on a bicycle (a shocking image at the time), and then decapitated it.

In the 1920s, over a thousand male Cambridge students marched through the streets chanting "we don't want women" and then laid siege to all-female Newnham College, smashing the windows and breaking the front gate.

Against this backdrop, Joan Robinson considered what really went on in job markets.

Are they really just about mathematical laws of supply and demand, or is something else going on? Oppression, suppression, perhaps everyday frictions that prevent us seamlessly sliding from one job to another?

In her words, "I never learned maths, so I had to think."

In 1933, she published *The Economics of Imperfect Competition*, in which she sought to explain why workers were paid so little. What Joan Robinson realised was straightforward and in retrospect pretty obvious: there are no free markets for jobs, and never have been.

The basic theory of *free markets* is that, left to their own devices, everything will find a natural equilibrium, so the price of everything – including wages – will be determined by supply and demand.

Joan Robinson's book was largely a critique of this view. There is a long history of preventing the working classes from earning more. In feudal societies, peasants were forbidden to leave the areas they worked in. From the early 1600s, the English Parliament allowed landowners to formally take control of what had been common land, forcing many poor rural people to work for landlords rather than themselves (the *informal* practice of "land enclosures" had been going on since the 12th century).

In the 1830s, anyone caught trying to set up a union in the UK was transported to Australia. In China, the "Hokou" system still categorises everybody as either "rural" or "urban" and restricts access to education and healthcare in cities for anyone deemed "rural".

American high schools are largely funded out of local taxes (no wonder schools in Bel Air are better than ones in Detroit). Remember that it took legislation to outlaw paying someone differently because of their skin colour or gender – a discrimination that couldn't exist without unequal power dynamics.

But according to equilibrium theory – the magic of supply and demand – free markets will reward people "correctly". That is to say, if people work harder or smarter or do jobs that are needed but no one else wants to do, then the market will pay them more.

Equilibrium theory – which underpins all of free-market mathematics – assumes that the prime motivator for supply and demand is *money*.

But is that true? To me it seems like madness. And I'm not the only one. Research by the Federal Reserve in America found that people frequently say an *interesting* job is more important than a well-paid one. Nurses and teachers are more motivated by *helping* people than by money.

Yet if people have different incentives then an equilibrium is never reached, because we're constantly playing a different game, with different goals.

And it's not just about different incentives. We don't all have the same access to education or healthcare or even encouragement or time to study. We have literal walls around our countries and forced deportations of immigrants. As we don't all have the same access to the same jobs it's not really a "free" market, in that we can't all simply choose to participate.

Which means minimum wages don't create unemployment for the simple reason that the market was never at an equilibrium price in the first place. All minimum wages do, Joan Robinson argued, is shift the power dynamic. No wonder that those in power so often hate them.

—

At a village fête last summer, I got chatting to a recruitment consultant who told me he had a stinking hangover after celebrating the reward of his annual bonus the night before. He told me that he found work for locum nurses in the NHS and, without prompting, told me that he was paid considerably more than the nurses.

"But it's right that we're paid more," he said, "as society values our work more."

Really? It struck me that I had two possible responses:

a) "Hmm. Care for some Pimms?"

Or b) something along the lines of, "Oh, I don't know, if you were in hospital, in a lot of pain because someone at a village fair had just swung a croquet mallet at your head, and a nurse was about to inject you with morphine, and then paused, and said, 'Actually, how much will you pay me for this?' I bet you'd discover how much you really value that nurse's work."

I mean, obviously I went with (a), but let's pretend that was due to politeness rather than cowardice.

—

I was aware that the history of science is littered with ideas that were mainstream until the moment they weren't. I'd read about how, in the 19th century, many scientists believed that the universe was pervaded by an *ether*, an invisible substance that allowed light to create waves through it. It was a theory that seemed to make sense – how could anything move as a wave unless it was travelling through another substance – but despite years of trying to detect it, it was never found, and eventually the idea was abandoned.

Perhaps the simple supply and demand diagram, with its precise equilibrium, was one of these things? Maybe I could begin my lecture with, "Here's a historic curiosity that people used to believe."

Yet clearly a lot of people still believe that their salaries, for instance, are a simple consequence of supply and demand – that we are all somehow paid the "right" amount. This really troubled me, as the only arena of thought where people refuse to abandon unproveable ideas is religion. As a newly anointed lecturer in economics, had I become a priest by mistake?

Still, I fretted that I must be misunderstanding something crucial about supply, demand and equilibrium pricing, that there must be a simple explanation for what I was missing. So I went to speak to one of the senior economics professors. He was a respected academic who had been teaching the subject for years, and rather marvellously looked a bit like Blackbeard the Pirate.

He had an office he hadn't tidied since before the electronic era and, as if to make a point, he carried a pencil tied around his neck with a string, that he sometimes poked into his beard for effect. I took an instant liking to him.

I didn't want to admit that I was confused by the first page of the textbook, so I casually asked him which examples he used for explaining equilibrium prices when he taught supply and demand.

He laughed. "Oh, not that rubbish! The Law of Supply and Demand was disproved in the 1970s. Have you not read Debreu, Mantel and Sonnenschein?"

I looked at my feet. "Um, not for a while."

He opened a drawer in his desk and rummaged around looking for something. "The maths behind the 'Law' of Supply and Demand is complete nonsense, the assumptions required to make it work are insane, and there's practically nothing in the real world that fits the model."

I hadn't expected him to be so blunt, or in all honesty that he might confirm my notion that the idea I was meant to teach on day one of my course might not actually be true.

"But why are we teaching it, then?"

He shrugged his broad shoulders and scratched his beard. "Because it's on the syllabus."

"But why is it on the syllabus?"

He laughed, shut the drawer without finding what he was looking for, and gave me a big, gold-toothed smile.

"Because we're all afraid of Henry George."

As I was new to the school, I assumed he was referring to someone in the department. Perhaps someone that I, too, should be afraid of. But he wasn't. It turns out that Henry George has been dead for a very long time.

6

THE THIRD MOST FAMOUS MAN IN AMERICA

"I took economics courses in college for four years, and everything I was taught was wrong."
Theodore Roosevelt, US President

Teaching economics at the business school turned out to be a lot harder than teaching tax. Partly it was because people go into a tax lecture expecting it to be boring, then discover it's mostly about conflict and the preposterous lies told by the vile super-rich, whereas my students turned up at my economics lectures expecting to learn how to become super-rich alongside tales of unabashed greed and what they actually got were endless fucking diagrams.

A student would come up to me clutching their textbook and stressily point at some exercise, asking, "So, like, does the *marginal propensity to consume* line cross the *average total cost* line from below or above?" I mean, *what?!* How the hell should I know? Except, of course, I was meant to know, because I was the teacher.*

---

* There is no diagram in which a marginal propensity to consume line crosses an average total cost line. They're two completely different concepts. It's like asking someone to explain the maximum air speed of eczema. All the same, my attempt at a sketch must have been pretty convincing as my student thanked me for clearing it up.

It wasn't just supply and demand. It felt like the entirety of entry-level economics was expressed in two dimensions. And none of the books I'd read about economics and nothing I was being exposed to at the think-tank bore any resemblance to the diagrams about *production frontiers* or *the Phillips curve* that I was meant to be explaining.

In one lecture, I was meant to demonstrate something called *Ricardian Equivalence*, a concept first voiced by David Ricardo that posits that people won't spend more if you cut taxes, as they'll predict future tax rises (so there's no point cutting taxes). It didn't sound true, and indeed when I looked it up, I discovered that the concept was called "sheer nonsense" by the economist Joseph Stiglitz and "total horseshit" by the economist Lars P Syll. So great, here I was, supposed to be teaching total horseshit.*

My week had a nice pattern, though. I went to the Institute for Fair Economics on Mondays and Tuesdays, had two days at home to write my sci-fi epic (and promote *Taxtopia*), then I'd hop on the train on Friday to the business school. Tax at 11 a.m., Economics after lunch. The management team had threatened to expand this to two days of teaching but luckily the lecturers were unionised, so the bosses didn't push their luck.

One lunchtime, I saw Blackbeard (my piratical colleague) looking for something on his hands and knees in the gravel next to the huge glass doors of the main entrance of the economics department, and when he saw me, he leapt up.

"Nothing," he said, as he brushed himself down, which was a bit odd as I hadn't asked him anything.

Slightly out of awkwardness, I asked him if he knew a professor of

---

* Apparently, David Ricardo didn't believe in Ricardian Equivalence either, but it experienced a revival in the 1970s and now often appears in the form *"if we assume that Ricardian Equivalence holds..."* It's usually expressed mathematically, like this: "As $c_t + c_f/(1+r) = f_t + y_t + y_f/(1+r)$, then if $U = u(c_t) + au(c_f)$ utility is maximised when $u'(c_t) = a(1+r)u'(c_f)$". I bet you skimmed that equation, didn't you? In which case good for you, it really is horseshit.

economics whom Ioannou had suggested I meet the following week. I think I just assumed that all economics professors know each other.

"Aren't you all on a big WhatsApp group, or something?" I asked, when he looked puzzled.

"A *what* group?" he said. I'm still struggling to work out if he was teasing me or not.

We got chatting as we headed inside the building and I confessed to him that I had struggled a bit with my first few lectures, and asked him whose fault he had said it was that all these graphs were on the syllabus.

"Henry George," he replied, very earnestly. "Come with me, I'll give you something."

—

On Sunday, 31 October 1897, flags across New York city were flown at half-mast. It was two days before the election of a new mayor, but all campaigning ceased. In Midtown Manhattan, a mournful silence descended, punctuated with the sobs of grown men. The police had to hold back the vast crowds that had come to walk past a funeral bier that lay beside a simple bust in the great hall of Grand Central Palace, on Lexington Avenue. Over a hundred thousand people shuffled in to pay their respects, another hundred thousand waited for their turn, but never got a chance.

The only comparable event was said to have been the funeral procession for Abraham Lincoln, some thirty years or so earlier. A few newspaper reports suggested that the attendance was even bigger here. An evangelical clergyman and then a rabbi took their turns to address the crowd, then excited murmurs broke out as the dead man's friend, the Catholic priest Edward McGlynn, rose to speak. Father McGlynn was a controversial figure – a famously brilliant orator and defender of the poor who had been excommunicated by the Pope ten years earlier for preaching about the unfairness of the American tax regime at meetings of the Anti-Poverty Society, before being surprisingly readmitted to the church after a committee of professors at the Catholic University of America, in Washington D C, advised the Pope that McGlynn's views on tax were not at odds with Catholic teaching, after all.

Cries of *"Hush"* went out as McGlynn, a huge man with a broad chest and now, here, tears running down his cheeks, delivered his eulogy:

> *He died in a struggle upon which he had gladly, enthusiastically entered… to fight for a cause which would make the magnificent truths of the Declaration of Independence something more than glittering generalities… he was not merely a philosopher and a sage; he was a seer, a forerunner, a prophet; a teacher sent from God.*

The New York Times referred to the atmosphere surrounding this funeral as "hero worship", then acknowledged "but its object really was a hero".

Breaking with the custom of the day, there are reports of "tumultuous handclapping" filling the funeral hall as Father McGlynn pointed a finger heavenwards and declared, "I believe that I mock not those sacred scriptures when I say: there is a man sent of God, whose name was Henry George."

All of this might come as a surprise, especially if, like I was when I joined the business school, you're unfamiliar with Henry George. Nowadays, if he gets mentioned at all, it's as the inspiration for the board game *Monopoly*.

—

"You can't really understand the history of economics if you don't know about Henry George," said Blackbeard, his eyes scanning his bookshelves and his gold teeth glinting.

This seemed implausible to me. I'd read a number of histories of economics, owned several books with titles like *The Great Economists*, and, with all due consideration to arrogance, was pretty sure I did know the history of economics rather well. I mean, come on, I was an economics lecturer who also worked at an economics think-tank.

"Ah-ha, here you go," he said, springing up from his chair with more nimbleness that his size suggested possible and hooking an old biography from a shelf. The book was creased and dog-eared, which I'll admit is always a good sign.

I must have looked a bit confused, but he was chuckling.

"That'll change the way you see things," said Blackbeard.

Not likely, I thought.

I skimmed the first few chapters. They were interesting, but were mostly bog-standard biography stuff that could have described the lives of millions of young American men in the middle of the 19th century.

Henry George was born in Philadelphia in 1839. He was forced to leave school while barely in his teens and went to work on a ship, then moved to California, got a low-paid job as a typesetter, and eloped with an orphaned Australian girl named Annie Fox.

I found myself flicking the pages. I wanted to read about economics, not trudge through a sob story. But I'd missed something significant, and indeed it's only when I come back to write about him now that I realise what that was. Almost every other economist's biography follows one of two stories, either *born into a wealthy family and surrounded by intellectuals, this classical economist blah blah blah*, or, for the 20th-century ones, *after scoring top grades at high school, he then attended Harvard before becoming a professor at the University of Chicago*.

Henry George's life wasn't like that. In 1864, a great drought ruined the harvest in California and led to a spiral of joblessness and hunger across the state. George lost his typesetting job and after the birth of his second child found himself reduced to begging. He admitted in later life that at one point he was so poor and hungry, and so desperate to provide for his family, that he had considered robbing a "well-dressed" gentleman he encountered in the street. Instead, perhaps demonstrating his art of persuasion, he explained his predicament to the man and was given five dollars (which would be worth about a hundred dollars today).

This was not the first economic depression George had witnessed. The ship he worked on had spent a month off the coast of Australia and he described the situation there as "very hard ashore, thousands with nothing to do and nothing to eat". Another recession in 1857 had been the main reason he left

Philadelphia for California. He was a smart and curious man and a thought stayed with him. Why do these recessions keep happening?

He began a career as a journalist, writing for the newly established *San Francisco Times* and eventually becoming the paper's managing editor, where he used the platform to campaign against corruption, making enemies as he did so. As a foretaste of his developing philosophy, one of his most successful early articles was called "What the railroad will bring us". In it, he warns that for all the rising prosperity that the railroads will usher in, they would also bring misery. He asks whether California really wants to be like New York, a place "ruled and robbed by thieves, loafers and brothelkeepers; nursing a race of savages fiercer and meaner than any who ever shrieked a war-whoop on the plains". (The eulogisers at his funeral in New York glossed over this description of New Yorkers.)

In the same article, he then points to the cotton mills of Massachusetts, "with their thousands of little children . . . being literally worked to death" and the pin factories of England, "where young girls are treated worse than even slaves on Southern plantations" and the coal miners of Belgium and France, "where the condition of production is that the laborer shall have meat but once a week". Personally, I'm guessing that being a slave on a Southern plantation was worse than only getting meat once a week, but I think I get the gist of what he was trying to say.

Despite his own experience of poverty, he highlighted the relatively decent wages in California as an indication that "the natural wealth of the country was not yet monopolized", and this thought – that "natural" wealth would become controlled by a minority of people – became the centrepiece of his big economic idea. If Blackbeard was to be believed, what Henry George did next may have profoundly changed the course of the 20th century.

—

The professors at the business school generally viewed teaching as an irritating distraction from their real job of researching, which seemed to comprise getting drunk, barking out random ideas and then getting their graduate students to do all the work. In other words, it wasn't that different a career to working in a think-tank.

But as, in theory, research required deep and undisturbed concentration, all the professors were given their own offices. Mere lecturers, like me, had to make do with a space to one side of the students' common area that was notionally off-limits to students but had no actual dividing barrier (like a door, or even a wall), just a few desks with tiny signs that said "staff only", where we could "prep" for our lectures. The thinking seemed to be that anyone who had to actually *prepare* for a lecture wasn't worthy of respect.

A professor called Alva found me at one of these desks as I was packing up my things for the day. I'd only had a brief interaction with her before, but I understood that she was ultimately responsible for the course I was teaching. Her face looked like she was trying to hold her nose without using her hands.

"Can I have a quick word?" she asked, in the same way that a policeman might say, "Would you mind stepping out of your vehicle?"

"Sure," I said, hoping that her next line was going to be, "We've just realised that we're one professor short of our quota, so would you like a promotion?"

"I'm afraid we've had a complaint from one of your students..."

"Oh really?" I'd barely taught anything. Maybe she was mistaken?

"Apparently, you teased her about her piercings."

I was pretty sure I hadn't. "I've not teased anyone about anything," I said, very genuinely.

"She said you claimed that 'Big Piercing' was behind the rise of septum piercings...?"

"Oh," I said. "That wasn't about one particular student. They *all* have septum piercings."

She frowned. "She also said you referred to TikTok as 'The Great Satan'...?"

"I *may* have done that. It made sense in context."

"Stick to the syllabus," she said, giving me the least friendly wink I've ever received.*

I felt rather deflated on the train ride home. I'd only taught a few hours of economics and already my students were complaining about me. I've since learned that this is pretty standard – if students are enjoying your class you could tell them that you want to drown their pets with your bare hands and they would brush it off as a quirky aside, but if they sense a whiff of hesitancy you only have to adjust the air conditioning to be accused of intolerance.

But I comforted myself with the biography of Henry George. I'd just got to the good bit.

—

After a failed bid to enter local politics, and with his newspaper not earning him much money, Henry George took on a job as State Inspector of Gas Meters.

Actually, sorry, that wasn't the good bit. But it was this undemanding job that gave George time to write his ideas down, which eventually became a book, which he called *Progress and Poverty*, which was published in 1879.

Almost unheard of now, it is hard to exaggerate what a sensation it was. Both George Bernard Shaw and Leo Tolstoy described reading *Progress and Poverty* as life-changing. The book was praised by Albert Einstein, who said he "couldn't imagine a more beautiful combination of intellectual keenness, artistic form and fervent love of justice" (and remember that Einstein could imagine a lot). Karl Marx denounced it.

Winston Churchill was such a fan that he briefly quit the Conservative Party to support the rival Liberal Party when the Liberals began promoting Henry George's ideas.

---

* The University of Chicago economist Leonardo Bursztyn conducted research in which he found that two-thirds of TikTok users would pay to *quit* TikTok, but don't quit due to addiction and a fear of missing out. His conclusion was that TikTok (and most other social media platforms) have a net *negative* value to their users.

In some years, it sold more copies than the Bible, and indeed it became one of the bestselling books of the 19th century. It is still one of the bestselling economics books of all time.

George claims that the inspiration for his book came in a flash, during a chance encounter with a teamster in San Francisco Bay, as they talked about the cost of land. "It came over me that there was the reason of advancing poverty with advancing wealth. With the growth of population, land grows in value, and the men who work it must pay more for the privilege."

With the publication of this book, Henry George became one of the most talked about people in the world.

The prevailing view of the day was the same one that the Reverend Malthus had set out to prove almost a hundred years earlier, that poverty persisted despite increases in wealth because populations were rising, so there simply weren't enough resources to go round. In other words, poverty was a grim inevitability.

There were, of course, conflicting views. A common explanation for poverty at the time was that the poor simply lacked financial self-restraint – if they saved their money instead of squandering it on alcohol and other vices then they would become richer.*

But *Progress and Poverty* tackled this problem in a different way: How is it that *despite* rising prosperity the poorest in society remain poor? Henry George believed he knew why.

The *reason* that poverty persists, he argued, is because our society misunderstands our relationship with *land*.

Land is valuable, he said, not because of the actions of the person who owns that land, but rather the actions of everyone else. Good schools, good transport links, nearby shops and parks, low crime, employment opportunities, all these things push up land values. All these things make the landowner richer. But the landowner doesn't pay for these things.

---

* This view lives on today as "of course the young could buy houses, but they're wasting their cash on flat whites and smashed avocadoes."

The workers do. People with jobs pay taxes, the taxes improve the neighbourhood, so the landowner gets richer.

As Henry George put it, we tax private earnings and private expenditure to pay for public goods that create private wealth. To George, this was the grand injustice at the heart of society, and would inevitably lead to a greater and greater concentration of wealth in the hands of a smaller and smaller number of people, all paid for by the exploited worker. A landlord need do nothing to earn their wealth – the working masses will be forced to hand their money to the landlord, twice over: once indirectly as taxes, and once directly as rent.

George saw this as a moral travesty, that led to a "shocking contrast between monstrous wealth and debasing want".

—

When economists talk about rent, they are usually referring to a concept called *economic rent*. This is not the same as normal rent – the kind you pay to your landlord in return for not being homeless. Economic rent is a (usually) undeserved *extra* payment because of something being monopolised.

For instance, imagine there was a field that anyone could graze their cattle on. How much could you charge someone to use that field? That question doesn't make sense – I just said anyone who wants to can use the field.

But what if I put a fence around it and insisted that I own the field. Now how much could I charge for access? If the alternative to the cattle farmer is that their cows die, then I could charge just short of the value of each cow.

It gets worse. If the farmers, now struggling to make money from each cow because they're paying so much in rent, decide to buy *more* cows, the *landowner* will get even richer – because they can charge for access per cow. But the landowner didn't do anything to deserve that extra money – they didn't work harder or graze their own cows, they merely monopolised the land, and received economic rent for it.

This *economic rent* was the issue that got Henry George most fired up.

—

At around this point I added *Progress and Poverty* to my reading list. I mean, if I was going to be an economics lecturer I should probably read one of the bestselling economics books of all time, right?

The enormous popularity of *Progress and Poverty* ignited a debate about landownership. Where previously Henry George had struggled to make much headway in politics, he suddenly found himself thrust into the spotlight. He toured first America and then the world, delivering lectures and inspiring a following. He was sometimes referred to as the Prophet of San Francisco. His critics complained that he was less an economist and more the leader of a religious movement.

Shortly after the release of *Progress and Poverty*, Henry moved to New York (despite his earlier observations about loafers and brothelkeepers) and befriended prominent members of the Irish community, accepting their invitation to lecture in Ireland. At the time, Ireland was entirely ruled from London and had, as British Prime Minister Benjamin Disraeli put it, "a territorial aristocracy, the richest of whom lived in distant capitals". In other words, if anywhere had a problem with land being owned by a tiny minority while the bulk of the population suffered, it was Ireland.

Huge numbers of people came to hear Henry George speak:

"Ownership of land always gives ownership of people!" he declared, to cheers from the Irish audience, who longed to hear an alternative argument to the prevailing economic view, that inequality, poverty and recessions were inevitable, and probably the poor's fault.

George's analysis of poverty in Ireland included the role of potatoes, which had been introduced to Ireland to lower the cost of food and thus alleviate the suffering of the poor, but paradoxically the improved harvests had resulted in higher rents and lower wages: "No matter how much productivity increases, rent steadily swallows up the whole gain (or even more). Thus, the condition of the masses in every civilized country is tending toward virtual slavery – under the forms of freedom."

George argued that all inventions or innovations that improved *productivity* – that is, that helped workers make more and better stuff in the same amount of time – really just increased demand for land, which increased rent, which made workers poorer.

"It does not seem to be one human being who drives another," he said, "but 'the inevitable laws of supply and demand'. And for this, no one in particular is responsible."

This was all a bit too revolutionary for the British, who promptly arrested Henry George. But far from stopping him, the arrest only increased his fame. At one point, only the author Mark Twain and the inventor Thomas Edison were said to be more famous than Henry George was.

You might be wondering at this point how someone could become so popular, and a book could sell so well, just by pointing out the unfairness inherent in a majority of land being owned by a tiny minority of people. Sure, whipping up some anger about all the injustice and inequality in the world might get you a few supportive cheers, but it's not enough on its own. It was the subtitle of *Progress and Poverty* that really got people excited. The subtitle was, simply, *The Remedy*.

At this point, I got pretty excited too. One of the reasons I'd quit my job working in tax was that I'd come to the deeply uncomfortable conclusion that we tax the wrong people and tax the wrong things, with disastrous consequences for both equality and the economy, and here in one of the most groundbreaking and popular economics books of all time was exactly that argument – that the root of society's problems lay in a dysfunctional and unfair tax system.

The Remedy that Henry George put forward, to fix all society's economic ills – inequality, poverty, booms and busts, and so on – was to scrap all taxes except one: a single tax on land values. He would tax away the economic rent that landowners received. His followers became known as Single-Taxers.

At first, this may sound a little bonkers, but the more you read George's argument the more convincing it becomes. Isn't it a little odd that in today's world you can buy some land, do nothing with it, but still get richer when land values rise? Surely no one should get richer by doing nothing?

Whereas if you had to pay an annual tax to own that land then you would have to do something productive with it – which probably means employing people to use or improve the land. If those people you employ aren't paying taxes themselves, then they can keep more of their wages to spend on things they need – making the employees richer and boosting demand for more produced goods.

George drew on the idea that land (like air and water and sunlight) was a natural resource and as such no one person should derive excess "economic rent" from it – meaning the ability to monopolise it and charge people to use it. So instead, whatever amount a landlord would be able to extract as rent from that land should be paid in its entirety as a tax to the government, to be shared among all people.

If you own a property, this might sound scary. But a crucial part of George's land tax idea was that it was only the *land* value that got taxed – not the value of the *property* that was built on the land. Thus, every landowner had an incentive to improve their land (and thus create wealth), or sell their land to someone else who would improve it.

This flipped incentives on their head. Under a single land tax system, government infrastructure spending would always be paid for by the people who benefited from it, via increased land values. So the government would always have the incentive to build more value-creating infrastructure. A private landowner could still get rich from building, well, *buildings*, but the land underneath those buildings would sell for (almost) nothing, as all the excess value would be captured by taxes to be used for the benefit of all society.

Land taxes are impossible to evade (unlike almost all other taxes) and don't distort the market, as taxing land doesn't reduce the supply or use of land. Indeed, it encourages the use of it. A landowner who had no productive use of land would be encouraged by the land tax to sell their land to someone who would make better use of it. So there's always an incentive to improve your own land, as it will make you richer to do so. "Land banking", where land is just owned in the speculative hope that its value increases, becomes impossible.

Under Henry George's *remedy* everybody ends up incentivised to use land efficiently and create wealth (and jobs), no business is curtailed by taxes on their profits, no employees are made poorer by taxes on their income, no products are made more expensive by sales taxes. Landowners can still get rich, but only if they improve their land.

And what's more, as speculators would disappear, there would be a dampening of the cyclical pattern of booms and busts that led to the sort of recessions that had cost George his typesetting job and left him so destitute he contemplated robbing someone.

Really strikingly, unlike pretty much every other radical economic philosophy that has been put forward over the centuries, Henry George's *remedy* is hard to label as either left or right wing. He believed that in creating a single land tax we would need neither income taxes nor taxes on capital. And with his land tax there would be enough money left over to pay a "citizen's dividend". What capitalist could be opposed to abolishing taxes on capital? What socialist would oppose a universal basic income?*

—

Once upon a time, the board game *Monopoly* was known as *The Landlord's Game,* and came with two sets of rules. One of them you'll be familiar with – buy up whole sections of town, drive up rents and force your friends into bankruptcy. The other set of rules was explicitly Georgist. Indeed, fans of Georgism would entice people to play the game to demonstrate his theories.

In the Georgist version of the game, rents were still paid to landlords who improved their properties by building houses, but a base rent – on the unimproved value – had to be paid by the landlord to a pool that everyone benefited from. There would still be a winner who made the most money by improving their land the most, but the game was only over when the *poorest* player doubled their money. So, in a sense, everybody would win.

The Landlord's Game was eventually renamed *Monopoly* and released by Parker Brothers, a company founded by a man called George Parker, who

---

* He also advocated for free bus passes, but perhaps that's a separate issue.

believed that games didn't need to be educational. Having had prior success with a game called *Banking*, Parker dropped the Georgist version.

—

Almost inevitably, given his legions of fans and his personal conviction that his ideas would improve the world, Henry George re-entered politics. A political movement of Single-Taxers sprang up around him, and in 1886 he ran to be mayor of New York.

But he faced a big problem. A corrupt political organisation known as Tammany Hall with links to both organised criminal gangs and the New York police force was notorious at the time for voter intimidation, harassing rival campaigners, stuffing ballot boxes with fake votes and doling out political appointments in return for bribes, and in this way controlling New York politics.

Tammany Hall's power base had long been among the Irish neighbourhoods of New York, but Henry George's popularity with working-class voters threatened to alter the political landscape along class divides, which could permanently weaken Tammany's influence. So representatives of Tammany Hall made George a secret offer – they would secure him a safe congressional seat if he agreed not to run for mayor of New York.

But George had spent the first half of his career writing about political corruption – he was not about to take part in it. He announced his candidacy for mayor as leader of the newly formed United Labor Party.

Afraid of splitting the Democratic vote (even though a lot of that vote was rigged), Tammany Hall agreed to support a non-Tammany candidate, the industrialist and lawyer Abram Hewitt. Seeing that a fight was on, the Republican Party put up one of their best candidates, future US President Theodore Roosevelt.

George had to rely on neighbourhood meetings and street-corner rallies to drum up support, as his ideas had turned the wealthy landowning elite of New York against him, which meant the newspapers were against him and almost no wealthy donors backed him. Tammany Hall even distributed leaflets two days before the election written by a senior member of the

Catholic Archdiocese of New York describing George's ideas as against the teachings of the church. I wouldn't of course want to speculate whether these anti-land tax leaflets were inspired more by biblical doctrine or the church's landholdings (thought to be over 170 million acres today).

The Tammany-backed Democrat candidate Abram Hewitt called George a communist, and implied that Georgism would result in a French Revolution-style Reign of Terror. So far, so typical American election, you might think.

In those days, votes were not cast in secret, as they are today, and contemporary satirical cartoons show factory owners and landlords standing over their employees and tenants, watching which way they voted, threatening dismissal or eviction if they picked the "wrong" candidate. Henry George was so incensed by the obvious corruption of *public* voting that he campaigned throughout his life for what he called "Australian ballots" or secret votes (Australia were pioneers in this regard). George also bucked the trend of the time and campaigned for votes for women.

In some ways, given the vested interests that he was up against, it's a miracle that George got any votes at all. Even more surprising is that he beat Theodore Roosevelt into third place. Although he didn't win.*

Yet the popularity of his movement marked the beginning of the "Progressive Era" of politics, a time of policies designed to alleviate the suffering of the poor and curtail the power of industrialist elites. Inspired by George, Land Tax initiatives were launched across America, as well as in Australia, Canada, Denmark and elsewhere. But it was in the United Kingdom where his ideas were perhaps to make the biggest impact.

---

* Ironically, the new mayor, Abram Hewitt, probably did more harm to Tammany Hall than Henry George ever would have. Hewitt eventually became a New York congressman and Chairman of the Democratic National Committee, and used his position to break the power of Tammany Hall. He even cancelled the St Patrick's Day parade.

I spent most of the weekend excitedly telling my wife about Henry George. I mean, I tried telling my kids, too, but they weren't so interested, even when I described it as like learning that the Space Race in the 1960s had really been between America, the Soviet Union and Malawi, and Malawi had been winning. "Imagine how you'd feel if none of your space books ever mentioned that?"

"Should we check?" asked my son, which then meant spending half an hour learning the names of all the dwarf planets.

Even after Covid, my wife and I had continued with our two-person cocktail society (largely because of the expense of babysitters), and over margaritas I told her that I'd been stalling a bit on my analogous sci-fi epic.

"Why don't you write about Henry George, then?" she asked.

I pondered it for a while. Or I'd addled my brain with tequila and it was running very slowly. One of the two.

"I've already written a *how to save the world by reforming tax* book," I said, though also thinking she'd made a good point.

She has a talent for noticing when I'm protesting too much, and she gave me a prod. "I bet there's a Henry George society you could speak to."

—

In 1891, members of the United Kingdom's Liberal Party (then one of the two main parties – the other being the Conservatives) met in the city of Newcastle, in the north-east of England, to discuss what it was that, besides power, they actually wanted.

This was a radical idea for a political party at the time – to actually draw up a list of policies. Top of their list was Irish Home Rule, but almost as prominent was Land Tax Reform, directly inspired by Henry George's *Progress and Poverty*. The Liberals struggled to push through their ideas until a landslide victory in 1906 enabled the introduction of what became known as the People's Budget. It was in the run-up to this election that future Conservative leader Winston Churchill quit the Conservative Party to join the Liberals, inspired by the writings of Henry George to advocate for the Land Tax.

The People's Budget is still a landmark in British political history, the first time that a budget was produced with the specific purpose of redistributing wealth, by shifting taxation away from labour and onto land. The House of Lords (who owned most of the land) vetoed the bill, the first time they had vetoed a budget in 200 years. Prime Minister David Lloyd George quipped of the dukes in the Lords that each one "costs as much to keep up as two dreadnoughts . . . [but] last longer". This constitutional crisis led to the Parliament Act of 1911, which shifted power away from the aristocracy and prevented the Lords from ever vetoing another budget.

In other words, had it not been for Henry George, British politics might still be dominated by aristocrats.

—

The following Friday, I returned to Blackbeard's office with the book about Henry George. I paused for a moment outside his door, as I could hear the sound of several people laughing coming from his room. Then the door opened and a number of students appeared, all smiling still, one saying something like "that was *amazing*". As I entered, Blackbeard was standing with his back against one wall and seemed to be struggling to tuck his shirt back in.

"Ah-ha, hello. Just having some fun with the undergrads. How are you?"

I noticed his fly was undone.

"Um . . . ?"

"I was just doing an impression. Do you know Dr Moray?"

"Er, no."

He finished dealing with his shirt then thankfully grappled with the zip on his trousers. "Ah, don't worry about it then. What can I do for you?"

"Henry George," I said. "It's compelling, but then what happened? Where are the Single-Taxers today?"

He laughed. "We might need to get a drink before we discuss that."

I half expected him to pull out a bottle of rum (he didn't, sadly). Instead, he patted himself down, pulled a pencil from his beard, then said in a tone that bordered on contempt, "Unless you need to *teach* or something?"

"There are two versions of how this story ends," Blackbeard explained, over a pint of bitter (of course he'd drink bitter) in a pub called, appropriately enough, *The George*. "The one you usually hear is that for all his rhetoric, Henry George's ideas were neither original nor practical – say, how would you separate land values from property values? The Liberal Party made such a complete hash of introducing a land tax in their People's Budget that they repealed it in 1922. And then, of course, Marxism promised more to the downtrodden than Georgism, so Marxism – *communism* – took over as the leading idea among the *Left*. And as a result, Henry George's ideas died when he died."

It was true that Henry George had died relatively young, from complications following a stroke at the age of 58, while running again to be mayor of New York (he was in ill health, ironically saying of the election, "I will make the race if I die for it").

Blackbeard swirled the end of his beer around the glass, as if looking for answers in the vortex. "But I don't buy any of that," he said.

"So, what's your theory?" I asked. I've learned that asking an economist "what's your theory?" will keep at least one of you entertained for hours.

He finished his beer, looked at me, then tapped his glass. Despite being a professor of economics it was not clear if he knew how the round system worked.

Once I'd bought him another beer, he launched into a story I'd never heard before in any of the economics books I'd read.

"My theory," he said, clearly pleased that he had someone to explain something so far off-syllabus to, "is that Henry George wasn't defeated intellectually. He pissed off a lot of very rich and very powerful people. I think the real story is this: he was deliberately, systematically, *silenced*."

7

IS THE ENTIRETY OF MODERN ECONOMICS ONE GIANT CONSPIRACY? AND IS DEATHLESS SOUL JELLY A REAL THING?

"Economics, it turns out, is not about discovering laws: it is essentially a question of design."
Kate Raworth, economist

Blackbeard fixed his dark eyes on me and lowered his voice, then asked, "What do you know about John D Rockefeller?"

"Um, he was rich?" I said.

"Oh, yes. And who do you think was the biggest threat to his wealth?"

I laughed, a little nervously. "Was it Henry George?"

Blackbeard slapped his thick hand down on the table. "Yes! This is where the fightback began."

Rockefeller's company, Standard Oil, was founded just a few months before Henry George had his revelation that monopolised land ownership was the source of poverty. By the end of the 19th century, Standard Oil had come to control 90 per cent of the American oil market and at his richest, Rockefeller was wealthier, in comparison to the size of the US economy, than Elon Musk, Bill Gates, Jeff Bezos and Mark Zuckerberg *combined*.

This was the era of the so-called Robber Barons, the immensely wealthy business owners, industrialists and financiers who, depending on whose side you're on, were either innovative entrepreneurs who spearheaded the economic boom of America, or were unethical monopolists who used their wealth and power to control politicians, destroy competition and exploit their employees. How different the olden days sound to today...

These were men like Cornelius Vanderbilt, who had more wealth than the US Treasury had cash; Andrew Carnegie, whose sale of his steel business is probably the largest sale of any business, ever, and John Pierpont Morgan, the financier who bought Carnegie's steel business and had change left over.

In Rockefeller's case, he had ruthlessly expanded his business from being one of many kerosene refiners in Ohio into a vast corporate empire that owned railroads, pipelines, refineries and oil wells across the country. He was an innovator – slashing the production costs of oil, pioneering the use of pipelines, even finding uses for oil's waste products (like using it to make chewing gum) and, by issuing tradeable certificates for the future delivery of oil, he helped introduce derivative trading to America.*

He was notorious for undercutting his rivals until they were forced to sell their businesses to him, at which point he could jack up his prices. He pioneered what today is called *Vertical Integration* – the ownership of every step from the wells extracting the oil, the railroads and trains transporting it to refineries, the refineries themselves, the pipelines, the local oil trucks, right the way through to employing the salesmen selling his chewing gum.

---

* A derivative is simply something that is valuable because *something else* is valuable. So, a piece of paper that can be exchanged for oil is valuable because the oil is valuable. Rockefeller's introduction of derivative trading meant it no longer became necessary to buy oil in order to profit from rising oil prices (as you could buy the *right to buy oil* – the derivative, instead), which is why oil traders today wear brogues rather galoshes.

He owned ships, mines, warehouses, timber yards, a beautiful 3,400-acre estate just north of New York City (his brother had a 1,000-acre estate nearby), as well as a dozen other homes and estates.

But he claimed that the best investment he ever made wasn't in any of these things – not his businesses, not his innovations in banking, not his dozen or so houses nor his 1,200-acre horse-training farm or his golf course in New Jersey. No, the man who said, "Do you know the only thing that gives me pleasure? It's to see my dividends coming in" stated that the best investment he ever made was a donation in 1890 to help found the University of Chicago.

Before the publication of *Progress and Poverty*, the bestselling book on economics was called *Political Economy for Beginners*, written by English uber-brain Millicent Fawcett. In it, Fawcett runs through what we would now call *classical economics* – the key concepts pioneered by Adam Smith and David Ricardo, including that the production of goods is only possible thanks to *Land*, *Labour*, and *Capital*.

Land includes all natural resources (so things like crops and timber and minerals), Labour is all of us workers, and Capital is things like tools and buildings and machines.*

But what's this got to do with Rockefeller's "best investment"?

Well, when the classical economists like Ricardo and Smith were writing, taxes were relatively light, at least compared to today. There were taxes on goods (like tea and candles, but also some weirdly specific things like wig powder or patterned wallpaper), and there were tariffs on most imports (like the Corn Laws), and stamp tax was paid on newspapers and certain legal documents (this was the main tax American colonists were complaining about when they chanted "no taxation without representation" in the run-up to declaring independence). There were also occasional other, sometimes wacky taxes (like on windows or fireplaces), as well as, in Britain, the Poor Laws that Ricardo detested so much.

---

* Though even this is contentious – Ricardo, for instance, said that food was capital.

This meant that the classical economists weren't living in a world with a comprehensive enough tax system for them to pay a huge amount of attention to taxation policies, other than to highlight the role taxation played in suppressing free trade, and to postulate on what ideal taxes would look like.

When Millicent Fawcett was reintroducing the classical economists' ideas to the masses, there were still no income taxes in America. In fact, other than a brief period during the American Civil War, the United States didn't levy what today we'd recognise as income taxes until 1913 (with the passing of the 16th amendment).

And that meant that ultra-rich industrialists like John D Rockefeller barely paid a bean in taxes. But now, all of a sudden, the bestselling book in America – Henry George's *Progress and Poverty* – is arguing that they should be. Instead of commissioning a rival book with a counter-argument (that actually no, the rich shouldn't pay more tax), Rockefeller commissioned an entire university.

It wasn't just Rockefeller. Steel magnate Joseph Wharton (who owned 100,000 acres of New Jersey) founded Wharton Business School in 1881 (two years after the publication of *Progress and Poverty*). Railroad tycoon Leland Stanford founded Stanford University in 1885. In 1888, the investment banker John Pierpont Morgan donated what was then the huge sum of $100,000 to Columbia University, allowing the economics department to expand from two members to almost fifty (a few years later its president, Seth Low, would run against Henry George in another New York mayoralty race).*

Directors from large corporations (which were often major landowners themselves) were brought in to sit on the boards of these new universities and the academic staff – especially in the economics departments – were expected to tow the party line: that raising taxes on landowners was a bad idea. Despite the Single Land Tax being one of the most talked-about ideas in

---

* In the 1970s, students at Stanford University were refused permission by the university administrators to change their sports teams' mascot to a Robber Baron on the grounds that it was offensive to the memory of Leland Stanford. The same administrators had been fine with the previous mascot, called "The Indian".

political economics at the time, not a single Georgist was invited to join the staff. Indeed, any professors caught promoting Henry George's ideas could expect to be marginalised or fired. In the words of economist Mason Gaffney, it was a culture of "placate or perish".

One victim of this culture was assistant professor Scott Nearing, who was fired from Wharton Business School for *going too far* by distributing Georgist pamphlets and for promoting radical views like "inequality is wrong" and "children shouldn't be forced to work."*

"Wait," I said to Blackbeard, a couple of beers into his story, "you're telling me that the Robber Barons founded business schools *and the University of Chicago* because they were worried about Henry George?"

"Oh yes," he replied, leaning forward over the table. "You bet they did."

"Really?" I was worried this sounded dangerously like a conspiracy theory. I wondered if I should ask him about the moon landings or whether pigeons are controlled by the CIA. "Surely, if anything, they'd be more worried about socialism than Georgism?"

Socialism, incidentally, originally meant simply the opposite of *individualism*. It was a French idea, that began life as the philosophy of "Utopian Socialism" – rather than all of us being self-serving and competitive, we should work together more, and be nicer and more helpful to strangers. That the word *socialist* has become so charged is almost certainly the fault of Karl Marx, who in 1848 published *The Communist Manifesto* which was *extremely* socialist – in the sense of everyone forcibly sharing everything, pretty much on pain of death.

Blackbeard wasn't so sure. "The timings don't make sense. The problem of socialism for the Robber Barons in the late nineteenth century was less about the threat of violent communist revolution and more about labourers

---

* It was largely thanks to Nearing's response to his dismissal that the *tenure* system was introduced, which protects academics from being fired due to their views (but which didn't protect Nearing from being kicked out of the Communist Party for being too radical).

demanding better working conditions – have you heard of the Knights of Labor?"

"Err...no."

"They were a huge international organisation, something like a fifth of all workers in the USA, Canada, Australia and the UK were affiliated with them – they made demands for a maximum eight-hour working day. Imagine the hit to the Robber Barons' profits if their workers only worked eight hours a day!"

I was conscious that, once again, I was being paid to sit in a pub, and would be home in the early afternoon. Academia is a tough life. "So, what happened?"

"In 1886, strikes were orchestrated across America in support of this demand for an eight-hour day, with possibly as many as half a million workers downing their tools across the country. Then a riot broke out at a rally held at Haymarket Square in Chicago after a bomb was thrown at the police. The violence became known as the Haymarket Massacre, and it doomed the Knights of Labor."

"Why?" I asked, not quite sure that I followed.

Blackbeard grinned. He seemed to have even more gold teeth. "It acted as a catalyst to anti-union arguments, along the lines of, 'See, whenever labourers call for better working conditions, it ends in violence. So, let's end the calls for better working conditions.' The real battle between socialism – or in its extreme form, *communism*, wasn't to come until the twentieth century. Towards the end of the nineteenth century, the big intellectual challenge of the day wasn't Marxism, but Georgism."

"So you're saying that the Robber Barons funded American universities to churn out anti-Georgist economists?"

"Not exactly!" He banged his glass down on the table, then, slightly out of sequence, closed one eye and pretended to shoot a pistol at a student at the bar, who gratifyingly pretended to have been shot. "They were far too clever for that. They didn't want to debate his ideas, they wanted to extinguish them. Henry George said that we need to tax land, so the Robber Barons' pet economists had to make us believe that land didn't exist."

For a moment I thought I'd misheard. "What?! That's insane."

"Isn't it? Yet that's exactly what happened. And they had a weapon up their sleeves that Henry George didn't possess: mathematics."

—

It might help to put some of this in context, so here's a very a brief tour of some of the other big names in 19th-century economics.

In 1844, the philosopher and leading political economist John Stuart Mill wrote that the theories of "political economy" *assumed* that people always desired and worked towards obtaining more wealth. Though Mill didn't mean that in a good way. He thought this assumption was nonsense, since as much as people liked having more wealth, there were lots of other things they liked too – like not working. But he didn't see this wealth-seeking assumption as a problem because "no political economist was ever so absurd as to suppose that mankind are really thus constituted."

Keep that thought in mind – that it would be absurd to assume people always work towards maximising their wealth.

In 1862, the English economist William Stanley Jevons published *A General Mathematical Theory of Political Economy*, a book often credited with introducing mathematics to economics (the clue is in the book's title).

Jevons observed that every *extra* item we purchase must be worth a little bit less to us, as otherwise we would never stop buying things, and he developed the first mathematically precise (though theoretical) "demand curve", to show that people would only desire more of something if its price fell. It's the logic of the second beer not tasting as good as the first.

For this logic to hold, Jevons had to ignore John Stuart Mill's warning that it was absurd to assume people only cared about money, rather than, say, not getting too drunk to cycle home.

Jevons argued that we all sought to maximise our "utility", by which he meant *personal wealth* instead of *happiness*. This was a mathematical simplification, necessary as wealth can be measured precisely, but happiness can't. He even demonstrated how his theory worked by imagining a hypothetical person he called "calculating man".

You may have spotted that possibly the most problematic assumptions in economics had just been introduced – we now have "wealth means happiness" and "man constantly calculates the wealth he gets from transactions", neither of which, of course, are true. So in other words, we're now measuring everything in terms of *money*, and ignoring actual human nature, which you would only normally do if you were in the grips of some form of *mania*.

But as this demand curve was based on mathematics, and as mathematics is always true, then, Jevons declared, this curve must be as good as a scientific law. Hence the *Law* of Supply and Demand.

Next up, in 1874, a romantic novelist named Léon Walras published a book with the seriously unromantic title *Éléments d'économie politique pure*. It wasn't just the title that lacked romance – according to economist George Stigler, the book contained a "depressing array of mathematical formulas". It also, as you might guess from the title, had the misfortune to be written in French, meaning it wasn't widely read outside France.

But it was this book that first laid out a complete *general equilibrium theory*. That is to say, the **X** of supply and demand – the idea on page one of every economics course: that producers want to sell more as prices rise, consumers want to buy less, and as these desires can be predictably quantified a magical equilibrium arises where these two mathematically precise lines meet, a point at which there is no wasted surplus of production nor shortfall of desired goods.

Jevons and Walras's ideas about supply and demand and general equilibriums were then built upon by another mathematical prodigy, Cambridge Professor of Political Economy Alfred Marshall – the one who argued that degrees shouldn't be given to women.

Marshall did more than anyone else to popularise the "Law" of Supply and Demand, in a mammoth textbook called *Principles of Economics*, in 1890. Tellingly, note that it's no longer *political* economics. From now on, economics would be mathematical, and there's no scope for politics in mathematics, right?*

---

* The **X** of supply and demand is often called the Marshallian Cross, even though Walras actually got there first.

"The idea of man as a calculating, money-seeking being struck many of the Robber Barons as self-evidently true," said Blackbeard, clearly enjoying himself. "And general equilibrium theory argued that markets for everything, from railroad tickets to labourers' salaries, were the consequence of a natural law which shouldn't be interfered with, which was wonderful news if you monopolised the railroads and paid subsistence wages."

I was enjoying hearing this too, but I don't know if I was convinced.

"All right, so economics becomes a mathematical science, not a political argument. But what's that got to do with making land disappear?"

"Adam Smith had recognised that land ownership was intrinsically unfair – as rent should be free since land costs nothing to produce, but rent never is free – and Henry George had instigated an intellectual revolution by calling for the taxation of land. But now we have a new breed of mathematical economists, the *neoclassical* economists, with Marshall's textbook as their bible."

"Okay," I said, still not sure where Blackbeard was going with this, but keen to understand how you can make land disappear. "So what did Marshall say about land?"

He took a deep breath in. "Practically nothing! In the nine hundred pages of his era-defining textbook, he only mentions 'land' on about three of them, and most of that is a whinge about how hard farming is."

I deflated a little. Ignoring something is hardly the same as making it vanish. I said as much to Blackbeard.

"But that was just the first shot across the bows. Meanwhile, a chorus of academics at the universities founded and funded by the Robber Barons repeated and amplified each other's dismissals of Georgism. Remember that before the Robber Barons, there were barely any professional economists in the world, now suddenly there were dozens, hundreds, all ultimately paid for by the land-owning elite, who wanted equilibrium theory to be promoted because it defended the status quo, and wanted land taxes to be crushed. And the loudest and most effective voice in this chorus was none other than John Bates Clark."

"Who the prize is named after!" I said, far too excited by having some evidence of knowing something about this. The John Bates Clark Medal is awarded annually to whichever American economist under the age of forty is judged by the American Economic Association to have made the biggest contribution to the field.

"Yes, it's ridiculous. As a young man, Clark was a socialist who argued that it was 'a dangerous mistake to extol competition', but after joining Columbia University he soon got the message that the real danger was extolling Georgism. He wrote dozens of works directed against Henry George."

"You'd think one good one would be enough."

"Quite! The crux of his argument, and you'll be forgiven for thinking I'm making this up, given how crazy it sounds, was that capital – literally things like tractors and shovels and warehouses – has an 'immaterial essence' that 'transmigrates' and 'transmutates' into land."

"Transmutates?" I asked, wondering if this was a clever economics word. (It isn't.)

"Yup. It's almost spiritual. What he's getting at is that land is just another form of capital, and consequentially not worth analysing separately. So, Adam Smith was wrong. It's not *land*, *labour* and *capital* that make an economy grow, but just *labour* and *capital*."

"And that means no land tax?"

"Worse! If capital is the type of wealth that creates more wealth, it follows that if you tax capital, the economy will shrink. He was arguing for the entire tax burden to fall on labour."

"I can see why the establishment named a prize after him."

"It gets even worse. He went on to argue that land on its own is not wealth. It only becomes wealth when it is appropriated – so by appropriating land, landowners are actually creating wealth. We should be thanking them! The landowners who ultimately paid his salary loved him to bits for it."

"And people accepted that theory?"

"Of course! All the top economists were saying it's true. All the newspapers were saying it's true. It's in all the economics textbooks. And economics is a mathematical science now, remember, so who can argue with it? Yet it's loopy! Clark even argued that not only does capital have a 'deathless soul', but is also like 'jelly', in that it's mouldable into whatever form it's required to be in."

"Deathless soul jelly?"

"On the one hand, deathless soul jelly, on the other Stanley Jevons's *marginal utility theory*, to say that both labour and capital receive an amount of wealth proportionate to what they contribute to production. Which is a just a way to say *you get what you deserve*."

"And you think this was deliberate?"

"At first, for sure. Why else would Rockefeller and J P Morgan and the rest have funded all these economics departments? They kicked out the vicars who used to sit on university boards and replaced them with land-owning businessmen. Then after a while neoclassical economics was the only game in town. Students of economics were forced to learn it and professors were forced to teach it. They still are."

As we walked (a little off-balance) back to the campus, a thought occurred to me. In 2015, the British government had introduced something into all education centres called the Prevent Duty. It's a brilliant plan to tackle terrorism: getting everyone from nursery teachers to university lecturers to grass up any students who start acting strangely (even though arguably that could be said to be *all* students). Specifically, I'd been instructed by the university administrators to watch out for anyone getting radicalised by dangerous ideas.

I wondered, while hearing about Henry George and the rise of the neoclassical economists, whether *I* was perhaps in danger of becoming radicalised. Did I need to report myself?

I got back to the main atrium of the economics department and looked up at the TV screen that told students where their next lectures were being held, and with whom. My vision was a little blurry and I had to concentrate. I had thought I was finished for the day, but there on the screen, apparently due to teach a class that started five minutes ago, was my name. Ah.

8

THE DUMBEST IDEA IN THE WORLD (AND OTHER THINGS THEY TEACH YOU AT BUSINESS SCHOOL)

> *"Economics is really a religion. So why should you be puzzled by the fact that [economists] cling to and never give up their views despite frequent falsification?"*
> Joseph Stiglitz, economist

My tax-evasion book, *Taxtopia*, was released in March 2023. I'd tried quite hard in that book to sound as apolitical as I could and was quite proud that both the right-wing newspaper *The Sun* and the left-wing magazine *The Big Issue* asked me to write articles for them.

In that book, I didn't say that we needed to *eat the rich* or to *get the scroungers off benefits*, instead my goal was merely to highlight the absurdity of the world's tax systems – from the little quirks like the boxes of snails used to dodge property taxes and the court case to determine whether the X-men superheroes were human or not, to the more fundamental absurdity that rich people tend to pay a far smaller proportion of their wealth in taxes than poor people do.

I wrote about how a greater chunk of my grandmother's wealth had been taken in inheritance tax than had the Duke of Westminster's, and I outlined exactly how Starbucks and Facebook and Elon Musk can avoid paying tax. I thought I was quite light-hearted about it, more a "isn't this ridiculous?" than "let's smash capitalism!" I even argued that companies shouldn't pay tax.

All the same, one reviewer called me a Marxist.

I did, in fairness, read both Karl Marx's *Das Kapital* and *The Communist Manifesto* at university, as a course requirement, though all I really remember about them was how angry Marx was all the time – the closest he ever got to a joke was the line, "the last capitalist we hang shall be the one who sold us the rope."

What I hadn't known before is that Marx's economic philosophy built directly on the work of David Ricardo, who was of course himself inspired by Adam Smith.

Smith and Ricardo had both argued that the value of a commodity comes from the labour used to produce it. Marx pushed that idea to its revolutionary conclusion: if all value comes from labour, then the profit that capitalists make must be the result of exploitation – or, as he put it, not being one for subtlety, "Capital is dead labour, which, vampire-like, lives only by sucking living labour."

All three of them – Smith, Ricardo and Marx – agreed that society was divided into classes of landowners, labourers and capitalists, and that land, labour and capital were the essential inputs to economic production. Marx referred to landowners as a "parasitic class" – a relic from feudal days who did not produce anything themselves but extracted incomes simply by owning land. He called labourers the *proletariat*, from the Latin for *children*, as in Roman times a *proletarius* was a Roman citizen so poor that the only thing he could contribute to the state was his children, to be future workers. And the capitalists were the *bourgeoisie*, literally "town-dwellers", who exploited the poor, and did whatever the 19th-century equivalent was of watching Apple TV, holidaying in Tuscany and making their own houmous.

Marx saw this exploitation as part of a sweeping historical inevitability.

He went even further than Henry George and suggested that private property both created and exacerbated class oppression and was part of an exploitation that would become intolerable to the proletariat, who would inevitably rebel, seize power and create a classless communist utopia.

Interestingly, given how much more well known Marx is than George nowadays, when Karl Marx died in 1883 it was said, according to the historian Roy Douglas, that "there must have been dozens of Englishmen who had argued about Henry George for every one who had even heard of [Marx]." It's known that Marx owned several copies of *Progress and Poverty*, while Henry George confessed that he'd never read any of Marx's works.

—

I managed to make friends with one of my colleagues at the Institute for Fair Economics. She was called Kanya and had recently finished a PhD in a niche area of *econometrics* (which is probably the most mathematical branch of economics). She had a high fringe, a larger septum piercing than normal, often wore a denim jacket with anti-dairy industry stickers sewn onto it and brought her pet dog to the office (I think it was a whippet).

The newspapers at the time were filled with analysis of ongoing trade negotiations between the UK and the USA, which had hit a stumbling block over Britain's refusal to allow imports of American chicken. The issue was hygiene standards: American chicken farmers soak their chickens in chlorine, a practice which is banned throughout Europe. A large number of more right-wing politicians had been arguing that Britain should lift the ban. This was about free markets, they said, *let the people decide if they want chlorinated chicken or not.*

Ioannou had suggested that our institute should write a "think-piece" about deregulation in the food industry, purely for the publicity, which is how Kanya and I ended up working together.

I almost blew it. Seeing her animal rights stickers alongside her dog, I blurted out the first question that came to mind.

"So... is your dog a vegan?"

She glowered at me, thought for a moment, then gave me a two-word answer, the second word of which was "you". But then she laughed.

"Nah, he keeps eating squirrels."

In the 1850s, British Member of Parliament Thomas Wakley used *The Lancet* – the medical journal he had founded – to publish an analysis of the adulteration of foodstuffs. He found that everywhere he looked, inedible and even dangerous chemicals were being added to everyday items like bread, coffee, sugar, milk and tea. Plaster of Paris and chalk were being added to bread, strychnine was added to beer.

Thanks to his influence, in 1860 the Adulteration of Food and Drink Act made it a criminal offence to knowingly sell food which endangers health. You can imagine the free marketeers were appalled – surely consumers would reject adulterated foods, which would consequently drive such vendors out of business, without the need for legislation? Typical government nanny state, telling us we can't add rat poison to the beer we sell.

I asked Kanya if she thought that free markets would discourage unhygienic practices.

This was clearly something she'd spent a long time thinking about. "It's much cheaper to fool people with advertising and lobby for deregulation than it is to raise a chicken in an environment in which it's not crawling with parasites."

"You're such a *Marxist*," I said.

She laughed, then she chewed the idea for a while and said, "I think the only people who are still Marxists haven't heard of the Solow residual."

"Ha, yeah, right," I said, in what I think may not have been a terribly convincing impression of someone who knew what she was talking about. I waited a few moments, then asked if she wanted a coffee. As the kettle boiled, I took out my phone and tapped into Google: *Solow residual*.

Amazingly, it seems that no one properly checked whether Adam Smith's holy trinity of land, labour and capital were really driving economic growth until 1956, when an economist at the Massachusetts Institute of Technology called Robert Solow decided to put the theory to the test with actual data.

Solow measured how the increase in wealth of various countries correlated with both their number of workers and with the amount of capital that each worker had access to (largely measured by investments in factories and machinery). He ignored land, as the amount of available land stays the same.

When Solow plotted these data points together what he found should have, in many ways, overturned close to 200 years of economic thought:

There was almost no relationship.

More precisely, in some countries only 13 per cent of economic growth seemed to be due to the combination of capital and labour. Meaning that the residual amount, the remaining 87 per cent of growth, came from something else.

Some economists had, by Solow's time, acknowledged that a fourth factor, "entrepreneurialism", was needed to glue the other factors together. Which is fine, but surely 87 per cent of economic growth wasn't just due to people saying, "You there, yes you on the tractor, start ploughing that field!"

Solow joked that "if God had meant there to be more than two factors of production, He would have made it easier to draw three-dimensional diagrams." In the end, he reasoned that the extra growth (his missing residual amount) must be coming from what he called "technical change" and is now known as *total factor productivity*.

By this, he meant improved education and new skills and organisational techniques, but mostly, new technology. After all, it's new technology that lets us do more, with less. If it used to take a dozen men to plough a field and now it's done with one man and his tractor, that's economic growth (especially if the other eleven men find something else to do).

It was like economists had just been looking at the farm labourers and the investment in a new machine, without recognising that it was the initial *invention* of the tractor that had been the important bit. It would be mad to study the Renaissance or the Age of Enlightenment while ignoring the role of the printing press, or to disregard the steam engine and the spinning jenny in the Industrial Revolution, yet by only focusing on "labour" and "capital", economists had done just that.

But if the vast majority of economic growth comes from technology, what the hell have economists been doing all this time? Shouldn't the majority of economics be answering the question "How can a society best organise itself to foster innovation?" To which the answer is probably *pour money into schools.**

In fact, it's really striking that when you read most histories of economics, they explain the wonders of increasing wealth by pointing to all the new technologies we have. The economic historian Andrew Leigh uses the example of the progression from wood fires to oil lamps to candles to light bulbs, and highlights a marvellous statistic that the earnings from work are 300,000 times higher today than they were in prehistoric times, as measured by the amount of artificial light it affords.

But . . . why is that a history of economics? Shouldn't that be a history of, well, technology? Sure, if one economic system fosters innovation better than another, that matters, but which one does? Should we let venture capitalists pick winners, or just give NASA a blank cheque? Every economist claims *their* version of economics is the best for fostering innovation, in much the same way that every parent claims their own child is gifted.†

You might think that the realisation that labour and capital make up a tiny proportion of economic growth would prompt economists to come up with a new theory. Instead, this is what I had to teach to my undergraduates (it's called the Cobb–Douglas equation):

Aggregate output [that's the size of the economy] *is equal to labour × capital × total factor productivity. Total factor productivity is everything that is not explained by labour and capital, such as technology.*

I really, really wish I was kidding – but I'm literally paraphrasing this from a textbook that's on my lap as I type. Again, perhaps I'm missing something, but

---

* And abolish INSET days.
† Other economists have pointed out a flaw of using *technology* as a stand-in for "total factor productivity": that once something is invented, everyone can get access to it. For instance, more than half of Bangladeshis have smartphones, four-fifths of Kenyan children have been vaccinated against common illnesses and both Algeria and Paraguay have put satellites into space. All four of these countries are still staggeringly poor.

isn't this nonsense? It's like a cake recipe that says *add flour to eggs and, um, other stuff*. I mean, sure, that's true – but the *other stuff* is what distinguishes one cake from another.

The *other stuff* of the equation are all the messy variables that go into economic growth – schooling, corruption, energy costs, taxes, gender norms, healthcare, natural resources, levels of trust, rental costs, road networks ... but they're much harder to measure, so economic models often simply assume they don't change and stick with Adam Smith's notion of "capital" and "labour".*

—

I didn't see Blackbeard at the university that week, but he emailed to invite me to a varsity rugby match later that month. I assumed he meant *watching* rather than *playing*, so accepted his offer. Unfortunately, I did see Professor Alva – the one who had somewhat indelicately informed me of the complaints I'd received from my students.

"How are you today?" she asked, with the echoing tones of an executioner enquiring what I'd like for my final meal.

"Good, thanks, I—"

She cut me off. "Listen, just a quick word, I'm sure you weren't, but I happened to overhear some of your students commenting that you were – like I say, I'm sure you weren't, but possibly a little tipsy in one of your lectures last week?"

"Oh," I said, trying to sound surprised. Bloody Blackbeard and his three-pint stories about John D Rockefeller. "I had a cold last week, maybe I sounded bunged-up?"

"They described you as 'shit-faced'."

"Um. I have a slight speech impediment."

"They said you were singing."

"Ermm ... It was more of a *rap*."

---

* Obviously, I don't mean *all* economic models. Some are incredibly sophisticated. But some are complete crap.

"I just thought I'd mention it." She gave me that weird hostile *wink* thing, again. "Perhaps no more rapping in class?"

"Sure," I said. "Sorry."

—

I think I can correlate my enjoyment of every job I've ever had to whether I had a decent work buddy, and once I found Kanya I started spending longer hours in the office. She was something of an enigma.

She was rude about every economic theory out there, but at the same time absolutely loved *economics* as a discipline. Her mathematical skills were off the charts, but she said she hated expressing economic ideas numerically, which given she'd just finished a PhD that was entirely about expressing economic ideas numerically seemed particularly bizarre. She was also responsible for teaching me something I didn't know about Adam Smith that has really stayed with me.

Most people's main takeaway from Smith's *The Wealth of Nations* is that free markets don't need to be centrally organised, as people will unintentionally benefit society if all they do is pursue their own goals. The magic of capitalism is that by simply trying to get what we ourselves want, we end up producing what others needed.

Indeed, about the most famous concept in all of economics is from *The Wealth of Nations*, when, during a discussion on where merchants should invest, Smith states that a person would be "led by an invisible hand to promote an end which was no part of his intention".

This providential *invisible hand* is often accepted as an article of faith: free markets will solve the world's problems without government intervention. To anyone who has done very well out of free markets it's become practically heresy to argue against it.

Smith never quite explained what he meant by the invisible hand, but it's perhaps best demonstrated by his oft-quoted line, "It is not from the benevolence of the butcher, the brewer or the baker that we expect our dinner, but from their regard to their own interest."

This is usually taken to mean that it's thanks to the butcher, brewer and baker having a *profit-motive* that we get to eat our tasty dinner. Though that's possibly not quite what he meant. Adam Smith saw himself as a moral philosopher – in the same year that *The Wealth of Nations* was published, his fellow moral philosopher Jeremy Bentham wrote: "It is the greatest happiness for the greatest number that is the measure of right and wrong."

Self-interest, to Adam Smith, didn't just mean *money*. It meant *self-worth*, more like what today we'd call "self-realisation". He actively argued *against* profit-seekers whose interests didn't align with those of the rest of society, and at no point said that markets are infallible or that selfishness always leads to beneficial outcomes or that governments should never intervene. Smith was very concerned about monopolies and corruption and the neglect of the poor.

One Sunday, Kanya and her partner invited my family round for lunch, and while I don't want to suggest that all we talked about was economics, she did mention that Adam Smith's famous quote about the *benevolence of the butcher* overlooks an important detail: Smith lived with his mother – who, among other chores, made him his dinner. Kanya had a framed poster hanging on the wall of her small kitchen, on which was the following quote, laid out like a poem:

> *It may not be for the benevolence of the butcher*
> *that we expect our dinner,*
> *but it was from the benevolence of Smith's mother*
> *that he could expect his.*

"That's funny," I said to her, when I saw it.

She scowled at me (though it didn't help that I'd asked for "real" milk in my coffee). "Do you think it's funny that unpaid labour is ignored?"

I had to think fast. "You're *almost* unpaid. I'm not ignoring you."

She weighed that up, then softened a bit. "All right, I'll tell you something that *is* funny." She put the lid on her carrot casserole, opened her laptop and started googling something as she spoke. "People obsess about Smith's *invisible hand*, like it's the hand of God or something, but do you know how often Smith used that phrase?"

"No...?"

"Three times. In all his books. And each time it meant something completely different. There's this Harvard history professor who reckons Adam Smith himself thought the invisible hand was just an ironic joke. Isn't that hilarious?"

I didn't want to confess that I didn't really get what was so funny.

"Imagine if he was still alive," she added, perhaps wondering why I wasn't smiling. "He'd be like, *What, my 'invisible hand' theory? You've spent two hundred and fifty years obsessing about that? Guys, I was kidding! It was part of my 'opaque foot' routine...*"

I did actually laugh at that, but more for the ridiculous voice she used for Adam Smith. She made him sound like a Scottish Bugs Bunny.

—

I thought about Kanya's comments about Marx and Smith, and Solow and chlorinated chicken, for quite a long time. She had been through almost a decade of academic study and had emerged from it deeply cynical, but she was still, and I think this is very important to say, completely enthralled by the ideals (if not the ideas) of economics – that, done right, it has the power to improve the world.

I especially thought about this as so little of what I was teaching at the university seemed to be about improving the world. More often than not, it was more about *gaming* the system.

I mean, shortly after Kanya and I wrote about food regulations, I was meant to deliver a lecture on pricing strategies. Despite the course beginning with an explanation of how supply and demand created an equilibrium price, without any sense of irony we then went through page after page about how businesses actually decide prices *in the real world*.

There was *product line pricing*, where you sell one product cheaply (like a flight) but then sell the add-ons expensively (like luggage and "speedy boarding"); a *loss leader*, where you sell something below cost, to entice customers to spend more elsewhere (Britain banned the sale of beer below cost in 2014, as supermarkets kept selling crates of beer for ridiculously low prices, knowing that shoppers would fill their trolleys with other things too).

Perceived value pricing (also known as "snob pricing") is deliberately setting a high price to suggest a higher quality – though a follow-on from this is the tactic used by beer brand Stella Artois, which ran an advertising campaign saying Stella was "reassuringly expensive"; to begin with, the beer was pricier than other beers, but over time the price fell even while the adverts continued, the idea being that consumers would say, "Oh wow, look, there's a great deal on this Stella Artois, it's the same price as Foster',s."

The list never seemed to end. It all involved trickery. It felt like the rotten end of capitalism but our textbook seemed to celebrate it. There was *decoy pricing* and *penetration pricing*, *market segmentation*, *freemiums* and psychological tricks like removing the £ or $ sign to remove any association with money, which is why restaurant menus sometimes say things like *soup 5, salad 7, steak 22*. You may have noticed that you'll see a higher price online when you are using your phone compared to when you are using a laptop. Economists helped come up with that idea.*

The problem I had with all of this is that none of it was about making a better product – it was purely about converting a "consumer surplus" (that idea that some customers would pay more, but don't have to) into a "supplier surplus" (that a business would be able to sell a product for less, but can get away with charging more). I asked Kanya what she thought of this.

"Yeah, depressing, isn't it? It's why so many restaurants are part of chains. They're not successful because their food is better, their economists have just worked out how to squeeze every last penny out of you. It's like when you get charged for condiments. Why are they fucking charging for condiments?"

"Aren't they just finding an equilibrium price for mayonnaise?" I asked, using a tone that I'm pretty sure indicated I was joking.

---

* Yes, always use a laptop to buy online, as many vendors will automatically offer you a lower price as they know you're more likely to shop around and compare prices if you're not on your phone.

She rolled her eyes at me. "I had a professor at university who used to joke that economics would be a lot better if Alfred Marshall had a thicker pen."

I laughed, but I wasn't sure if I was meant to. "What does that mean?"

"Here," she said, pulling out a sheet of paper, "I'll show you."

And then she drew this:

"So what's the bit in the middle?" I asked.

"The real world," she said. "Messy, isn't it?"

—

I asked Kanya for her opinion about whether it mattered that I was supposed to teach economic ideas that I didn't necessarily believe in.

"Relax... no one takes all that fundamentals stuff seriously," she told me.

"Then why are we still expected to teach it?"

She gave the same sort of shrug as Blackbeard had. "I dunno. I guess we just always have. I suppose it just provides a framework for other ideas."

That gave me the chills. Especially as one of those *other ideas* that I was meant to teach was something called *shareholder value maximisation*. I really struggled to contain myself as I walked through the theory with my students.

—

In 1970 the economist Milton Friedman (the one who didn't like minimum wages) wrote an enormously influential article with the title "The social responsibility of business is to increase its profits". In this article, he stated explicitly that the managers of a company had no duty to care for anyone other than shareholders. A company's money ultimately belongs to the company's shareholders, so managers at that company should not do anything to reduce shareholder wealth.

So, for example, when I recently overheard two shelf stackers at my local supermarket complaining that they were no longer given tea and biscuits at breaktime, Milton Friedman would say, "Good. Those weren't their biscuits, they belonged to the shareholders."

This view was not unique to Friedman, though it became known as the Friedman Doctrine, and was part of the business philosophy called "shareholder value maximisation".

The earliest recorded mention of shareholder value maximisation pre-dates Milton Friedman's article by a few years. In 1962, a US textile company called Indian Head Mills announced that their objective was not "to grow bigger for the sake of size, not to become more diversified, not to make the most or best of anything, not to provide jobs, have the most modern plants, the happiest customers, [or] lead in new product development" but "solely to improve the inherent value of the common stockholders' equity". In other words, the company would do everything and *anything* it could to boost its share price.

In 1981, during a speech at the Pierre Hotel in New York, Jack Welch, the CEO of General Electric, then America's largest industrial company, argued that all companies should adopt shareholder value maximisation. All that matters is share prices. Companies should charge as much as they possibly can, while squeezing suppliers, reducing employee pay and selling a shoddier product.

This was an era when American Airlines is celebrated for *removing an olive* from their in-flight meal – supposedly saving the airline $40,000 per year. Their passengers were still paying for that olive, of course, but now the shareholders were getting to eat it.

Imperial Chemical Industries (or "ICI") was Britain's largest industrial company when I was growing up – at its peak it employed 130,000 people. Where once their stated aim was "to be the world's leading chemical company", by 1994 that had changed to "our objective is to maximise value for our shareholders."

In the short term, shareholder value maximisation transfers an enormous amount of wealth from employees, suppliers and customers to shareholders. But in the long term it just pisses off the company's employees, suppliers and customers.

Take it to its extremes – and a worrying number of executives have – and it's actually *ethically correct* to sell a dud product to someone if you think you can get away with it.

It's *morally good* to renege on a contractual agreement if you think your counterparty doesn't have the resources to sue you, and it's worth companies borrowing heavily if it facilitates paying bigger dividends in the short term, because in the short term all of these things boost profits . . . until they don't.

Part of the appeal to directors of shareholder value maximisation is that share prices are always based on future profits rather than historic ones, and are especially skewed towards profits made in the near future, so if you can boost profits over the next few years at the expense of profits after that period, share prices will usually rise.

But then those few good years go by and you're stuck with staff who've quit, suppliers who don't want to deal with you, no new innovative products to sell and customers who have gone elsewhere. It turns out that those other stakeholders are important.

Many analysts came to realise that, in the long term, shareholder value maximisation doesn't maximise shareholder value.*

Even Jack Welch, the CEO of General Electric, has conceded this, calling

---

* I thought about this when Netflix started cutting back on new content, raising prices and showing adverts. It was done to keep shareholders happy. But I'm not sure "let's sell a worse product at higher prices" is a good long term business strategy. Time will tell.

shareholder value maximisation "the dumbest idea in the world". Both Indian Head Mills and ICI have now gone out of business.

It was still on my syllabus, though.

—

I realised that I was having a crisis of faith. Deep down, I still want to be that card-carrying capitalist that I was as a teenager, and fundamentally I realised that I still believed in the power of free markets and free trade to improve the world, but I began to wonder if it really was a faith more akin to a religious belief than anything based on actual, sound facts, let alone science. My faith was certainly not helped when my washing machine broke.

I assumed that with the right YouTube video I would be able to fix it. After an hour of careful dismantling, I discovered that the plastic cam belt had slipped off the drum, but there seemed no way to get it back on. At that point, I did what I should have done to start with, and phoned an expert.

"If the cam belt's gone you'll need to replace the whole machine," he said. *Typical*.

A cam belt in a washing machine is just a loop of plastic, so I can't believe a new belt would cost more than a couple of pounds, but no, the machine was designed in a way that meant the entire thing needed replacing if one small part broke. I think I knew who to blame: a man called Bernard London, who in the 1930s had moved from Russia to New York and had tried to make a name for himself by writing pamphlets about how to save the economy, which he self-published.

These pamphlets shared a theme. To pull America out of recession the government needed to *break things*. To literally smash what we owned to pieces, in order to force us to buy new goods.

As he put it, "Factories, warehouses, and fields are still intact and are ready to produce in unlimited quantities, but the urge to go ahead has been paralyzed by a decline in buying power." This decline would be fixed if the government bought up old machines and old goods, and destroyed them. This would force consumers to buy new goods, which would mean factory owners had to employ people to make those new goods, so the economy would spring back to life.

Each pamphlet he wrote used the same phrase in their titles, words that had never been seen in print together before: *Planned Obsolescence*.

Flash forward 20 years. By the 1950s, the US car industry had a problem – virtually everyone who needed a car had bought one. The industry had been too successful for its own good. So what to do? Leading industrial designer Brook Stevens stumbled across Bernard London's pamphlet and a light bulb lit up (a light bulb which, since the 1920s, had been designed not to last).

What if car makers brought out new designs every few years? Couple the release of new models with heavy advertising campaigns and everyone will want a new car, even if their current one isn't broken. The new cars could include new gizmos to make your neighbours envious. *Oh, your car doesn't have a cigarette lighter? How old fashioned!*

The strategy worked so well that by the 21st century everything from smartphones to frying pans were designed not to last, or at least to *feel* outdated.

Some economists (and my industrial designer friend) claim that planned obsolescence is a myth. *Of course the screw in your frying pan is cheap – the whole pan is cheap – that's a good thing.* But so worried is the European Union about planned obsolescence that they've introduced a law that both outlaws the deliberate shortening of a product's lifespan and requires products to be repairable.

Free market advocates are horrified – imagine making it cheaper to fix something rather than buy a new one! Unfortunately, this law has come too late for my washing machine. (And Brexit means it won't apply in Britain.)

But then, like Gideon asking for a supernatural sign from God to prove His existence (take that, Father Nicholson, who thought I wasn't listening in Sunday school), I stumbled on a fascinating example of one of the world's most successful businesses turning its back on both shareholder value maximisation and planned obsolescence.

—

In 1914, newspaper headlines in America carried stories of a new "gold rush" – the car-making industrialist Henry Ford had decided, seemingly out of nowhere, to *double* his factory workers' wages.

To explain the motivation behind this move, he published a 41-page pamphlet explaining that "The sole and simple aim of the entire scheme is to better the financial and moral standard of each employee and those of his household." He referred to the deal as "profit sharing".

The pamphlet explains that employees are expected to put aside some of their pay to save for the future (though Ford acknowledges that employees with six children might save less than those with only two or three). The pamphlet also advises that employees should use the pay rise to buy a house in a nice neighbourhood and send their kids to school. Several pages of the pamphlet are about how employees should use soap and brush their teeth.

As an exercise in benevolent, or perhaps patronising, paternalism it's incredible stuff – the pamphlet has photos of the kind of houses the workers were expected to buy, and even what their bedrooms and bathrooms should look like (very Edwardian chic). After a few months or so of earning these higher wages, the pamphlet suggests, they should add an extension to their homes, after a year and a bit they should add an extra floor.

I mean, hell, I'll use soap for that sort of pay.

To qualify for the "profit share", Ford's employees had to be over 22 years old, unless they were married (Ford warned against younger men marrying "hastily" in order to qualify for higher pay). More significantly, they also had to be sober, hard-working and "clean", and the Ford Motor Company employed investigators to check that employees weren't spending their bonuses on "riotous living".

Sure, it's patronising, but reading this pamphlet more than a hundred years later, and especially looking at the photos of the fantastic houses you could buy on a Ford salary, it's hard not to be moved. Ford states that this profit-sharing arrangement will "provide for families in sickness and health and in old age and to take away fear and worry. To make a well-rounded life and not a mere struggle for existence . . . to implant in the heart of every individual a desire to Help the Other Fellow . . . to help uplift humanity."

This is what nowadays is called *stakeholder* value maximisation, the idea that businesses should ensure the wellbeing of everyone connected to that business – the suppliers, the staff, the customers, the bank, the neighbours, even their rivals, not just because it's morally right, but because in the long run it's better for everybody (including the shareholders).

At the time of his death, Henry Ford was one of the richest people in the world. So it turns out you can pay your staff well and still be a billionaire.

I was reminded of Henry Ford when I read that Elon Musk had laid off 14,000 employees at Tesla due to falling demand for their cars, but had also gone to court to argue that he personally deserved a $56 *billion* bonus. A quick bit of maths, and you'll see that $56 billion could have kept those employees in work for about a hundred years.

Musk has said that "capitalism is not just successful, but morally right." It must be easy to think that when you're the richest man in the world, and you need a justification for why it's okay to lay off thousands of your staff while paying yourself a bonus.

There's an irony here that Tesla has received around $38 billion of government support. Governments across the world have subsidised buyers of Tesla's cars, and at their peak in 2024 a US government carbon-trading scheme meant that *half* of Tesla's profits were due to the sale of carbon emission credits to other car-makers.

Fortune magazine published an article titled "The true genius of Elon Musk is his 'subsidy harvesting strategy'". Musk himself has acknowledged that Tesla came close to bankruptcy several times, including in 2010, when crisis was only averted after the Department of Energy loaned them $465 million. That's not free-market capitalism, that's Big Government intervention – the sort of state subsidies you encounter in socialist countries. Still, I hope he enjoyed his bonus.

9

THE SECRET CAT AND THE UN-SECRET SOCIETY

"The problem of the modern economy is not a failure of a knowledge of economics; it's a failure of a knowledge of history"
John Kenneth Galbraith, economist

I told Ioannou that I would leave the office early on Tuesday as I was having lunch with two members of the Henry George Foundation.

"The *what* foundation?" he asked.

"Henry George. They promote his ideas."

Ioannou looked at me, puzzled. "I don't know who that is," he said.

I'd arranged to meet at a restaurant attached to a trendy theatre near Waterloo Station in London. One of the foundation's members, David, had arrived before me and as I shook his hand he gave me a big smile and asked if I had *seen the cat*. I looked around the restaurant, which was large and high-ceilinged but mostly empty. There were a couple of waiters and an ancient couple struggling with their soup. But no cat.

"Um, no?"

It turned out that there were quite a number of Henry George societies to pick from. The Foundation I'd got in touch with was founded in 1929 and is now affiliated to the School of Philosophy and Economic Science, which

I'd seen posters for on the London Underground but didn't otherwise know anything about.

I sidestepped the *cat* question and asked David how he got into economics.

"I'm not an economist," he said, a bit surprised that I'd asked. "I'm an engineer. I used to work for Thames Water."

At one point in his career, he explained, he worked on a project to clean up the Ganges River in India, and the BBC had made a documentary about him, called *Thames Wallah*, narrated by Kenneth Branagh. This was not quite the biography I was expecting, but then I'm not sure what I was expecting.

David told me that, as part of his work at the Henry George Foundation, he hands out flyers about land taxes at political party conferences, and he gave me one of the flyers. I looked at it, politely, not really getting the point of it.

It didn't feature a slogan or graph or any traditional economic bit of data, but instead a hand-drawn picture of a farmhouse with a tree in the foreground and a couple of animals sitting on the grass. Was one of the animals a cat?

"Erm...?"

But then I saw it. Hidden within the empty spaces of the branches of the tree was the outline of an impossibly large cat. It was one of those optical illusions where at first nothing seems amiss, but once you see the cat you can't unsee it.

Right, I thought, *a metaphor. Gotcha.*

We were soon joined by Andrew, a research fellow at University College London who had been a business owner and now taught at the School of Philosophy and Economic Science.

The restaurant was wonderfully relaxed and both David and Andrew spoke in an almost hypnotically measured way. I began by asking Andrew about a letter he had written to *The Economist* magazine on the subject of Singapore.

—

Singapore is one of those places that really stands out from the competition, but its success often seems enigmatic. It has a free education system that is frequently judged one of the best in the world, it has free universal healthcare that is ranked in the top five globally, and it is richer, per person, than the United States. Its crime rates are so low that a Singaporean client (from my tax advisory days) once laughed at me when I worried about leaving my laptop on an outdoor table as we crossed a busy square to visit a food van. As in, "why would anyone steal a laptop?" Such an attitude would be unthinkable in London.

But not only are crime rates among the lowest in the world, guess what else is? Singapore's tax rates.

Companies pay minimal taxes on their profits, sales taxes are tiny, there's no capital gains tax or inheritance tax, and income taxes start low and barely push above a 20 per cent rate, and even then only for millionaires.

So... what explains this puzzle? How can a country have both low rates of tax and world-leading public services?

—

Andrew's letter to *The Economist* magazine had pointed out that the Singaporean government has a virtual monopoly on *land*, thanks to a piece of legislation introduced in 1966 by Singapore's first prime minister, Lee Kuan Yew, called the Land Acquisition Act, which allowed the Singaporean government to purchase land for any state purpose.

"This wasn't a land grab," Andrew explained, "landowners were paid for their land, though nor was it an opportunity for landowners to extort the state, as the Act allowed the government to buy land at its *existing* value. This meant that any uplift in the value of land that arose from public infrastructure projects, or even other landowners' private developments, was captured by the state, and not by individual landowners. By 2002, 90 per cent of Singapore's land was in public ownership. This meant that the government had an enormous source of income: rent."

I thought of all the rent I'd paid in my own life, and all the interest I'd paid on a mortgage. None of it had gone to my government. It had made me poorer, and made my landlord or my bank richer. I said as much.

"Imagine if instead of paying landlords and banks you'd paid the government rent, instead?" said Andrew. "The government could spend their income on world-class healthcare and education and infrastructure that makes everyone not just richer, but happier."

"And reduce taxes?"

"Yes. Because the government has all this extra income from its monopoly on land, the government can now *massively* lower taxes, so you end up richer, *twice over* – you're paying less tax and receiving better public services."

That didn't seem so bad. In England, half of all the land is owned by less than 1 per cent of the population, including 30 per cent that is still owned by aristocrats.*

"But has Singapore eliminated poverty?" I asked.

Andrew laughed. "Oh no, there's some terrible inequality in Singapore – the best land is still in private hands."

In my tax career I'd often thought of Singapore as a tax haven. Taxes there, as a percentage of national income, hover around 12 per cent, compared to about 25 per cent in the USA, 29 per cent in Australia, 35 per cent in the UK and 44 per cent in France.

But rent paid to the government is not tax, it's rent, so isn't included in these figures.†

"The biggest mistake Henry George made," said Andrew, "was the words he chose to describe his solution. He shouldn't have called for a single tax on land, he should have called for the abolition of tax. People could carry on paying rent, but it now goes to the government."

I could see how that would be more popular.

"All right, but wouldn't a land tax force little old ladies out of their childhood homes?"

---

* It's even worse in Scotland, where more than half the land is owned by just over 400 people.
† Indeed, while it looks like there's much less tax in the USA than the UK, the US figures don't include health insurance premiums, which aren't necessary in the UK because of the National Health Service. If instead of saying "tax" we said something clunky but more internationally equivalent, like "compulsory deductions from income plus payments for services usually provided by the state", then the US has a "tax" burden closer to France's.

"And orphans," replied Andrew, with a smile. "You could always defer the land tax until death. Or you could argue that large homes should be lived in by large families."

I was determined to pick holes in their argument. "But what if I wanted to go and live off-grid in the wilderness – wouldn't I be forced to pay an annual tax?"

"Not if it really was the *wilderness*," said David. "If the land wasn't wanted by anyone else, the tax could be zero."

"Wouldn't it be too complicated?"

"America already has land taxes. In some cities, local tax rates are deliberately split between a *land* proportion and a *property* proportion. Places that have raised land taxes and lowered property taxes have seen derelict lots restored, and increased employment and lowered crime."

"But doesn't it mean that if a trendy new restaurant opened next to this one then the owners of *this* restaurant would have to pay more tax – because suddenly the local area is more popular?"

"Why would that be a bad thing? If this restaurant got more customers because of the actions of someone else, why shouldn't they pay for it?"

I was struggling to find holes in their argument, so I decided to change tack.

"What do you do at the School of Philosophy and Economic Science when you're not promoting Henry George?" I asked.

"We meditate," said David.

I laughed, assuming he was joking.

"Meditation is part of all of our courses," said Andrew, with a smile. "Some of our students find it a bit strange."

I wondered how my students would feel if I said, *Right, put away your textbooks, let's meditate.*

Actually, they'd probably love it.

"Cool," I said.

Eventually, we got up to leave. Just as I was putting on my coat, Andrew thought to add, "Just one more thing. We're not a cult."

I laughed. And then he added, "Just in case you've read that we are."

I felt my journalistic instincts kicking in. "Um, where would I have read that?"

He waved his hand casually as if gently swatting away a troublesome fly. "Oh, there were some allegations made by the *Evening Standard* years ago. Silly stuff. You know, dominant personalities, all blown out of proportion."

That evening, I told Henrí that the Henry George duo had claimed not to be part of a cult, *which is exactly what a cult would say*. "And they meditate!"

"So do I," she said. "So does your dad."

"Yeah, but..."

She gave me a look.*

I wasn't entirely convinced by Blackbeard's story about Rockefeller being responsible for the decline of Georgism, but at the same time *something* had to be responsible for it. I mean, in 1927 the esteemed American philosopher and educational reformer John Dewey was saying that no one had the right to call themselves educated unless they were acquainted with Henry George. Georgism was still being discussed in the British parliament in the 1940s.

In 1946, the novelist Aldous Huxley wrote in his preface to *Brave New World* that he wished he'd included a genuinely utopian alternative – he referred to it as the *possibility of sanity*. In that utopian world, he wrote, economics would be "decentralist and Henry-Georgian".

I was still busy promoting *Taxtopia*, and on the podcast circuit I got chatting to the *Sunday Times* journalist Rob Dix, who is the author of a brilliant book called *Seven Myths About Money*. He happens to host his own podcast, called *The Property Podcast*, so I thought he might be an ideal person to speak to about Henry George,

"I envy your anonymity," Rob said, when I explained about the number of different fake names, dodgy voices and "burner" email addresses I had to use to conceal my true identity. "What an exciting life."

---

* For the record, no, I don't think either the Henry George Foundation or the School of Philosophy and Economic Science are cults. Both David and Andrew were lovely and really helpful, the robes they gave me fit well and the ritual sacrifice after our lunch was a right lark.

I laughed. "Yup. Nothing says *exciting life* like being an anonymous accountant."

I asked Rob if he thought it was true that powerful landowners had suppressed Henry George's theories. He wasn't so sure.

"The reality is even more depressing," he said. "So many people have their net worth, retirement plans and identity tied up in their homes that it's easy for politicians to turn a majority against land value taxes. Besides, land value tax is simple and efficient – which probably explains its total lack of popularity among politicians and bureaucrats, who feel personally threatened by any policy that doesn't require a five-hundred-page implementation manual and a sprawling new department to administer."

I laughed again. That was certainly my experience of taxation. There's no particular reason for tax law to be complicated, other than the hundreds of thousands of accountants who benefit from its complexity, and lean on politicians to keep it that way.

"There is, though, one genuinely good reason to fear land value taxes," he continued. "Henry George envisioned them as a 'single tax' – elegant, self-funding, and capable of replacing all others. But that was a hundred and fifty years ago, when today's extent (and cost) of government involvement in our lives would have been unimaginable. If we see land value taxes in our lifetimes, we can safely anticipate it being yet another additional layer rather than a replacement for anything."

That, again, certainly chimes with how most, if not *all* new taxes work. No government ever says, "We've just introduced a plastic packaging tax, so we'll scrap inheritance tax." I'd vote for land taxes as a replacement for other taxes, but I couldn't see myself voting for just *extra* taxes.

—

Eventually, I developed my own theory about why Henry George got forgotten. I'm not so sure it was just the Robber Barons, though they played their part, or just the rise in home ownership making us all wary of land taxes. Instead, I think we can trace the origin of Georgism's demise to a single event, at a single place, in April 1947.

Economists and politicians from all over the world were meeting in Geneva to thrash out an agreement on international trade – part of the long disarming of the tariff wars of the 1930s (that included the Bretton Woods conference). The Austrian economist Friedrich Hayek used the gathering as an opportunity to invite several dozen leading economists and philosophers to the Hotel du Parc, beneath the mountain of Mont Pelerin, on the other side of the lake to the trade conference.

Friedrich Hayek was a tall, lean man with a neat moustache, wire-rimmed spectacles and the bearing of a fastidious professor. Softly spoken and impeccably polite in person, he nonetheless wrote with the intensity of someone convinced that the wrong footnote could end civilisation. He began his career in post-imperial Vienna and by the 1940s had moved to London and made a name for himself in academic circles. His polite manner disguised a fiery conviction that economic freedom was inseparable from political freedom. He received international attention with his 1944 book, *The Road to Serfdom* (published in America by the Rockefeller-founded University of Chicago), in which he fiercely argued against state intervention in free markets, and in particular that governments should not interfere with the ownership of property.

The backdrop to this meeting (and Hayek's book) was the spectacular failure of neoclassical economics to predict the 1929 Wall Street Crash, nor deal with its aftermath.

Stock-market jitters had begun in the spring of 1929, and then exploded (if jitters can explode) on Thursday 24 October, when panic-selling swept the stock exchanges, wiping 90 per cent off the price of most investments. What followed was a period of mass unemployment and widespread bankruptcies. The stock market didn't recover their losses until the 1950s (though obviously the Second World War didn't help).*

---

* The *Brooklyn Daily Eagle* remains my favourite record of "Black Thursday", as the first day of the crash became known, for use of the headline: "Wall St. in panic as stocks crash, attempt made to kill Italy's Crown Prince." I'm still trying to work out how the two events were linked.

Central to the neoclassical economics of the Robber Baron-funded economics departments (especially at the University of Chicago) was the idea of equilibriums – that, if left alone, markets would naturally find the "correct" price for all goods. People are *rational*, after all, so if they saw that share prices were shooting upwards despite no underlying increase in company profits, they would hardly rush out to buy *more* shares, would they? They certainly wouldn't be so irrational as to borrow money to buy those shares, thus risking bankruptcy if the share prices fell, would they? And surely banks wouldn't gamble with their depositors' money by speculatively investing in bubbling stock markets, right?

Yet that's exactly what had happened in the build-up to the crash.

To the free marketeers – people like Friedrich Hayek – the joblessness and poverty that followed the Wall Street Crash was just a market correction, a "necessary evil". Give it time, and the market will recover. Sure, a global depression followed in the wake of the crash as people lost their life savings, companies shut down, and massive unemployment and resentment fuelled the rise of fascism in Europe, but relax – in the long run everything will be okay.

Well, step forward Cambridge economist John Maynard Keynes with his famous retort: "In the long run, we are all dead." Remember that he was the one who argued that whenever there was a recession, the government should step in to get us out of it: if there was unemployment, then the government should make jobs; if there was not enough spending in the economy, then the government should spend more. It was only central government that could boost demand across an entire country.

Keynes's belief in government intervention was, to Hayek and his neoclassical economist colleagues meeting in the Hotel Du Parc, terrifying.

Following Keynes's advice, President Franklin Delano Roosevelt spent enormously on infrastructure projects, like the Hoover Dam, La Guardia Airport and the Lincoln Tunnel, introduced the Social Security Act (which provided unemployment payments for the first time) and created the Securities and Exchange Commission to regulate the stock markets and investment banks. Roosevelt's New Deal in 1933 promised Americans that they should be "free from want" and "free from fear" – freedoms as important as freedom of speech and religion. He even repealed prohibition, though that was more about finding something to tax rather than *freedom to drink beer*.

To Hayek, a government dictating which infrastructure projects are needed, handing money to unemployed people and regulating markets was dangerously close to socialism. Or, as he put it in *The Road to Serfdom*, when "economic power [is] ... centralised as an instrument of political power it creates a degree of dependence scarcely distinguishable from slavery".

I don't know what it is about all these economists talking about *slavery* (Lenin thought freedom in capitalist countries meant "freedom for slave-owners"), but Hayek did it again when he welcomed a hand-picked group of 39 economists, historians and philosophers to the Hotel Du Parc – among them the Chicago School economist Milton Friedman and the philosopher Karl Popper. Hayek began by quoting the French aristocrat Alexis de Tocqueville, who put it simply: "socialism is slavery".*

Interestingly, once again "socialism" meant the same thing as "communism". To Hayek, "socialism means the abolition of private enterprise, of private ownership of the means of production, and the creation of a system of 'planned economy' in which the entrepreneur working for profit is replaced by a central planning body." To me, as a 21st-century north European, "socialism" means high progressive taxes and high government spending, but not a dictatorship of the proletariat. Hayek argued that I was wrong (despite having never met me), as progressivism would inevitably result in a communist dictatorship.†

Crucially, Hayek believed that "the system of private property is the most important guarantee of freedom". The idea of taxing privately owned land was thus, to him, a stepping stone to tyranny.

---

* My kids have a similar attitude when they're forced to share their toys.
† To his credit, Hayek recognised that the same term can mean very different things to people – he picked up on the fact that a "liberal" in America means someone who is left wing (so probably a bit socialist), but in Britain (historically, at least) means someone who believes in individual liberty (so is probably not a socialist). And neoliberal has come to mean the political branch of neoclassical economics, so pretty right wing. It's almost like everyone wants to claim that their own side are liberal.

This is where Hayek's plan came in.

Together with Chicago School economist Henry Simons and Cambridge professor of economic history Sir John Clapham, he wanted to create a society of free-market thinkers who could use their influence to dismantle the principles of the New Deal and the economics of Keynesianism (though they would keep the legalised beer drinking).

Hayek proposed they call the society the Acton–Tocqueville Society, after the British Lord Acton (of "power corrupts, and absolute power corrupts absolutely" fame) and the Count de Tocqueville, who as well as his disparaging remark about socialism being slavery, had said that "inequality is necessary to make the poor desire to be rich" (which was easy for Tocqueville to say, given he had an inherited title).

One of the people present was Chicago School economist Frank Knight, who suggested that naming their society after two Catholic aristocrats might be a bad idea. Instead, they decided to use the name of the place they were meeting in, and thus the Mont Pelerin Society was born.

It would become the closest thing the world has to a secret society of powerful behind-the-scenes influencers . . . or at least it would be, if it wasn't so entirely *un*-secret. They actually have a pretty good website, you can attend their meetings (or read the transcripts), and anyone can join, provided you "share their aims and values".

Funding from the society came from the Bank of England (thanks to the influence of another aristocrat called Lord Grantchester), the Swiss bank Credit Suisse (which has since collapsed following a string of fines for facilitating money laundering and tax evasion), the William Volker Fund (a charity founded in the US, which disbanded in the 1960s after the founder's nephew appointed a neo-Nazi to run the fund), and the libertarian American think-tank the Foundation for Economic Education, which was set up in 1946 to oppose the New Deal, social security, minimum wages and the Marshall Plan (which was the enormously successful project to rebuild Europe after the Second World War).

The Mont Pelerin Society's stated aims were to restore human dignity and freedom, and that they believed the best way to do this was via competitive markets and the defence of private property.

The core beliefs of the Mont Pelerin Society were that big governments were dangerous to freedom and dignity, and that free markets would solve the world's problems. In other words, let the rich get rich without interference, and as that's better for freedom and dignity, we will all benefit. You can imagine how delighted the aristocrats and bankers who supported the society's foundation were to hear that their wealth should be untouchable.

Ironically, Hayek himself wrote that it was his enthusiasm for Henry George that led him into economics, but he had later been radicalised at university to a libertarian position.

The society's plan was to set up lobby groups and think-tanks around the world to promote the curtailing of government control, as well as spreading their ideas throughout university departments and into political corridors, with the aim of controlling the narrative.

That narrative had no place for notions like *land taxes*. Instead, wherever possible, taxes were to be cut, social security programmes reduced and regulations to prevent corporate excesses would be torn up. This was ideologically driven – Hayek didn't (and indeed, couldn't) present data to show that cutting taxes would lead to greater prosperity, instead he argued that doing otherwise would lead us down the "road to serfdom".

Friedrich Hayek quickly won support from the wealthy businesspeople who would benefit most from reduced taxes. Early on, he convinced the battery-farming pioneer Anthony Fisher to found the Institute for Economic Affairs (IEA) in London, a think-tank that to this day promotes low taxes, low regulation and "freedom" in healthcare (which seems to mean abolishing the National Health Service). The IEA has a controversial history of receiving funding from tobacco companies, casino groups, tax havens and the oil company BP, and coincidentally has published literature promoting tobacco, gambling and tax havens, as well as denying climate change.

One of the most striking developments in the aftermath of the Mont Pelerin Society's foundation was the establishment in 1968 of the Sveriges

Riksbank prize for economics, which was probably the biggest marketing coup ever for neoclassical economists. You probably know this prize by a different name – the Nobel Prize. It's an odd name, as when this economics prize was created, Alfred Nobel had been dead for over seventy years.

Alfred Nobel died in 1896. His inventions – most famously of dynamite – made him extremely rich, but he was no enthusiast for free markets. According to economic historian Avner Offer, he once wrote in a letter that he "hated business with all [his] heart" and was deeply wary of financiers. He left his wealth to a foundation to fund the award of prizes in physics, chemistry, physiology or medicine, literature and peace. There was enough money in the foundation that each prize is still worth 11 million Swedish Kroner (about $1.22 million dollars) per year.

Then, the Sveriges Riksbank (Sweden's central bank) decided to honour its *own* 300th anniversary by creating a new "Nobel" prize for economics. Worse, it's not even actually a prize for *Economics*, it's a prize for *Economic Sciences*. See, economics isn't political, it's not moral philosophy, it's a *science*. You can't argue with *science*. Alfred Nobel's own great-grandnephew Peter Nobel said that "Nobel despised people who cared more about profits than society's well-being. There is nothing to indicate that he would have wanted such a prize."

To complete the marketing coup, in 1974 the prize was given to none other than Friedrich Hayek himself, which led to a resurgence of interest in his work.

All these think-tanks, prestigious prizes and cultivated professors had a serious aim: to influence a whole government. In fact, why stop at one? By the end of the 1970s, almost a third of Ronald Reagan's campaign staff were Mont Pelerin Society members, as was Reagan's future Secretary of State George Schultz and the Chairman of the Federal Reserve, Arthur Burns. New Zealand's finance minister Roger Douglas was a member, as was Australian Treasurer and future prime minister John Howard.

In the UK, Prime Minister Margaret Thatcher set up her own think-tank, inspired by the Mont Pelerin Society's ideas, which was almost called the Hayekian Society (Thatcher had read Hayek's *Road to Serfdom* as a teenager and bought into its key messages). Thatcher's Chancellor of the Exchequer, Geoffrey Howe, was also a member of the Mont Pelerin Society.

And the last thing any of these people wanted to talk about was Henry George.

—

The rugby match that Blackbeard had invited me to was an annual affair where our best student side played against (what I was surprised to learn was) our rival university. I don't think there was a single economics student on either team, and Blackbeard didn't seem that interested in the rugby, and he barely fitted on the fold-down plastic chairs, but he clearly loved the tradition of it all. The main tradition was, it became apparent, drinking pint after pint of Guinness.

Blackbeard has a natural confidence and a swagger and a charm that gives him an aura of intellectual prowess that wouldn't normally be associated with constant drunkenness, but I started to wonder if he had a drinking problem. Still, it didn't stop his students trying to impress him, and I think I fell into that trap. I was, perhaps, a little *conspiratorial* in how I expressed my theory that it was the influence of the Mont Pelerin Society that ensured that free-market economic thinking dominated the second half of the 20th century.

"I've been to some of their conferences," he said, which surprised me more than it should have. "Their members are far too diverse to be . . ." He looked for the word.

"A conspiracy?"

He chuckled. "The truth is always simpler. If you want to know why Henry George isn't on the syllabus, I can *show* you, with just one picture. Have you got a phone on you?"

"Of course," I said. *Who doesn't have their phone with them?*

"Google *Samuelson family tree of economics*." And then he cheered loudly.

"Did we score?" I asked.

"No. That winger just got ploughed into the turf by that enormous brute!"

"Our winger?"

"No idea," he said. "I don't know which team is which."

In 1945, a young economist at the Massachusetts Institute of Technology named Paul Samuelson was commissioned to write a textbook for a compulsory economics course taken at the university. The story goes that the existing students *hated* their economics classes and the instructions given to Samuelson were simply to keep it all clear. He was told that he could include or leave out anything he wanted.

He decided to include John Bates Clark's view that land was just another form of capital and also Alfred Marshall's diagram of supply and demand. He included Ricardo's arguments for free trade and Smith's invisible hand.

He decided to leave out Henry George. This was particularly pointed as he included a "family tree of economics". It was this family tree that Blackbeard had told me to google mid-rugby match.

The tree showed the links from early forms of mercantilism to the *classical* economists Adam Smith and David Ricardo, all the way through to the time he was writing. As far as Samuelson was concerned, there were only two schools of economic thought remaining in the 20th century: Socialism and *Neoclassical* Economics.

The book came out in 1948 and was titled, simply, *Economics*. Samuelson's particular interpretation of economic history – and who the key players were – would not have been especially significant but for one fact: his book was enormously successful.

Actually, *enormously successful* may be an understatement. Samuelson's *Economics* became just about the most successful textbook in the entire world. It is currently on its 20th edition and has been translated into 41 languages, with each edition selling around 300,000 copies.

Samuelson was obviously delighted – not just with the sales, but with the influence he had on generations of impressionable young minds. "I don't care who writes the nation's laws," he said, "as long as I can write its economics textbooks."

Blackbeard jabbed his finger at my phone. "Generations of student economists couldn't pass their exams unless they faithfully reproduced the Laws of Supply and Demand as set down by Alfred Marshall and repeated, parrot fashion, the insignificance of land and the importance of free trade." He would have looked a bit like a triumphant barrister in court, had he not been wedged into a small plastic chair with a half-drunk pint of Guinness in one hand. "Sure, they might have realised that not *every* assumption was true, and that there might be more to economic thought than just neoclassical economics and socialism, but that didn't matter in order to become expert economists. And once they were experts themselves, they repeated the theories to their own students."

Samuelson, Blackbeard explained, dismissed land taxes as a "political issue" (implying that the rest of economics wasn't), then justified the rents charged by landlords using the "Marshallian Cross" of supply and demand.

I flicked through the various versions of Samuelson's family tree – different editions featured a slightly different tree. The combined wisdom of John Maynard Keynes and the neoclassical economists, particularly Alfred Marshall, was sometimes referred to as the *Neoclassical Synthesis*.

"There's your conspiracy," said Blackbeard, looking pleased with himself. "If it isn't *socialism*, by which he meant *communism*, then it's supply and demand and Keynes. And that's it! That became economic orthodoxy for thirty years. Actually, longer."

"Why longer?"

"Because Keynes got sidelined in the 1970s when we found ourselves with unemployment *and* inflation, which Keynes thought shouldn't happen. So then we were left with just your Mont Pelerin crew. But there's two great ironies here."

He was interrupted by a student I'd never seen before handing him another pint of Guinness. He fired his finger pistol at her, and she pretended to be shot, then she returned to her friends. As he already had a Guinness in his other hand, he passed it to me.

"What were the ironies?"

He downed the rest of his pint then took back what I thought was *my* Guinness. "Thanks ... the first is that neoclassical economics is *rubbish*. But because the textbook says that's what economics is, it became orthodoxy. Rather than teaching generations of students to ask *why* the world is as it is, they were just taught *it's because of supply and demand*, and worse, *here's the maths to prove it*."

"But that's not still the case, is it?"

"All these impressionable young minds – they believe anything we tell them. You know what I learned the other day?"

"What?" I asked, laughing a bit. A slight slur had entered his speech.

"Guess how long it takes the Earth to spin once on its axis."

"Is it not twenty-four hours?"

"No! We're told that at school and then believe it all our lives. We need to *question* things, not just be told 'this is a fact'."

"Like Pluto being a planet?"

"Exactly. Or why is healthcare free, but not legal services?"

It seemed polite not to mention at that moment that I'd heard from another colleague about Blackbeard's impending divorce. I imagine the cost of legal services was near the front of his mind. Instead, we paused for a while, pretending to enjoy the rugby. Then I asked him what the second of his "ironies" was.

He scratched his beard, as if in deep contemplation.

"The second irony is the really big one: that Samuelson wrote his book, claiming that the battle of economic ideas was between neoclassicists and socialists, at the exact same time that a violent war was waging between two ideological forces that affected hundreds of millions of people and had already cost millions of lives. And I'll tell you this. It wasn't a war between socialists and neoclassicists."

I was a bit stumped. I thought I knew all the big wars of the 20th century.

"Who was it between then?" I asked.

He turned and looked at me, suddenly appearing sober, even if that was statistically very unlikely.

"It was a war between communists and Georgists."

10

THE RISE OF NEOLIBERALISM, THE GEORGIST CIVIL WAR, AND AN UNLIKELY VENDOR OF PLASTIC DUCKS

"Economics, as it has been practised in the last three decades, has been positively harmful for most people"
Ha-Joon Chang, economist (writing in 2010)

In 1644, the Manchu people of north-eastern China conquered the Ming state and established their own "Pure" or "Qing" dynasty. Over the next two centuries, this dynasty flourished, greatly expanding the size of the empire and overseeing a golden age of culture, architecture and art (a good Qing dynasty porcelain bowl could set you back $25 million these days).

But, by the dawn of the 20th century, the Qing dynasty was losing its dynamism. The population of China had grown enormously, but wealth was becoming ever more concentrated in the hands of the Manchu elite, which imposed higher and higher taxes and was seen as foreign and corrupt.

The Qing emperors had lost a series of wars against Britain over the right of the Brits to sell drugs to the Chinese and had been severely weakened by the Taiping Rebellion – a civil war that ended at roughly the same time as the

American Civil War, but in which about thirty times as many people died (the leader of the losing side claimed he was the brother of Jesus Christ).

China had failed to industrialise. Local warlords were consolidating power. The country was in the grip of an opium epidemic. Resentment against the ruling regime resulted in another rebellion at the end of 1899 by a secretive organisation known as the *Boxers* in Britain but more excitingly as the *Society of Righteous and Harmonious Fists* in China. The Boxers claimed that their martial arts made them invulnerable to gunshots, though an alliance of eight nations (including the UK, USA, Russia and Japan) proved that wasn't true, and suppressed the uprising.

The Qing dynasty was now hanging on by its fingertips. Sure enough, just a few years later, another rebellion of revolutionary groups known as the Tongmenghui swept the Qing dynasty from power in the Xinhai Revolution, ending 2,000 years of imperial rule.

At the head of the Tongmenghui, and now invited to become the first president of the first ever Republic of China, was committed Georgist Sun Yat-sen.

Sun Yat-sen was clear what direction he wanted to take China in: "The teaching of Henry George will be the basis of our program of reform," he declared. "On it we will found our new system."

Sun Yat-sen was born in Guangdong province, but grew up in Hawaii. He was 13 years old when *Progress and Poverty* was published and was entranced by its ideas. Inequality and poverty were even worse in China than in America, and he dreamed of combining Western ideas of democracy and liberalism with Henry George's single tax on land values and bringing them to a Chinese nation free from foreign domination.

To this end, he created the *Three Principles of the People*, a philosophy to guide the new republic. The principles were nationalism (meaning Chinese people should rule China), democracy and welfare rights. This last principle was explicitly Georgist.

Sun Yat-sen declared that a single land tax was "the only means of supporting the government [that] is an infinitely just, reasonable, and equitably distributed tax". He proposed a land tax on all *unimproved* land, exactly as Henry George had. Cleverly, he suggested that landlords could determine the value of that land themselves, but with one proviso: the government had the right to purchase the land at that particular price. So a landlord couldn't avoid the tax by deliberately undervaluing their land, as they'd risk being forced to sell at that undervalued amount.

The tax collected from land would then be redistributed for public benefit. Had Sun Yat-sen succeeded, China would have become the world's first Georgist nation.

Other people in China had different ideas.

In 1923, Sun Yat-sen invited the newly formed Chinese Communist Party to form a united front with his party, which had now been renamed the Kuomintang, or *Nationalist* party. The aim was to create a military alliance that would defeat the many warlords who had, since the aftermath of the Taiping Rebellion, held sway over vast swathes of the country.

Not to trivialise it, but it turns out that arming two ideological revolutionary groups to the teeth and setting them off on a military endeavour did not end well. By 1927, the two parties were in open conflict with each other, following a massacre of Communist Party members by the Kuomintang.

Blackbeard looked awfully pleased with himself as he reached his conclusion:

"Because the Kuomintang called themselves the *Nationalists*, the Chinese Civil War is normally remembered as a contest between communists and nationalists. But that doesn't really make sense, as the Communist Party were also nationalists. The Kuomintang were guided by three principles, and nationalism was just one of them. They could just have equally called themselves the *Democrats*, or the *Georgists*, or the *National Democratic Georgists*."

Whatever they may have called themselves, the civil war continued to rage, on and off, for the worst part of 22 years. In the end, the Kuomintang, now led by Sun Yat-sen's disciple, Chiang Kai-shek, retreated to Taiwan, a territory which had only recently been seized from the Japanese Empire at the end of the Second World War. Taiwan was then and remains now, effectively, a separate country, though the Chinese Communist Party are loath to admit it.

Taiwan had been occupied by the Japanese since the Sino–Japanese war of 1895, so when the Kuomintang took over, Chiang Kai-shek had a perfect opportunity to implement the land reforms proposed in Sun Yat-sen's Three Principles (though he quickly forgot the "democracy" principle and ruled via martial law, which was only lifted in 1987).

Against the advice of American neoclassical economists, Chiang Kai-shek broke up large landholdings to provide land to a great number of smaller landowners. The neoclassical economists argued that this was a mistake – larger landholdings would be more efficient, which would create more wealth, which would (eventually) trickle down into the hands of the Taiwanese population.

But against the expectations of neoclassical economists, the small landowners were more motivated and more entrepreneurial than they had been as mere farmhands, and food production soared. This lowered food prices, which meant the Taiwanese could spend money on other things besides food.

The excess food was exported, which created foreign currency to buy machines that would further increase productive efficiency and form the basis of new industries, which now had available labourers to work in, as improved efficiencies in farming meant more food could be produced with fewer people.

The Kuomintang then went even further and *again* rejected the advice of neoclassical economists by protecting their nascent industries with tariffs on imports and subsidies for exporters.

Over the decades, the emphasis on land reform and land taxes drifted away (land taxes are now effectively insignificant in Taiwan), but they formed the basis of a successful nation. Today, the average Taiwanese person is three times richer than the average Chinese person, and wealth is far more equally divided among the population.

—

We had an academic staff meeting every so often, which gave Professor Alva the opportunity to restress the importance of sticking to the syllabus.

At a meeting a few weeks after the rugby match, she made what she pretended was a general point, but I'm pretty sure was directed at me.

"Could I just remind everybody that as much as I'm sure we all appreciate *meditation*, we don't have capacity in our timetables to include it during our seminars."

One of my colleagues gave me a nudge.

"Also, please don't set off fireworks in the lecture theatres."

All eyes turned to Blackbeard. He made a play of looking behind him, as if someone else was to blame.

Professor Alva waited for a few giggles to die down. She had one more agenda item. "And we're still looking for volunteers for the financial placements team. Anyone?"

The room went strangely quiet. I didn't know what the "financial placements team" was, but everyone was suddenly looking at their fingernails or seemed overly interested in the ceiling tiles. I had a colleague called Stan who I'd had a slightly frosty exchange with the previous week when I'd tried to (economically) justify my buying of a lottery ticket and he'd accused me, baselessly, of falling into a trap called the *gambler's fallacy*.[*]

"You used to work in the City, didn't you?" he asked, loudly, from across the room, using my name, and with an expression of innocence.

Professor Alva turned to look at me.

"Oh, of course," she said. "You'd be perfect for the team. Thanks for volunteering."

—

When I was born, Margaret Thatcher was the prime minister of the UK, Ronald Reagan was American president, and across the world the most

---

[*] I'd merely pointed out that if a lottery ticket cost £2 and the odds of winning were 50 million to 1, then as the jackpot had reached £160 million it made mathematical sense to buy a ticket. The gambler's fallacy is unrelated to this – it's the belief that because the last three spins of the roulette wheel landed on red, the next spin is more likely to be black, as it's "overdue".

famous and possibly most influential economist of the day was Milton Friedman – one of Hayek's original 39 picks for the Mont Pelerin Society.*

It wasn't just the UK and USA that were influenced by Friedman – the 1980s saw the adoption of policies inspired by Friedman in Canada, Australia, New Zealand, West Germany and Japan that are collectively often referred to as *neoliberalism*.

Margaret Thatcher became prime minister of the United Kingdom in 1979, almost exactly a hundred years after the publication of Henry George's *Progress and Poverty*. What arguably began as a Robber Baron-funded mission to avoid paying taxes by wiping Henry George's ideas from the Earth had now reached its apotheosis. The communists had defeated the Georgists in the East, and now the free marketeers, led by Milton Friedman and the University of Chicago, were about to be unleashed on the West.

—

The 1970s had been a time of *stagflation* – high inflation *and* high unemployment, which as Blackbeard had pointed out was something that Keynes said shouldn't happen. The root cause was political: Middle Eastern nations had imposed an oil embargo due to Western support for Israel, and as a result oil prices had quadrupled.

To deal with this stagflation, Milton Friedman argued that what was needed were "supply side" reforms. Governments should not be managing *demand*, as Keynes suggested, but manipulating *supply*. If you buy in wholesale to the thin-line mathematical equilibrium model of neoclassical economics, both approaches make sense.

---

* Ronald Reagan had campaigned on a promise to "Make America Great Again", so really Donald Trump's slogan should have been to "Make America Great Again, Again".

i.e. Keynes said do this:

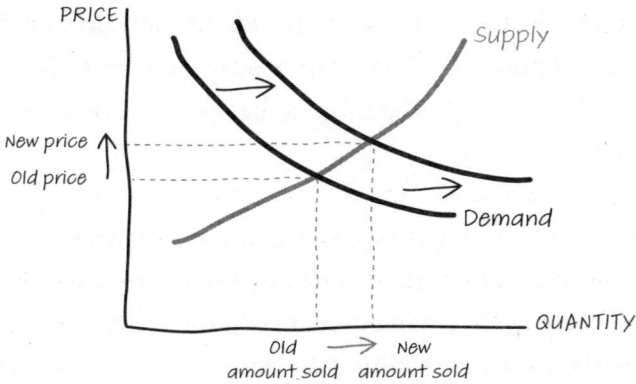

Which shows more stuff being sold but prices rising, while Milton Friedman said do this:

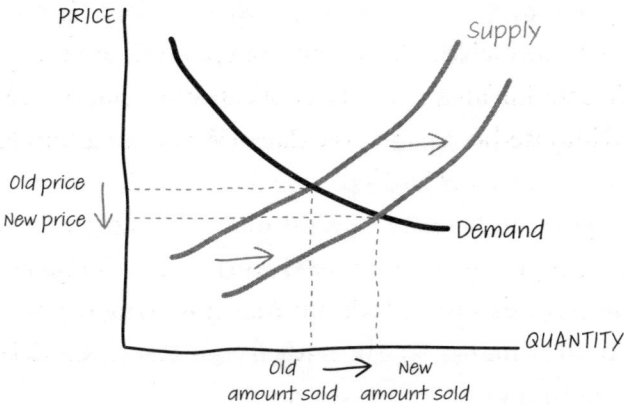

Which shows more stuff being sold (i.e. the economy doing better), *and* prices falling.

Wonderful stuff! Sveriges Riksbank, I mean, *Nobel* prizeworthy, even, but how do you actually get an entire economy to increase its *supply*?

For Reagan and Thatcher, the answer was obvious: cut taxes on rich people to free up their capital, raise taxes on poor people (and cut welfare payments) to encourage them to work harder, erode the power of trade unions, allow big businesses to move production to cheaper foreign countries, reduce government regulations and, crucially, control the money supply. This last step was known as *monetarism*, and was the centrepiece of Friedman's thinking.

—

It may just be worth taking a moment to comment on where money actually comes from, given we're about to talk about the *money supply*, because it's one of those things that seem obvious at first and then turns out to be not what most people are expecting, a little bit like the answer to, *when you lose weight, where does the weight go?**

Very little money is actually printed or minted. Instead, and I'll forgive you if you think I've gone completely mad, most money is created whenever someone *borrows* it.†

But how can this be? How can you *borrow* money if the money doesn't already exist? It sounds completely crazy, but bear with me.

Say you go to a bank like HSBC and ask to borrow some money. HSBC won't hand you physical cash. Instead, HSBC will simply *record* the transaction as having occurred: *your* account will show that you now have the amount you requested and a corresponding *debtor* account at the bank will show that you owe HSBC that money.

Literally, with a few strokes of a keyboard *and nothing else*, you will have access to your borrowed money. It hasn't really come from anywhere. You could now use that money to, say, buy a house. But this is where things get really wild.

---

* I'll give you a hint: you don't turn it into energy or defecate it. Answers at the back.
† In the USA, it costs more to produce both pennies and nickels than those coins are actually worth. You'd think that the government would just stop making them, but according to the "assiduously nonpartisan" (and massively libertarian) think-tank the Cato Institute, a small zinc company called Artazn has spent $3 million since 2006 lobbying to keep the pennies in circulation. Artazn, not coincidentally, has received over $1.2 billion since 2002 as the sole provider of the metal in US pennies.

If the person who sells you that house also banks with HSBC, then HSBC can simply record that you no longer have any money in your account, but this other chap does instead.

Whereas if this other chap banks with some other bank, say, Santander, then HSBC will have to transfer the money from your account at HSBC to the other chap's at Santander ... but here we hit a problem – this money is so far just an accounting entry created with keystrokes.

To transfer your payment for the house to the account at Santander, HSBC will have to use what are called *reserves* – effectively a kind of interbank money. If HSBC don't have sufficient reserves they can borrow some, either from another bank, or, as a last resort, from a central bank (like the Bank of England, European Central Bank, Federal Reserve or the Reserve Bank of Australia).

I appreciate this is all pretty loopy, but in short, this all means that the vast majority of money circulating today is created by commercial banks *lending* to their customers. The real limitation on how much the banks can lend is how much their customers can afford to pay back (though there are regulatory restrictions as well). Try not to think too hard about where the customers paying back their loans get *their* money from (though it's mostly from other people borrowing money).

Most of the rest of the money in circulation is created by central banks. And where does the central bank get their money from? Well, pick whichever metaphor you like: it comes from out of thin air or is plucked from a magic money tree or emerges straight out of their pinstriped backsides. The central bank just goes, *Shazam, here's the money you need.**

And that means that central banks can control the money supply by reducing the amount of money they themselves create or restricting the

---

* Central banks do impose limits on the total amount of money they create, and new money can also be created when governments spend more than they collect in taxes and central banks fund the difference, which might sound like a dry, technical point, but is part of just about the most contentious issue in modern economics, as we'll see in a bit.

amount that banks are allowed to lend. Though the easiest and most common way to control the money supply is to intervene at the very first step: stop people wanting to borrow money. If people don't want to borrow money, say, because interest rates are too high, then new money doesn't get created.

—

The logic of monetarism is based on an equation made famous by the American neoclassical economist Irving Fisher, who had been awarded Yale University's first ever doctorate in economics in 1891 and by the 1920s was considered America's leading economist. (Though his reputation suffered when he publicly declared, just days before the Wall Street Crash, that "Stock prices have reached what looks like a permanently high plateau.")

Among a long list of achievements (including campaigning against corsets), Fisher refined an equation known as the "equation of exchange", or, more commonly, "MV=PT". It's probably one of the most famous equations in all of economics.

This equation shows that if you multiply the amount of money (M) in an economy by the frequency with which that money gets spent (called *velocity*: V), this has to equal average prices (P) multiplied by the number of transactions (T).*

Milton Friedman considered Fisher to be "the greatest economist the United States has ever produced", and he took Fisher's equation to heart. Friedman argued that if we assume *velocity* and the number of *transactions* stays the same, then price increases (that is to say, *inflation*) must be directly related to the money supply.

So, Friedman argued that the way to reduce inflation is simply to reduce the money supply, proclaiming that "inflation is always and everywhere a monetary phenomenon."

Economists don't like inflation for a number of reasons – the obvious one is that it erodes the spending power of money, so anyone on a fixed income

---

* Though, just to be awkward, the "T" is sometimes substituted by a "Q" or a "Y". It all means roughly the same thing.

(like pensioners) will see their wealth levels fall. But inflation also discourages saving and makes investment decisions more difficult, and risks resources being misallocated (as it becomes hard to say if prices are rising due to increased demand, or just general inflation). In worst-case scenarios, inflation could lead to *wage–price spirals*, where increasing prices results in demands for higher wages, which leads to higher prices, and so on, possibly ending up with *hyperinflation*, when money effectively loses all value.*

And now here was Friedman with a solution. Governments could control inflation by restricting the money supply.

There's an old joke, though, about how economists open a can of beans – they just *assume* they have a can opener. Friedman's confidently proposed monetarism would only work if the assumptions he had made were true. Were prices simply a reflection of the amount of money in an economy? Or might increases in interest rates lead to people hoarding money, fearing uncertainty, and thereby reducing the *velocity* of money? Would people delay big purchases because they're spending more on their mortgage payments, which would reduce *transactions*? Or perhaps businesses facing rising interest rates would simply raise their prices to pass the increased cost on to their customers?

"Who cares?" said Thatcher and Reagan. "Let's do it!"

—

"Did you really set off a firework in a lecture hall?" I asked Blackbeard as we walked across the campus back towards the railway station, the sun already setting.

He chuckled. "Of course not. It was one of those *snapdragons* – you know, you throw 'em on the ground and they go 'bang'. I got given a whole box by my Secret Santa." He rummaged in his coat pocket. "Do you want some?"

---

* Inflation got so bad in Zimbabwe between 2008 and 2009 that a hundred trillion Zimbabwean dollars would not pay for a bus ticket across town and toilet paper was more likely to be accepted for payments than the official currency. Some enterprising Zimbabweans hung on to their hundred trillion-dollar bills, though, and now sell them as souvenirs for about five American dollars each.

"Thanks," I said. You never know when small explosives might come in handy.

"I also got given a joke book by one of my students." He tapped another pocket. "Do you want to hear a joke about *trickle-down* economics?"

"Sure."

"Actually, never mind," he said, already chuckling at his punchline. "You probably won't get it."

—

Neoliberalism wasn't just about tax cuts, monetarism and deregulation. Something much more sinister lurked just beneath the surface.

I remember as a kid in the 1980s not understanding how anyone could be unemployed when there were so many jobs that clearly needed doing, like sweeping streets or fixing potholes or rewinding the VHSs at Blockbuster. Why didn't the government just pay people to do those things, rather than paying them unemployment benefits to do nothing?

I know now that there are two answers to this.

The first is *yes*, the government should do exactly that. When President Roosevelt introduced the New Deal in 1933, he argued that people had a right to work. If the private sector couldn't provide a job for them, then the government would, especially on all the new infrastructure projects. This was an era when artists were paid to paint murals on public buildings and writers and musicians and actors were paid to enrich culture and foster pride in communities.

The second answer, though, is one of the most depressing things I've ever come across in all of economics. Introduced as a concept by Milton Friedman in 1968 – around the same time that he was arguing against minimum wages – it was originally called the Natural Rate of Unemployment, and is now catchily rebranded as the Non-Accelerating Inflationary Rate of Unemployment, or NAIRU.

Friedman's theory was that a healthy economy *needs* unemployment. If too many people have jobs, the theory goes, then just like if too much money is floating around, inflation will get out of hand.

No one actually knows how much inflation is too much. And no one knows how much unemployment is "needed" to get there. But the idea that somehow unemployment was a good thing appealed very much to politicians like Reagan and Thatcher, especially when their policies directly caused unemployment.*

By coincidence, high unemployment rates also act as a threat – if you quit your job, there might not be another one for you to get, so you better not act up (or ask for a pay rise).

When employee-controlled companies are faced with job losses, employees will usually elect to reduce their hours (and pay) across the board rather than let a few people go. You might think that this argument would hold for the whole economy – how about we have full employment, but everyone works a four-day week?

Indeed, John Maynard Keynes made a famous prediction in 1930 that technological improvements, and the efficiency gains that came with them, would mean that by 2030 we would all be working just a 15-hour week.

The NAIRU believers rejected the notion that we should reach full employment by working fewer hours. They argued that if we had full employment then employers would have to compete more to attract staff, which would mean paying higher wages. Higher wages would mean higher costs, which would push up prices, which would give rise to that never-ending "wage–price spiral".

I find this very odd. The same economists who argue for the importance of free markets and competition argue *against* full employment on the grounds that it might encourage competition for employees. I suppose it's different if competition affects how much you have to pay your own staff.

But the really depressing bit is that in America and Australia, at least, the NAIRU has won.

---

* Thatcher famously cut subsidies to state-run industries like shipbuilding and steel; Reagan cut support for some agricultural and manufacturing sectors; and high interest rates in both countries reduced borrowing for investment, which contributed to unemployment rates above 10 per cent of the working-age population, more than double what they are today.

The American Federal Reserve and the Reserve Bank of Australia are mandated to minimise inflation and maximise employment. But *maximum employment* is not defined as *everyone who wants a job has one*, but as the amount of employment that can occur without too much inflation . . . which is another way of saying that the central banks have a legal duty to ensure that there are permanently some people out of work.

—

Unusually for him, Blackbeard got the train with me back to London. He was very coy about why, and given that he was wearing a new shirt and had taken the pencil out of his beard I wondered if he had a date. Something was clearly making him nervous, because he grumbled the whole way, mostly about how he couldn't believe how expensive the train ticket was.

"They laid the bloody track a hundred and fifty years ago, and the train must be thirty years old . . . how many people do you think are on this train? Maybe a thousand? So what's that, maybe ten pence *each* for electricity and the driver's wages? So why am I paying a pound a mile?"

The train was, indeed, pretty busy and I was conscious that everyone could hear our conversation – not that I think many people disagreed with his sentiment. We were wedged into our seats opposite a mother with a young girl sitting on her lap, with a table between us and them. The kid was engaging me in a staring competition, which I felt eagerly keen to win.

"Do you think everyone who teaches economics is left wing?" I asked. (To Blackbeard, though I suppose *physically* towards the child.)

He gave a sort of *ha* noise that failed to startle the child out of her staring. "Of course. All the left-wing economists go into academia, all the right-wing ones go into banking."

I sort of blurted out what I said next, without thinking. "I've never understood how you can have a left- or right-wing economist."

He gave a weird sort of snort, like I'd said something completely moronic. I mean, obviously I appreciate that *everyone* sits somewhere on a political spectrum from left to right, but that's not really what I was getting at. He didn't seem to know how to respond without saying something rude, not that being rude would normally stop him. So I added, quickly, still staring at this small child, "I mean, it's not like you get left-wing *astronomy* or right-wing *particle physics*."

He thought about that for a moment.

"I knew a Marxist physicist once," he said. "He told me that he didn't believe in gravity. He said the masses were rising up."

I laughed, then realised something. "Was that in your joke book, too?"

I also realised, as I stuck my hands into my trouser pockets and felt the cluster of snapdragons Blackbeard had given me, that I knew how to win this staring contest.

—

Thatcher had the good fortune that North Sea oil production took off just as she came to power in 1979. In her belief that free markets know best, Thatcher allowed commercial companies to extract the oil, with a revenue-sharing agreement with her government. She then used this oil revenue to finance her tax cuts for the rich, halving the top rate of income tax and reducing inheritance and capital gains tax, while doubling the value added tax that is added to most goods sold (and which poorer people normally pay a greater proportion of their incomes on).

Similarly, Ronald Reagan cut taxes on billionaires (there were only thirteen of them at the time), reduced inheritance tax and capital gains tax (which only wealthier people pay), while raising the pension age and cutting social security payments. He did also reduce income taxes for poorer people, but these cuts were largely offset by higher excise taxes and the removal of deductions for things like student loan interest.

Famously, Thatcher also introduced a highly regressive poll tax – a tax charge of around £400 per year that everyone had to pay. For the rich, this was peanuts, but it was a tenth of the annual incomes of Britain's poorest 10 per cent of people.

Ironically, given Hayek's fear of governmental tyranny and belief that free markets would ensure dignity and freedom, the poll tax led to massive protests and rioting in the street and, ultimately, Thatcher's resignation.

She must have been gobsmacked – did the protesters not realise they were protesting against their own dignity and freedom?

Indeed, Hayek lamented that his generation – the one after Roosevelt's New Deal and Keynesianism – had forgotten that "the system of private property is the most important guarantee of freedom". Reagan took these words and ran with them. Where Roosevelt had argued for freedom from want and fear, Reagan promised freedom to work and freedom to own your own property.

Though, during his two terms in office, wages for average Americans fell and housing became much less affordable.

—

A few months into 2024, something happened that I'd secretly prepared for. I still managed to fluff it.

The institute was quiet and I was having lunch alone at a desk when Kanya sat down next to me. She noticed that I was reading a book about Milton Friedman and, in what I hope was a friendly way, called me a nerd for making little notes in the margins in pencil.

"What are *you* reading?" I asked her, to deflect, and she unzipped her hemp backpack and tossed down a paperback next to my sandwich for me to look at. I recognised it instantly.

"I picked it up in the airport. It's really good. Did you know you can save tax by buying a yacht?"

When I'd practised this moment, I always came across as cool and mildly interested, before wittily steering the conversation away from whether I'd read my own book. But now, faced with exactly this scenario, I just went red and failed to stop my voice breaking a little.

"I don't think that's true," I said, to put some distance between me and this *Rebel Accountant* fellow.

Ioannou was still obsessing about the rise of China. Some of the reports I'd been writing for him had received positive coverage despite not just being about tax or tariffs, so he suggested I write another "think-piece", this one about what's sometimes called the *Beijing Consensus* – a loose term used to describe China's mix of authoritarian political oppression, state-directed industrial subsidies and export-driven growth.

"Isn't it just a rehash of Colbertism?" I suggested.

He looked at me blankly. "I don't know what that is."

"Mercantilism," I offered, cautiously. "Jean-Baptiste Colbert was Louis the Fourteenth's finance minister. He could pretty much have written China's current economic policy."

He still looked at me blankly, in as much as anyone whose face was so wrinkled can look blank.

"It all ended in revolution," I added. At this he visibly relaxed.

"That's great! Include that, then."

—

The term "Beijing Consensus" was coined in 2002 by the journalist Joshua Cooper Ramo. He introduced it as a deliberate contrast to the "Washington Consensus", a package of free-market policies that the IMF, the World Bank and the US Treasury strong-armed developing countries into adopting during the 1970s, '80s and '90s if they wanted a loan.

The term Washington Consensus was itself coined in 1989 by the English economist John Williamson, and it's in this consensus that we see just how far Friedrich Hayek's ideas had travelled – from a discussion with Milton Friedman and others in a Swiss hotel room beneath Mont Pelerin to dictating terms to half the world's economies.

To be eligible for loans, poorer countries had to cut spending on social programmes, such as public healthcare and poverty alleviation projects, and "broaden the tax base", which is a fancy way of saying "raise taxes on poorer people".

They also had to cut taxes on businesses and privatise state-owned enterprises (even natural monopolies, like water or rail). They had to open up markets to international competition, cut regulations on workers' rights and product standards, and allow their currencies to weaken, making it cheaper for rich countries to buy their resources.

To free-market purists, this would result in some short-term pain – they called it "shock therapy", but in the long term these countries would get richer, so surely it was worth it?

To say that the Washington Consensus has had its critics is to put it mildly.

In practice, these reforms shifted power on a massive scale. In many cases, poverty and inequality soared. Newly privatised monopolies were snapped up by small elites and used to concentrate wealth. Political decisions were often surrendered to multinational companies, which at the time were being urged by Friedman to adhere to shareholder value maximisation, which meant they only had to care about their shareholders, not workers, customers or the planet.

Unsurprisingly, environmental degradation followed close behind. The IMF and World Bank pushed for soybean cultivation in Bolivia and Brazil, which meant clearing vast tracts of forest. In Ghana, a deregulated gold-mining sector led to the poisoning of entire ecosystems. Their push for aquaculture in the Philippines saw mangroves replaced with shrimp farms, while foreign fishing fleets were given access to West African coastal waters, depleting once well-managed fish stocks and devastating local livelihoods.

The most dramatic case of this "shock therapy" came after the collapse of the Soviet Union.

Transitioning from communism to capitalism was never going to be easy. The Soviet Union was formally dissolved on Boxing Day 1991, and within weeks the new government turned to the International Monetary Fund for help.

Many economists argued that reform should happen gradually, with international financial support and the creation of robust legal institutions, but the US was wary of offering too much to their former enemy, and Boris Yeltsin, the new president of Russia, believed that time was not on their side. So instead, spurred on by American economists, neoliberal reforms unleashed free-market forces almost overnight.

The result was chaos. The removal of price controls led to hyperinflation, meaning ordinary Russians' savings were wiped out. State-owned industries were rapidly privatised by a scheme devised mainly by University of Chicago economists in which almost all Russians were given vouchers, which they could exchange for shares in these newly privatised companies.

But with savings gone and trust in government shattered, most people sold their vouchers as quickly as they could, so privatisation ended up handing control of what had been state-owned resources to a new class of oligarchs, who used their new-found wealth for personal enrichment rather than societal benefit.*

In 1995, Boris Yeltsin auctioned off shares in the largest remaining state industries in exchange for loans. The auctions were effectively rigged by the oligarchs, and another vast transfer of state wealth to a few private individuals was complete. Roman Abramovich, who had first made his money selling plastic ducks (yes, really), bought a share of the oil company Sibneft for a little under $200 million, which he later sold back to Putin's government for almost $12 billion.

But remember what the free marketeers said – privatisation, deregulation and free markets are good for growth, right? In the case of Russia, it was mostly just good for a new breed of billionaires.

In 2011, the Moscow-based Higher School of Economics found that around half of Russians were poorer than they had been before the collapse of the Soviet Union.

Thatcher's private secretary for economic affairs, Tim Lankester, examined the effect and legacy of monetarism in a book called *Inside Thatcher's Monetarism Experiment*. His verdict, as an insider, was damning. Monetarism "promised much but completely failed to deliver".

He argued that monetarism fundamentally misunderstood how the economy worked, yet politicians stubbornly stuck to it, even as their policies caused real harm. It's almost as if politicians were driven by ideology, by pure *belief*, rather than actual evidence.

John Williamson, for his part, later admitted that he regretted including *Washington* in the name of the Washington Consensus, seeing as how,

---

* Richest of these was Vladimir Putin, now estimated to *personally* control over $200 billion of what was once Russia's wealth.

"Audiences the world over seem to believe that this signifies a set of neoliberal policies that have been imposed on hapless countries by the Washington-based international financial institutions and have led them to crisis and misery." Whatever would give people that idea?

He denied that the Washington Consensus had a neoliberal agenda (which he considered "an intellectual swearword"). By 2004, perhaps with the benefit of hindsight, he acknowledged that "the other new ideas of Reagan and Thatcher . . . notably monetarism, supply-side economics, and minimal government intervention, had by then been discarded as impractical or undesirable fads." It seemed like an odd choice of words. I mean, I think of an impractical or undesirable fad to be something like meme coins or platform shoes or Metaverse real estate, not screwing over the entire world.

The International Monetary Fund and the World Bank have, since around the turn of the century, put more focus on building robust institutions and curtailing corruption as a condition for bailouts.

—

It's hard not to look back at the 1980s and see that a kind of mania had taken hold. The world's most powerful people – Thatcher and Reagan, the IMF and the World Bank, finance ministers from Canberra to Caracas – all caught the same fever. Hayek's paranoid conviction that even the smallest hint of state intervention would send us goose-stepping into communism had leapt from the pages of obscure think-tank pamphlets to the summit of global power.

The cure for every ailment, real or imagined, was the same: deregulate, privatise, cut taxes and shrink the state. And in fairness, the results were impressive, but only if you were already rich. For everyone else, inequality ballooned, public services withered and discontent simmered just below the surface. Yet politicians pressed on, clinging to the simple faith that an invisible hand would bless us all, provided we stopped helping the poor, slashed taxes on the wealthy and unshackled the powerful.

That this made about as much sense as treating a fever by bloodletting took a while to sink in, and the biggest consequence of this economic faith was still to come, in a world where money itself is the product.

11

IS FINANCE HIGH? AND WILL A SIMPLE EQUATION LEAD TO THE END OF THE WORLD?

> *"The stock markets predicted nine out of the last five recessions."*
> Paul Samuelson, economist

I hadn't set foot in the office of a venture capitalist since my unsuccessful attempts to raise money for the start-up that made underwater acoustic equipment. On that occasion, it had been pretty much a humiliation.

There's often an air of mystique around the various players in the world of high finance, but in truth you can get involved yourself quite easily. I mean, venture capitalists are just people who invest in, well, *ventures.* Meaning *businesses,* usually new, private ones. So if your kids are selling lemonade outside your house and you agree to buy them the lemons in return for a slice of the business, then, congratulations, you're now a venture capitalist.

The only real difference between what you're doing with the lemons and what someone who calls themselves a venture capitalist is doing is that the "VC" has got formal approval from a financial authority and is probably playing around with a lot more money.

For most of history, economists have largely ignored the role that high finance plays in creating (or destroying) wealth, which given the gargantuan scale of the financial sector does make me wonder if it's the economists who are high. The scale of it all is astonishing: bond markets deal with debts with a combined value of over a $100 trillion; on a good day global stock exchanges list companies worth over a $120 trillion; and then there's trillions of dollars' worth of insurance contracts, derivatives, gold and the like also being bought and sold annually. You only have to skim off a small fraction of all that action and you'll find yourself with a pretty tidy income.

It's a similar story with hedge funds – in principle, you could set up your own hedge fund, as the whole point of them is that, unlike, say, an investment bank, they are private, lightly regulated and don't require too much disclosure about what they get up to. A hedge fund is not that different from getting your mate to trust you with a few bucks, and investing the money in literally anything.

Their name comes from the pioneering work of an Australian émigré named Alfred Winslow Jones, who had joined a Marxist Workers School in Germany, hung out with Ernest Hemingway while honeymooning in Spain during the Spanish Civil War, and became the US embassy's Vice-Consul in Berlin during the rise of Hitler.

He later received a degree from Harvard and a doctorate from Columbia (in sociology) and ended up working as a journalist for *Fortune* magazine, where in 1949 he wrote an article called "Fashions in Forecasting" which became the kernel of what is now a $4.5 trillion industry.

In his analysis, Alfred Winslow Jones realised that it should be possible to create a portfolio of investments that was indifferent to whether the entire stock market increased or decreased in value, by buying and selling equal numbers of shares. In other words, he realised he could *hedge* his bets – the losses on some shares could be offset by gains on others, meaning the success of his portfolio depended only his ability to pick shares, and not on the general performance of the economy.

To test this theory, he pooled together $40,000 of his own money and another $60,000 from four friends (at a time when an average American house would cost less than $8,000), and started using this *hedging* strategy in the US stock markets. He charged his friends a fee of 20 per cent of any profits he made, plus 2 per cent of the funds he managed, and his fund was small enough to avoid official regulation.

His hedged investment strategy was enormously successful. Winslow Jones consistently outperformed the market, which led to a flurry of imitators looking for novel ways in which they, too, could beat the market. Not all of them used the same "hedging" tactic, but the name stuck, and so did attempts to limit the number of investors in each fund in order to avoid official scrutiny.

Rather quirkily, the fee he charged of 20 per cent of any profits wasn't based on any particularly clever mathematical idea – Alfred Winslow Jones said he picked 20 per cent because that's what ancient Phoenician sea traders had done. Nevertheless, this "2 and 20" fee structure is still common in the hedge-fund industry.

Today, many hedge funds use a "leveraging" strategy, where they borrow huge amounts of money to magnify their gains, meaning they can make a fortune from small shifts in the price of their investment, but blow up spectacularly if they make the wrong call.*

The founder of the underwater acoustics start-up I used to work for was called Remy, and looked disconcertingly like Elizabeth Holmes, the Theranos founder who had been jailed for defrauding investors, and as we'd taken the lift up to the venture capitalist's office on the tenth floor of a building overlooking the Thames I remember her telling me not to describe what they did as a *fish disco*.

"I don't want to lose credibility," she told me.

She'd hired me because the venture capitalists had asked her to provide an NPV of her acoustic projects, and she simply had no idea what they meant.

—

NPV, or Net Present Value, is one of the most common investment appraisal techniques in the world. It's used to value shares in companies and to justify infrastructure projects and price-up government bonds. It's based on a pretty

---

* The maths of leveraging is just like buying a house with a mortgage – if you have $1,000, borrow $99,000 then buy a $100,000 house and you'll only need a 1 per cent increase in house prices to double your money . . . but try not to think about what happens if the house price drops.

simple concept, called the time value of money, which is really just asking, *Would you like some money now or a bit more money later?*

The answer, of course, is *it depends*. If inflation is high, you'd need more money *later* to forgo money *now*. If you owed mobsters some money and one of them was outside your door threatening to break your legs if you don't pay them this instant, you'd probably always opt for *money now*.*

Part of the time value of money is *opportunity cost*, meaning the profits you'd make if you invested the money elsewhere. Awkwardly, those *elsewhere* profits also depend on the *time value of money*, meaning that to find a time value of money we need a time value of money.

One way round this is to consider the profits offered by a "risk-free" investment and use that as an opportunity cost. Or at least, it would be a way round it if such a thing as a "risk-free" investment existed. American short-term government debt is often assumed to be the safest investment out there, but annoyingly the return you get on US debt can actually fluctuate quite a lot, and that's before you consider the odds of another civil war or thermonuclear exchange giving the US government an excuse not to pay their debts.†

Anyway, once you've settled on an opportunity cost, successfully predicted inflation and worked out the odds of mobsters breaking your legs, the really tricky bit is adding a "risk-premium" to reflect the likelihood that your profits will differ to what you're expecting. Most of the time, professional investors will look at how much the profits on similar investments have varied in the past, in much the same way as you might guess a football score by looking at previous matches (which, as we all know, is an infallible technique).

So, add together your guess about inflation, an opportunity cost that fluctuates unpredictably, the unquantifiable risk of your investment, your

---

* The time value of money is a weird combination of mathematical practicalities and emotion. If I ask my kids if they would like to watch an hour of television now or an hour of television later, they will always pick *now*, simply because deferring gratification is not fun, or to phrase it a different way, there is a time value of television (or TVTV). This *emotional* part is often inconveniently forgotten by financial analysts.

† I just googled what those odds are. They're terrifying.

immediate need for cash (because of mobsters) and your unwillingness to wait an hour to watch *Paw Patrol* (which will make no sense if you don't read footnotes) and you have the time value of money. Multiply this wildly imaginative number by some finger-in-the-air estimates of future profits while ignoring the odds of a nuclear war and, hey presto, you have the official best basis for assessing investments. That should make you worried.

If you express your time value of money as a percentage you can convert any future cashflows into a *present value*, which is effectively what you would pay for those future cashflows today. It was this present value that Remy's venture capitalists had asked her to provide.

"Well . . ." I had told Remy, in her small WeWork office, trying not to channel too much of what I'd learned advising the amoral rich at the Mayfair wealth management company into my tone of voice, "how much do you *want* your profits to be worth today?"

The mathematics behind present values are straightforward: you just need a predicted future cash amount and that time value of money, and you (more or less) multiply one by the other. I gave her some examples:

"If you think you'll make a profit of £5 million in ten years and your time value of money is 20 per cent, that profit is only worth about £800,000 today, but if the time value is 5 per cent that profit is worth over £3 million . . ."

She thought about this, scrunching her face up as she played around with my spreadsheet. Then it clicked. "But this is absurd! I could make up any numbers at all for my cash flows and use a low time value of money and my business would be worth millions!"

"Yup." I smiled. "Though, um, you can't say anything too outlandish. There's a line somewhere between a semi-rational superabundance of optimism and, you know, fraud."

She swayed her head a little, still toying with my spreadsheet, feeling the joy that inputting data in a small box can give you. "Sure, sure . . ." she said. "I don't want to pull the wool over anyone's eyes. There's of course a chance that our equipment isn't watertight. But if it was . . ." She tapped in another couple of forecast numbers and leaned back in her chair. "How about we go with this?"

I almost laughed. "That's a big number."

"But believable, right?"

—

Actually, while we're talking about Net Present Values and what a nonsense they are, it may be worth mentioning that all life on Earth might be destroyed due to some shady *time value of money* calculations.

In 2018, the Nobel Prize in Economics was awarded to a University of Yale professor named William Nordhaus, for his work on integrating climate change into economic models.

Nordhaus has a somewhat polarised fanbase. On the one hand he has been instrumental in getting economists to consider how a warming planet could affect economic growth, but on the other he has argued that we shouldn't overly worry about fixing problems caused by climate change *today*, as in the future we'll all be much richer.

Economic growth, he reasoned, would make the cost of action more affordable later on. So sure, it might be more expensive to suck carbon *out* of the atmosphere rather than just not put it *in* in the first place, but by the time we get round to it, we'll be so wealthy that we won't even notice the bill.

This is the same logic as maxing out your credit cards in your twenties because you assume you'll be a millionaire by your forties, but with, you know, the chance of global devastation if you're wrong.

To make this argument look respectable, Nordhaus demonstrated it mathematically, using a suspiciously precise time value of money of 4.3 per cent to show that we should spend no more than $1.48 today to avert $100 of climate damage one hundred years from now.*

The obvious flaw here is that the same logic will hold in the future. The people of the 22nd century could say, "Well, sure the ice caps have melted, the Indian subcontinent is too hot to live in and palaeolithic viruses unleashed

---

* The maths of this is called "discounting", and it's the same as compound interest, only backwards. i.e. if you invested $1.48 now and earned 4.3 per cent interest on it for 100 years then you'd end up with $100.

from the no-longer-permafrost have made my face break out in boils, but think how rich our grandkids will be – let them deal with this mess."

Implicit was the idea that the economy will continue to grow. But if the damage from climate change is cumulative – if rising temperatures trigger food shortages, social collapse or global conflict – then growth stops. In fact, a more realistic model would use a *negative* discount rate to reflect the risk of decline. And that same model would then tell us to spend a fortune today.

Worse still, Nordhaus's analysis assumed that only a tiny part of the economy actually depends on the climate – just little, insignificant things like *farming*. Since agriculture only makes up about 1 per cent of economic activity in developed countries, he reasoned, climate breakdown won't hurt the economy that much. How important could food possibly be? We can all just sit in air-conditioned offices and carry on with our Zoom calls. I guess, similarly, since we don't pay to breathe, breathing can't be that important to the economy.

One professor of environmental science referred to Nordhaus's recognition as "The Nobel Prize for Climate Catastrophe".

—

A tanned man in, I guess, his forties, with an open shirt and tight jeans, had met me and Remy in a reception area that had abstract art on the walls and giant bouquets of flowers on every table. I wondered if the flowers were related to a flower delivery company they'd invested in, but maybe it was just to prove that they had money to burn.

He kept joking about windsurfing (I honestly have no idea why) as he led us to a small glass-walled office where he introduced us to his colleague, an implausibly young woman, also wearing an open white shirt and tight jeans (I think this may be the uniform of venture capitalists). This small office was where we were to make our "pitch".

I'd spent about three days justifying Remy's proposed NPV by constructing an impressive interlocking spreadsheet filled with upwards swooshing graphs. It was, frankly, a little erotic, and at the end of my part of the presentation I rather proudly pointed to the final valuation figure.

There was a pause, as the VCs wondered if I was joking.

"Twenty-five million pounds?!" I understand that a question mark next to an exclamation mark is called an "interrobang", and I swear I could hear it as a separate word. This tanned windsurfer had a point. You can buy an underwater speaker on Amazon for about £30.

He then folded his arms and said, bluntly, "What if we offered you eight million?"

Remy folded her arms, too, trying to look nonchalant. "Well, sure, it's not ideal, but we could probably negotiate around eight million."

His face was fixed in his best poker expression. "What if we offered you one million?"

Remy's own attempt at a poker face couldn't hide her disappointment. "That would be too low."

The VC laughed, putting his hands behind his head and glancing triumphantly at his colleague. "Right then, so your price is between one and eight million."

I rather admired his negotiating skills, though I wish I'd realised that his asking for a net present value was a ploy.

Anyway, two days later he sent Remy an offer for a quarter of a million, which she rejected.

—

The official purpose of the university's financial placements team was to "cultivate relationships within the financial sector to better understand the roles our economics graduates could fill". Professor Alva had implied that it would involve going out for expensive lunches with department heads at flashy investment banks, as part of a symbiotic exchange of ideas.

In reality, it meant sitting alongside suckers from other universities in basement meeting rooms in the City listening to a 23-year-old HR manager explain how their graduate recruitment scheme was identical to every other bank's graduate recruitment scheme.

Most of the banks were *investment* banks – the really big hitters of high finance, businesses like Goldman Sachs and Morgan Stanley that help big companies raise money, advise on mergers and acquisitions ("should we buy that company for $10 billion?"), and, not that I'm bitter, pay much higher salaries than accountancy firms. When I qualified as a chartered accountant, one of my colleagues quit our firm to join Goldman Sachs and he told me that his salary was four times higher than it had been at our firm, and that his first-year bonus was higher than his salary, which wasn't bad for someone in their early twenties. That said, it's not a patch on Goldman CEO David Solomon, who received a $39 million payout in 2024.*

There are differing opinions about the contribution that investment banks make to society. Goldman Sachs's former chief executive Lloyd Blankfein claimed they were doing "God's work" by helping companies raise money, whereas *Rolling Stone* magazine journalist Matt Taibbi famously described the bank as "a great vampire squid wrapped around the face of humanity, relentlessly jamming its blood funnel into anything that smells like money". Maybe they're both right?

At one particularly dull recruitment presentation at a bank, I happened to chat to one of the representatives from another university as we were herded out into street. I mentioned that I was going to an almost identical recruitment "seminar" at a private equity firm in three hours' time, and he told me that he was going to it too.

"What are you going to do for the next three hours?" he asked.

"Shuffle around aimlessly contemplating which awful life decisions led to me being here today," I said.

"Cool." He nodded. "Can I join you?"

He was called Nguyen, and we drifted around the Square Mile comparing our experiences of our respective business schools. As we walked, he periodically took a dainty little paper bag from his blazer pocket, from which he plucked irregularly shaped chocolates that he chewed on thoughtfully. We headed for a public roof garden on Fenchurch Street and ended up sitting on a

---

* Though this is eclipsed by top hedge fund managers – in any given year, around two dozen hedgies are likely to take home over $1 billion *each*.

bench there with our sandwiches, and once I'd finished mine he looked at this dainty bag, then looked at me.

"Sorry, I haven't offered you any of these," he said.

"That's quite all right," I replied. I mean, I love chocolates, and he had loads, but honestly, that's fine, you keep them all to yourself.

"It's just . . ." He seemed unsure how to tell me. "I bought them off a drug dealer."

He then softly explained that he hated attending these recruitment seminars so much that he microdosed himself with psilocybin to get through them. Then he extended the bag to me.

"Would you like some?"

—

Back when I was a trainee accountant, I remember once how a senior manager had offered me a chocolate from a fancy-looking box (I doubt very much these were also laced with magic mushrooms, just to be clear). I politely shook my head and said, *No, thank you.*

After she had walked off, another manager scolded me.

"That's very rude, to decline her offer," she told me.

I was really taken aback. I hadn't meant to offend anyone. Is it really rude to decline a chocolate when you're offered one?

—

The building the private equity firm was based in was something else – astonishing curving concrete and reflecting glass and carpets that swirled as we walked over them. There were lime trees on the street outside that twinkled above a row of identical Porsches. At the front desk, a receptionist gave a smile that levitated towards us as she handed us our temporary visitor badges. Mine looked like a butterfly.

"Fourth floor," she said, with a voice that melted into air.

Nguyen gripped my hand in the lift and suppressed an infectious giggle. I think he was lying when he said *micro*dosing.

—

When I mentioned Goldman Sachs and the whole "vampire squid" thing, I may have given you the mistaken impression that investment banks are somehow the bad guys of high finance. That accolade surely belongs to the corporate raiders and asset strippers of private equity.

Equity just means ownership, and "private" simply means that *you* are not invited. Their game plan is simple: buy up companies, squeeze them dry, then move on. They usually do this by laying off staff, flogging the real estate and cancelling the Christmas party.

They're usually not very good at actually running the businesses they buy (I mean, logically, why would they be better than the current managers who actually know the industry?), so what they really specialise in is – how should I phrase this? – *alternative* means of extracting profits.

Typically, a private equity firm use a target company's own assets to buy that company. That might sound strange, but it's a bit like buying a house with a mortgage. But now imagine the house already has tenants, you double their rent and sell the roof when they're not looking.

Once in charge, the private equity firm typically sells off assets the company needs to operate, forcing the company to lease them back, and on top of that drains cash out through "management fees" and "special dividends".

So, in the end, what was once a large, independent company is left burdened with debt, rent payments and fewer staff, while its owners cut every corner they can find. But hey, the private equity firm walks away richer, so let's chalk it up as a success.

—

There were three executives from the private equity firm giving the presentation. They were wearing beautifully cut suits and they all had amazing hair and purred seductively.

"We offer the highest starting salaries in the Square Mile," said one of them, stroking his long, thin beard, "and in return, all we ask is for your so—"

Nguyen gave me a little tap, then leaned in and whispered, "Look. Look at their hair."

I shrugged and turned my hands palms up, to indicate I didn't know what he meant. I seemed to have more fingers than usual.

"What about it?"

He looked panicked.

"They've got *horns*."

—

Private equity firms have been accused of targeting sectors where their corner cutting and risk-magnifying activities fall upon the already vulnerable – nursing homes, children's care homes, trailer parks and, in America, prisons. It almost always follows the same pattern: load the acquired company up with debt, lay off staff, sell the assets, cut expenditure, extract a management fee.

The New York Times summed this up in 2023 with the headline, "Private Equity is gutting America – and getting away with it".

Ever wondered what happened to Toys "R" Us? I used to love it; I expect many of you did. Well, in 2005, private equity firms bought the company and loaded it up with unmanageable debt. Then, because of their *expertise* at running businesses, they then charged Toys "R" Us a "management fee".

This is a bit odd as, according to Mark Cohen of Columbia University's Graduate School of Business, the private equity-owned chain was "guilty of serial mismanagement". But maybe it was a small fee?

Oh no, actually, the management fee was $470 million. You might think that would've paid for a lot of top-flight managers, but it didn't work out that way. Toys "R" Us declared bankruptcy in 2018.

It's a similar story at Thames Water, which has a monopoly on all piped drinking water and sewage treatment in London, and which was privatised in 1989 in the hope that private investment would create a better service. It wasn't a hard sell to the private sector, as their product literally falls from the sky in England *all the bloody time*.

In 2006, Thames Water was purchased by Australian asset manager Macquarie and a group of private equity investors, who then used the company's own assets to borrow £7.3 billion.

It would be reasonable to imagine that some of the £7.3 billion they borrowed could have been used to improve their service, but since privatisation, £7.2 billion has been paid out as dividends to their private owners. So now, saddled with debts and discharging raw effluent into rural streams, the new owners of Thames Water want to raise bills by 40 per cent, otherwise, they say, they'll go bust.

—

At least all these high-finance firms that manage hundreds of trillions of dollars' worth of assets are filled with super-bright economists who know what they're doing, right?

In the run-up to the 2008 financial crisis, the big banks had a buzz-phrase: *diversifying risk*. Alan Greenspan, the chairman of the Federal Reserve, said that financial innovation had enhanced "the ability to differentiate risk and allocated it to those investors most able and willing to take it".

His vice-chairman, Donald Kohn, said that the financial system was now "more resilient and flexible – better able to absorb shocks without increasing the effect of such shocks on the real economy".

The innovation they were referring to was a system of "collateralised debt obligations" and "credit default swaps", which is finance-speak for mixing everyone's loans together and insuring the loans against the risk that they won't be paid back. These new innovations were, like so much of finance and economics, based on complex maths and absolutely bananas assumptions.

The most significant assumption was that the probability of one person's loan not being paid back was unrelated to any other loan not being paid back.

In reality, though, if two people work at the same factory then they could both lose their jobs at the same time, so will both be unable to pay back their loans. In other words, these financial innovations were based on a mistaken assumption.

This flaw was hidden in the complexity of the statistical analysis. Even the credit-ratings agencies (whose entire reason for existence is to verify the maths) failed to verify the maths.

When the 2008 financial crisis hit, it was the biggest downturn since the 1929 Wall Street Crash. A vast housing bubble, blown up by reckless and often downright predatory lending, finally burst. The "innovative" collateralised debt obligations and credit default swaps that were meant to manage risk failed to do so. The fallout was brutal. One in four American households saw three-quarters of their wealth vanish. Eight million Americans lost their jobs. Lehman Brothers, once the fourth-largest investment bank in the United States, collapsed overnight. As panic set in, banks around the world scrambled to dump toxic assets, triggering financial crises, emergency bailouts and a torrent of freshly printed money like nothing ever seen before.*

A global recession followed, and for most people living standards didn't claw their way back to where they'd been before the crisis until nearly a decade later.

Politicians who had been glorying in the "end of boom and bust" wanted answers. Famously, so did Queen Elizabeth, who asked the economists at the Bank of England why they didn't see it coming. Mervyn King, the governor of the Bank of England, told the Queen that it was a "collective failure of imagination".

Prime Minister Gordon Brown acknowledged that "we didn't understand how risk was spread".

In 2009, one senior banker is said to have reassured Chancellor of the Exchequer Alistair Darling that "from now on we will only lend when we understand the risks involved". Darling pointed out that the government was now the majority shareholder in that bank, following a bailout.

Alan Greenspan expressed his own shock. He acknowledged to Congress, with a degree of understatement, that there had been a "flaw in the model".

It was a flaw that led to over $10 *trillion* of monetary injections by central banks around the world in a mad scramble to save the financial system. As Sveriges Riksbank Prize-winner Paul Krugman put it, economists

---

* The investment bank Bear Stearns also collapsed. Their chief economist, David Malpass, wrote in 2007 in *The Wall Street Journal* that, "Housing and debt markets are not that big a part of the US economy." Malpass was rewarded for this, erm, *foresight* with a new job as president of the World Bank.

"went astray because . . . they mistook beauty, clad in impressive looking mathematics, for truth".*

It turned out that far from risk being prudently diversified and managed, it was being offloaded on to people who understood it even less than the bankers who were selling it.

—

Towards the end of the academic year, the university put on a careers fair. Representatives from different businesses gave short presentations in our lecture theatres and then put up stands in the sports hall, where wide-eyed third years were suddenly hit by the reality that their lives would no longer have structure. I involuntarily shuddered at the sight of the accountancy firms luring the unwary young towards them, like angler fish in the abyss.

Due to my role in the financial placements team, Professor Wilding had asked me to help facilitate, especially as one of the banks that heavily recruited from our university also sponsored a large amount of our business school, so we had to "endeavour to support them".

My "support" didn't really stretch further than making cups of tea, but I got chatting to one of the investment bankers at his stand.

"Do you enjoy your job?" I asked.

He nodded. "Mate, it's all hookers and blow."

"*Really?*" I asked, but then he grinned.

"No. But then I've only been doing it a year. Maybe in a couple of promotions."

One of the first students to talk to him was a young woman with green hair and a Nirvana T-shirt. I wasn't sure I recognised her from the economics department, but then she blended in pretty well. She looked the investment banker up and down and asked him what he did at the bank.

"I work in the liquidity coverage ratio analysis team," he said. It probably sounded sexier in his head.

---

* What's less commonly reported is that he wrote this in an article that was mostly about babysitting.

"So what would happen if your team didn't exist?" she asked, which I thought was a cracker of a question to ask at a careers day.

"The world would end," he replied, with the same deadpan delivery as his *hookers and blow* line.

She smiled at him involuntarily. "That's hot," she said.

Blackbeard, as usual, approached the end of the academic year differently. He was sprawled on one of the sofas in the common area of the economics department, between the pool table and the vending machines, half snoozing and occasionally dealing with students who wanted to appeal their exam grades. I took a break from the careers fair and went to sit down next to him. I told him I was thinking about becoming an investment banker so that students would think I was hot. I think he knew I was joking. At least, I think I was joking.

"I've just been reading about Equatorial Guinea," he said, which was the kind of way he responded to most of what I said to him.

"In Africa?"

"No, Finland." He rolled his eyes. "Of course, in Africa. Apparently, they've pumped enough oil since the year 2000 to give every one of their citizens around $50,000."

"Oh yeah?"

"They haven't done that, though. Instead, the ruling elite has misappropriated the money. Here, look –" He passed me a folded up magazine, and pointed to a picture of a yacht – "the president's eldest son, Teodorin Obiang, is thought to have amassed a $300 million fortune, more than the country's combined health and education budgets. He's bought himself a $120 million yacht that has been seized by Dutch authorities as part of a money-laundering investigation."

"What, so I shouldn't be an investment banker, I should be the son of a corrupt dictator?" I struggled to see the parallels between where I lived and Equatorial Guinea. It's not like Britain had a tiny elite who kept all the money... *wait a minute...*

He looked up at a student as she approached us.

"Sorry to interrupt," she said. "The administrator said I could talk to you about my exam result?"

"What did you get?" asked Blackbeard.

"Forty-seven."

"And what should you have got?"

"Fifty?"

Blackbeard looked at a printed-out list of student exam results he had on the low table in front of him, found this particular student, took a pencil from his beard, crossed out 47 and wrote in 50.

"Thanks!" she said, and skipped off, probably to make wild love to the apprentice investment banker in the sports hall.

"No," he said, returning the exam scores to the table in front of him. "We might not export as much oil nowadays, but we export financial services. It's like…ten per cent of the UK economy. It's where the highest paying jobs are. So, we have a brain drain from other industries into the one sector that doesn't actually make anything, then we sell our services overseas, which strengthens our currency, which makes it harder for the rest of British business to export anything. It's a vicious cycle, no wonder we're not growing."

"You think financial services are our 'Dutch Disease'?" I asked. This is the name often given to the idea of a "resource curse" – the fact that countries that strike oil (or, in the Netherlands' case, gas – hence their particular disease) end up with overvalued currencies that weaken their domestic industries and ultimately lead to a weakened economy, rather than a stronger one.

"I really do. It means our government depends on tax receipts from both the banks and their employees, so they relax banking regulations – which only ever leads to bigger mortgages and then…disaster. And what's more, all the money has flowed to London, where the banks are, at the expense of the regions."

It seemed plausible enough, but something about the way he was talking made me suspicious.

"Didn't you used to work for a bank?" I asked him.

He looked surprised that I knew. "It was a long time ago."

"Why did you leave?"

He returned the pencil to his beard. "I got fired."

—

Michael Hudson, professor of economics at the University of Missouri, likens the financial sector to the feudal barons in agrarian society, who got rich without having to get their hands dirty. No wonder all the peasants were poor when a single powerful *rentier* owned all the land. Nowadays, he says, "investors, financiers and bankers are the largest *rentier* sector of today's financialised economies."

The economist Sir John Kay, a professor at both the London School of Economics and Oxford University, makes a similar point – that high finance "can appear to be inordinately profitable, [but] that profitability need bear no relation to the value added from financial activities". In other words, sometimes financiers aren't creating wealth, they're just taking it from away from you.

One problem, as Hudson puts it, is that economists have long ignored the financial sector because loans and interest payments cancel each other out. If I owe you $500 and pay you $25 of interest on that debt then you are owed $500 and have an income of $25 – merge it all together and no new wealth has been created, so what's there for an economist to measure?

Hudson points out that "credit and its counterpart, debt, have shaped our economic systems since prehistory, [so] understanding how credit is used is therefore a sine qua non for understanding our economy". In 2004, Hudson argued that "a fundamentally different model" was needed to analyse the economy. Sadly, not enough people listened to him – most economists largely stuck with the old model, or at least did until the 2008 financial crisis.

I say *most* economists, but not *all* economists. There was, in fact, one economist tucked away in St Louis who managed to predict the 2008 financial crash almost perfectly, which was all the more impressive as he had died in the mid-1990s.

His name was Hyman Minsky, and he specialised in linking financial markets with the economic cycles of boom and bust. He had been born in Chicago in 1919, so had witnessed first hand the effects of the Wall Street Crash and depression that followed. During his lifetime, his research was admired but largely ignored by mainstream economists, yet his description of how banks create financial crises precisely predicted the crash that began to unfold in 2008.

He proposed that bank *lending* followed three stages:

First, money was lent to people who could afford to pay both interest and *repayments* of their loan (like a standard repayment mortgage).

This lending puts more money into the system, which pushes up house prices.*

Due to higher house prices, new borrowers can no longer afford the *repayment* parts of their loan, so the next stage is when banks offer *interest-only* mortgages, which can only be paid off by taking out a new loan.

New borrowing means house prices continue to rise, so next would come the "negatively amortising loan". This is the third stage, in which the interest itself is never paid over, but is instead added to the outstanding loan. Minsky called this last stage the *Ponzi Phase*.†

In America, such loans were incredibly rare before 2002, but then, with houses becoming ever more expensive, their use skyrocketed.

These mortgages were often called an "option adjustable rate mortgage", the "option" being to not pay the interest "rate" on the mortgage.

Not having to pay interest seemed too good to be true for many borrowers. In 2005, one in fourteen new mortgages in America was of this *optional* interest rate variety. In 2006, one in seven new mortgages was. By 2007, some $750 billion of option adjustable rate mortgages had been issued.

But it was too good to be true. Unpaid interest became household debt, *minimum* monthly payments were still required and were getting larger, and when borrowers couldn't even manage these, mortgage delinquencies soared. In 2008, more than 2 million US homes received foreclosure filings,

---

* Technically, not just house prices, but all "asset" prices, but it's easier to see what happens just by looking at houses.

† After Charles Ponzi, who in 1920 conned Americans out of $1 million per day by paying old investors with new investors' cash. He claimed to have found a way to make risk-free profits out of pre-paid postage stamps, which was ludicrously untrue, but he sued everyone who said so. When his scheme collapsed, six commercial banks collapsed with it.

and nearly 900,000 were repossessed. As house prices fell, panic spread, and the cycle violently reversed – just as Minsky predicted.

Stability, said Minsky, is itself destabilising. The housing market is one big pyramid scheme, with new buyers needing to be willing to pay ever higher amounts in a process that grows and grows until – in what is now posthumously known as a "Minsky Moment" – the whole thing collapses.

—

Blackbeard told me that he was going to spend the holidays doing research for a paper he was submitting for publication. It was going to be about Ottoman sultans.

"Sultans?"

"Yup," he said. "I think the Ottoman sultans had it right."

"Do you mean the harems?"

He chuckled, paused to give my point some consideration, then explained: "They effectively had a one hundred per cent inheritance tax, as they periodically murdered the nobility to redistribute wealth to the people."

I can imagine it was exactly that kind of attitude that got him fired from the bank.

—

After the Wall Street Crash in 1929, the US government passed the Glass–Steagall Act, a law designed to separate *commercial banking* (that is, making loans and taking in deposits) from *investment banking* (which is mostly buying and selling things, especially shares in companies). The goal was to prevent excessive risk-taking in order to bring stability to the financial system, by walling off the part of banking that created money and managed deposits from speculative and risky investing.

But in 1999, Republican senators Phil Gramm, Jim Leach and Thomas Bliley, with financial backing from Bank of America, Morgan Stanley, Credit Suisse, Citigroup, Goldman Sachs, Merrill Lynch and Lehman Brothers (spot the connection) introduced the Gramm–Leach–Bliley Act, which repealed and replaced the Glass–Steagall Act.*

The argument put forward by the bankers, sorry, I mean the *senators*, was that banks were over-regulated. Innovative new risk-managing products like *collateralised debt obligations* and *credit default swaps* were changing the financial landscape. Without deregulation, American banks were operating with one hand tied behind their back.

The new legislation allowed insurance companies, commercial banks and investment banks to merge, it removed conflict of interest provisions and denied regulatory authorities the right to regulate large investment bank holding companies. *Nope*, can't see any problems here.

Oh no, wait. In Sir John Kay's wonderful phrase, banking profits are often "borrowed from the future". It took all of nine years for the banking system to run wild with their deregulated lending and implode the economy.

As the economist Joseph Stiglitz put it, "Most of this innovation involved devising better ways of scamming others, manipulating markets without getting caught... and exploiting market power."

Jim Leach later regretted his involvement in the repeal of the Glass–Steagall Act, and joined the Democrats. Phil Gramm, on the other hand, joined the board of investment bank UBS.

When the 2008 financial crash started to unfold, the Chief Financial Officer at Goldman Sachs, David Viniar, claimed that they "were seeing things that were 25-standard deviation moves, several days in a row". Twenty-five standard deviations from the average means something that occurs only once per ten

---

* In the run-up to the vote on repealing the old Act, the big players of high finance contributed more than $86 million to members of Congress. The research group Open Secrets, which tracks money in US politics, noted an unsurprising correlation between the politicians who received the most funding from the banking sector and the politicians who voted to repeal Glass–Steagall and replace it with the Gramm–Leach–Bliley Act.

thousand trequadragintillion times (that's a number with 137 zeros). And apparently this was happening *several days in a row*. Wow.

Of course, it's always possible that the financial crash of 2008 wasn't something that should happen less frequently than once per *the entire history of the universe*, but that actually financial crashes come about fairly often, and Goldman Sachs's mathematical models were wrong.

I discussed all of this recently at a lunch with Adrian Bell, a professor of the History of Finance at Henley Business School. He explained it rather succinctly. In his view (though obviously a professor of financial history would say this), a big problem in the financial world is that neither financiers nor economists are taught any history.

So, when a banker says, "this is the first time we've ever seen anything like this", what they really mean is that this is the first time *they* have seen anything like this.

—

The tiny country of Iceland was one of the places hardest hit by the 2008 financial crash.

In the 1990s, Iceland embarked on a series of free-market reforms and, like the US, had deregulated its banking sector, which resulted in the rapid growth of Icelandic banks. By 2008, the assets of Iceland's three largest commercial banks reached 11 times the size of the Icelandic economy, financed by borrowing on international markets. Without regulatory oversight, there was nothing to stop bankers taking risks, and even, in some cases, lying about those risks.

In the crash, the Icelandic stock market lost 90 per cent of its value, the three largest banks collapsed and unemployment tripled. Many British and Dutch local government bodies, including police and fire services, had deposited cash in Icelandic banks and a huge legal wrangle began over whether they would ever get their money back. The Icelandic government put their ambassadorial residences in New York and London up for sale in a desperate effort to raise money and then went cap in hand to the International Monetary Fund.

But what happened next in Iceland was different to elsewhere.

Where other countries bailed out their banks, Iceland held their bankers accountable. Hundreds of bankers were investigated for financial irregularities and thirty-six were jailed (which, given Iceland's tiny population, is a *huge* number – the equivalent of about 32,000 bankers in America).

The economist Ellen Brown has a solution to all this which is less drastic than putting bankers in prison: nationalise the banks. She points to the fact that economic miracles occurred in places with nationalised banks, especially China, Taiwan and South Korea. Both the world's largest banks and the world's safest are state-owned. Profits from state-owned banks belong to the citizens of the state, and while losses from state-owned banks are borne by those same citizens, that's often true of *private* banks too, especially now they're "too big to fail" because the state, more often than not, ends up bailing them out.

She has argued that banking should be seen as a public utility, like water or the electricity grid – the government has the ultimate responsibility for managing money, so why does it outsource that responsibility to private companies? As she puts it, we need to *democratise money*.

Ellen Brown isn't the first person to suggest nationalising the banks, and thus ensure that the money we pay in interest every year would go to the state instead of *rentier* private companies.

Another economist got there before her. No prizes for guessing that his name was Henry George.

12

THE IRON LADY, THE LETTUCE AND THE INEQUALITY MACHINE

"Buy land. They're not making it anymore."
Mark Twain, not an economist

In October 2022, I wrote a prescient tweet. I was quite proud of it. A new Chancellor of the Exchequer was about to be appointed in the UK. His name was Jeremy Hunt, and he was to be the fourth politician put in charge of setting taxes and spending that year, replacing an Old Etonian named Kwasi Kwarteng.

A lot of newspapers described such churn as "unprecedented". But was it? With my nerdiest thinking cap on, I tweeted that *actually* it had happened before, though not since 1827. We were also on our second prime minister of the year, Liz Truss having replaced Boris Johnson in September. What I spotted was that 1827 was also the year that held the record for the shortest-serving prime minister. Was history about to repeat itself? I asked my four followers on Twitter.

My tweet did not go viral. It didn't help that *everyone* was predicting the same thing. It was obvious to even the densest of saplings that Liz Truss's days were numbered. *The Economist* magazine had speculated that her premiership would have the shelf life of a head of lettuce and to ram the point home the tabloid newspaper the *Daily Star* was live-streaming the wilting of a real lettuce (wearing a blonde wig).

And why was it obvious? Because on 23 September, Liz Truss's Chancellor of the Exchequer, Kwasi Kwarteng, had stood up in parliament and had, with the full support of the new prime minister, given an absolute masterclass in political and economic incompetence.

Following the Covid pandemic and Russia's invasion of Ukraine, inflation rates had started to rise across the world as production dropped, supply chains seized up and energy costs rose. Traditionally, the way to tackle inflation is to take money out of the system, which governments can do by raising taxes or cutting spending.

So what did Kwasi Kwarteng do, while Liz Truss smirked behind him? He announced not only the biggest tax *cuts* Britain had seen since 1972, but also a £60 billion subsidy for household fuel bills. For context, the entire annual defence budget of the United Kingdom that year was about £68 billion.

It was like throwing (subsidised) fuel on to a bonfire and expecting the flames to die down. Some hard-right members of parliament cheered, but as Kwasi Kwarteng excitedly read out his sweeping reforms, many of his own colleagues sat in stunned silence.

"I actually think she had the right idea," said Chris, a recently retired government economist Ioannou and I had gone for lunch with in Hackney, East London, to see if he could help with our latest project. Ioannou had chosen the restaurant – we sat on old pub garden furniture, they did a beer and burger deal for £10 and each beer was accompanied with notes about how far away they had been brewed. Our waiter wore his trousers so low that I was almost put off my food.

"*Really?*" I asked, struggling not to spit out my Foster's (brewed in Manchester). The budget had reduced welfare payments for 120,000 of Britain's poorest people, funded by giving a 5 per cent tax cut to the highest earning 1 per cent. Joe Biden, who at the time was US president – hardly a country that shies away from giving tax breaks to the rich – said that Kwarteng's budget was "a mistake".

"Yes, absolutely. Reagan and Thatcher did the same thing in the 1980s and huge economic growth followed. They cut taxes, reduced welfare spending, and deregulated. And the economy boomed."

"Not for everyone," I said. "And it's hardly booming now."

Kwarteng had refused to allow the Office for Budget Responsibility to scrutinise his plans, turning down their repeated offers to do so – despite the entire point of the Office for Budget Responsibility being to make sure that budgets are – you guessed it – responsible.

When Tom Scholar, the Permanent Secretary to the Treasury, warned of the economic shock that their dipstick ideas would cause (though phrasing his concerns more politely, I imagine), Truss fired him.

To avoid scrutiny, Kwarteng even refused to call his announcement a "budget", despite it being the biggest overnight economic change made by any British government in decades, referring to it merely as a "fiscal event", presumably because "Special Fiscal Operation" sounded too Putinesque. When he finally finished outlining the details of this *fiscal event*, Kwasi sat down with a smile on his face.

And then the markets reacted.

Almost immediately, the value of the pound started to tank, as currency traders realised the colossal level of borrowing that the UK government was going to need and the inflationary pressures that Kwarteng's plans would let loose. There's often a lot of hyperbole when journalists write about market movements – so I'll just state the fact: over the next three days, pound sterling hit an *all-time low* against the dollar. That's *all time* as in "since 6 July 1785, when the US Congress authorised the issuance of a new currency, the dollar".

Investors sold off UK government bonds so fast that the value of the bonds plummeted, entering into what City analysts called a *doom loop*. The Pensions Regulator hadn't been informed of the contents of Kwarteng's budget in advance and called it an "extraordinary shock", beyond anything they had thought possible. Some of these pension funds, responsible for paying for the retirement of millions of Brits, were so heavily invested in UK bonds that they came within hours of collapsing.

The Bank of England took emergency measures, offering to buy tens of billions in bonds to stop the rout. Exasperated, one former member of the Bank of England's Monetary Policy Committee described the actions of Truss and Kwarteng as "raging incompetence".

The International Monetary Fund broke convention and openly criticised Kwarteng's budget. The credit-rating agency Moody's lowered the UK's economic outlook to "negative".

Our rival (and much more successful) think-tank the Resolution Foundation calculated that the budget cost the UK government £10 billion in increased borrowing costs alone. That's enough to provide free school meals to every child, repair every pothole in the UK's roads, and double the number of police in London, with enough money left over to buy the *Mona Lisa*.

"It was a failure of communication, not of principle." Chris took another gulp of his beer (brewed 12 miles away). He spoke incredibly quickly with a slight East End geezer-y twang, which Ioannou told me was affected. "The mistake they made was not announcing their plans beforehand. If they had prewarned the Pensions Regulator, and the markets, and the Bank of England..."

"And not fired the Treasury Secretary?"

"Mweh, that was a political decision."

I imagine I didn't look too impressed. The Bank of England had reacted to Liz Truss and Kwasi Kwarteng's *political* decisions by hiking interest rates in an attempt to counter inflation. This had hit me particularly hard, as I'd recently doubled the size of my mortgage when I moved house.

I appreciate that middle-class financial sob stories are never that moving, and you might just think *well at least you have a house*, but as our personal circumstances have an inevitable impact on our economic beliefs, I thought I should share this information with you. You know, transparency and all that. Where the previous year I had been paying an interest rate of 1 per cent, after that salad-headed budget I was now paying 5 per cent, on a loan that was ten times the size of my income.

The papers were filled with similar stories – people who had saved for years to buy their dream home and were now faced with financial ruin, young couples moving back in with their parents, all because of higher interest rates. These stories had stayed with me (or at least, my nut-crushing interest payments had stayed with me), and eventually, about a year and a bit into my time at the Institute for Fair Economics, I approached Ioannou with a suggestion: our think-tank could champion a *heterodox* idea – that the root cause of all society's economic problems was that house prices were too high.

—

"The Bank of England raised interest rates because it has an official target of keeping inflation below two per cent" explained Chris. "But do you know why it's two per cent?"

"Because a little bit of inflation encourages spending, but too much destabi—"

"No. It's all because of some random fuckwit in New Zealand."

I hadn't heard this version before. "Go on," I said, intrigued. "Fuckwit" wasn't a term I'd heard many economists use before.

He checked something on his phone. "Yeah, here. 1988. New Zealand's Finance Minister, Roger Douglas, was being interviewed on television about his country's persistently high inflation rates..."

I perked up at the mention of Roger Douglas. As you may recall, I've already fingered him as a Mont Pelerin member.

"Then he says that *of course he would like to see inflation rates fall*. His interviewer pressed him to say what level he would like the rates to fall to. And at that point, Roger Douglas did something extraordinary – something no finance minister anywhere in the world had ever done before. He gave a numerical answer. *Ideally zero to one per cent*, he said. The crowd gasped. His interviewer fainted. Front pages were held across the world. Well, not quite – but they should have been, because this was momentous. That unplanned, unscripted, off-the-cuff remark is the origin of your mortgage payment quintupling."

"I'm not sure I follow."

"This was the first time that any finance minister *anywhere* had suggested an actual numerical target rate for inflation, rather than merely aiming at an ill-defined "low" rate. So the economists at the New Zealand treasury ministry scrambled to react to this new proclamation, and eventually decided that as real-world inflation was usually lower than "official" inflation, the official target would need to be bumped up a bit, which resulted in the world's first government-backed target of two per cent."

"What?" I said, clearly adding intellectually to the progression of this history lesson. "Is there not some empirical study of how inflation interacts with employment levels and, you know, *growth*, that has concluded two per cent is an ideal target inflation rate?"

"No!" He was laughing. "Not a bit of it. This minister in New Zealand, slightly panicked by a question he hadn't prepared for, went *err, how about 1 per cent?* And his underlings went *let's round it up a bit*, and then the rest of the freekin' world went, *oh great, someone's got a target rate, let's use that*."

I checked this afterwards. New Zealand announced a 2 per cent target inflation rate in 1990. The Bank of Canada adopted a 2 per cent inflation rate target in 1991. When the Bank of England got their independence in 1997, they also latched on to a 2 per cent inflation target, so did the European Central Bank and the Bank of Japan. Australia adopted a 2–3 per cent target (they couldn't be exactly the same as the Kiwis, after all) and Ben Bernanke officially adopted a 2 per cent inflation target for the United States in 2012.

I'd always imagined besuited, respectable, probably insanely boring policy analysts examining the minutiae of economic data and using clever statistical techniques to create convoluted financial models, but no, it turns out it's more, *Hey, Bernanke, last one to 2 per cent is a loser!*

"There's no real rationale for this two per cent target, it's like these beer miles," Chris swept his hand to the board where they were all proudly displayed. "It's better for the environment for a barrel to be cycled thirty miles here on a rickshaw than driven five miles in a van, but everyone likes a target, even a meaningless one."

"But surely it's not *meaningless*?"

"No one knows. When I was a student, I was taught that inflation rates of five to seven per cent were the *natural* rate. Some economists argue for inflationary targets being four per cent or six per cent or even higher, but the fact is that your mortgage is ruinously expensive because some bloke in the eighties in New Zealand picked a random number out of thin air."

"*Bastard*," I said.

—

Ioannou was fully behind the idea of our institute making its name as the *anti*-high house price think-tank. "At least, until we get paid to say otherwise."

He and I sat down to talk through some ideas as to how we could go about it.

"No one's ever found any strong evidence for the wealth effect," he suggested. "Perhaps we could start there?"

As it happened, I'd pretty much come to the same conclusion, but couldn't possibly tell him that. I hadn't revealed to him that I was secretly an author, so telling him that I'd already written a book about house prices would have started a conversation I didn't want to have. It would also have been, technically, not entirely true, as I'd never actually finished the book.

My aim had been to write a mathematical detective story – an exploratory narrative where our novel's protagonist (a young and devilishly handsome accountant) tried to uncover a secret equation known only to a powerful hedge fund. The equation predicted precisely what house prices were going to be in the future, which the hedge fund used to make a killing – figuratively, and later, literally (the corpse was hidden under the flower beds of the fund's rooftop gardens).

After all, prevailing economic wisdom is that house prices must be determined by some interplay between the supply of houses and the total demand for them, so on that logic it should be possible to mathematically determine that price. The twist was that I really would include that equation, or at least the closest approximation I could find to it. But about halfway into the book I realised both that the equation was beyond my mathematical skills and that sentences like "he inserted the quadratic function into the denominator and let the numbers do the talking" sounded far more exciting in my head than they did on the page, so I had abandoned the book to write a memoir about tax instead.*

—

When I'd first encountered the *wealth effect* as a lay person my immediate reaction was that it was, possibly, the most godawful theory in the entirety of economics (which might explain why no one particular economist has claimed credit for inventing it). The idea is simple: if you own a house and house prices rise, you'll *feel* richer, so you'll spend more money. In the worst case, you could always sell your home if you needed to.

This, of course, runs counter to most people's experience of buying a house. If houses become more expensive you have to spend more money to get one, leaving you with less to spend on everything else.

I mean, I've never met anyone who has said, "I've lost my job and just had a new baby but we're all going to Cancun on holiday because our house has gone up in value."

And if you do run out of money and have to sell your house, where the hell are you going to move to? All the other houses are now more expensive. And then throw all the costs of moving into the mix – monetary and social and psychological – and I couldn't see how the theory had any grounding in reality. I mean, at best, at absolute best, a downsizing childless old person might spunk on a cruise, but that's it.

Or at least, so I thought. Now that I was pretending to be a respectable economist, I figured that I should actually look at the evidence. It's all well and good for me to sneer at politicians ignoring the warnings of their economic advisors, but I couldn't then do the same myself with the wealth effect just because I'm cross with Liz Truss for quintupling the cost of my mortgage.

---

* Frustratingly, it was only after I started hanging out with economists that I discovered the equation is beyond *anyone's* mathematical skills, as the only way to make it work is to introduce simplifying assumptions, and the whole point of my plot is that there would be no assumptions (except the location of the corpse, due to some unusually spectacular peonies).

Besides, every time I tried to get a straight answer on why high house prices are good for the economy, the stock reply is, "Let me tell you about a little thing called the wealth effect." Surely everyone couldn't just be parroting some phrase they learned from an outdated textbook, right?

Digging into the economic literature, I discovered that I was being too cynical. Of course there was plenty of detailed analysis of real-world wealth effects.

But Ioannou was right. Some of the analyses reported small negative correlations (meaning you spend less on other stuff if house prices rise), some of it small positive correlations.

There wasn't anything terribly decisive, and even when the correlations looked statistically significant, they came with acknowledgements that it's very hard to isolate the *"wealth* effect" from the *"I can't afford to move so I bought a new car instead* effect".

It occurred to me that maybe I wasn't finding conclusive evidence of the wealth effect because I didn't want to find a link. Perhaps my own innate bias against needing a massive mortgage to buy a decent family home was clouding my ability to interpret the findings? I asked Ioannou how he dealt with this problem.

"Who cares?" he said. "We're all biased. So go with your gut."

My *gut* told me that maybe economics was not quite the precise science I thought it was.

More surprising was just how much of economic theory ignores *homes* almost entirely. For instance, the average size or quality of someone's house does not even feature in measures of national wealth – in fact, it's quite the opposite.

Around 10 per cent of Gross Domestic Product – the normal measure of a country's income – is made up of "Imputed Rent", which is the rent that a homeowner would be paying if they didn't own their own home. It means that if house prices rise then imputed rents rise, so GDP rises, so a country is said to be richer *even though nothing new has been made and no money has changed hands*. This feels like mercantilism, only with house prices instead of gold.*

At the same time, increases in house prices are not included in inflation figures, despite the fact that buying a house is the most significant financial commitment any of us are ever likely to make.

The Bank of England describes housing as a "small . . . part of how we measure the output of the economy". A "small part"? The thing you'll spend a lifetime saving for? Despite the fact that the kind of property you live in and *where* you live will affect every aspect of your life – your work prospects, your family size, your health, your education, your exposure to crime? If that's *small*, I'd hate to see what counts as *big*.

I didn't understand this at all. Shouldn't the size and quality of your house be the *main* part of how we measure an economy? It seemed like the most important aspect of our personal finances was being routinely ignored by economists. Surely there was more to it than this?

—

It is possible that at some point in my conversation with Ioannou I may have started ranting. And like I say, it's equally possible that the eye-bleedingly high interest payments I was now making were affecting my judgement, so let me just stick to facts for now. Here's one: the average British person is richer than the average American.

You read that right. In 2023 (which is the most recent year for which

---

* Gross Domestic Product adds up all the transactions that have occurred in a country in order to see how much economic activity there is. It has its problems. It ignores anything that isn't paid for, like breastfeeding or Google Maps, but does include expenditure on things we'd rather not spend money on, like repairing potholes or building tanks, and it certainly doesn't measure any of the things we care most about, like health or friendships or crime. Indeed, GDP was largely created by an economist called Simon Kuznets, who disapproved of governments latching on to it as a measure of welfare (as they still do).

I can get complete data), the average American adult has $112,000 of wealth compared to the average Brit having $163,000.*

That's a massive difference, but it conceals a bigger issue: the average house in the UK is about $40–50,000 more expensive than the average house in the USA, which accounts for pretty much all the difference in wealth between these two places. But if you take this analysis further, a troubling picture emerges.

The average new home in the UK measures just 800 square feet, compared to over 2,300 square feet in America. I appreciate that size isn't everything, but it underlines one of the biggest problems with mainstream economics: that the price of something isn't the same as its value. When we say that house prices are rising, what we really mean is that we're getting less house per pound (or per dollar). British homes aren't *better* homes, they're simply more expensive. That's a bad thing.

I hadn't seen Kanya for a while, so I sent her an email asking if she wanted to help on my new housing project. She didn't reply.

I saw her the next day in the office and asked if she'd seen my email.

"Has Ioannou not told you?" she asked. "I've handed in my notice."

This was devastating, obviously.

"Where are you moving to?" I asked, partly just curious and partly really asking, *Should I be coming with you?*

She gave me a sly sort of smile. "I'm going to be a teacher."

We hadn't discussed this at all.

"An economics teacher?"

---

* There is, as you probably know, more than one type of average. These numbers look at the person exactly halfway between poorest and richest – the *median* richest person. If we look at total wealth divided by total people – the *mean* average wealth – then Americans are actually way ahead of the British, with $564,000 of wealth per person to the average Brit's $350,000. This tells us that not only does America have more wealth overall, but that it's far more concentrated in the hands of the wealthy.

"No." She gave a slightly embarrassed laugh. "I'm going to teach music."

I felt her absence. The closest I came to finding someone to replace her was a young *lad* called Dil, but I struggled to bond with him as he usually worked from home due to his two-hour commute. Until recently, he had rented a tiny one-room place with his girlfriend in Slough, west of London, but after his landlord had raised their rent they decided to move to Hastings on the south coast.

On one of the rare occasions that we were both in the office, I made the mistake of saying that it must be nice to have a view of the sea, and he dejectedly told me that, despite living in a seaside town, he could not afford a view of the sea. "But we do get attacked by seagulls sometimes."

Dil took a keen interest in the anti-high house price project. To him, there was something terribly conspiratorial about it.

"Did you know that the Russians call mortgages *slave debts*?" he said. "Think about it – higher house prices mean you need a bigger mortgage, and that means you have to work harder for longer to pay it off. I'm not saying there's a secret cabal of financiers and politicians conspiring to make us work long hours for our entire lives just to afford a roof over our heads, but if I was in a secret cabal and I wanted to force people to work harder for their entire lives this is exactly how I'd do it. Americans can't quit their jobs because of health insurance, we can't quit ours because of rent or mortgages."

"I think Americans pay rent or mortgages too . . . ?"

"They do now the cabal's in control," he said, with a wink. "But imagine the alternative – houses so cheap that we could all have several. Here, let me show you this."

He swivelled his laptop round and pulled up a website called economicsfromthetopdown. "There's this brilliant Canadian economist called Blair Fix who is, like, an analytical guru. Read these articles."

The articles were about inflation, and hierarchies, and peak oil, but also the half-life of a Spotify hit and a satire entitled "The Voldemort Index" (in which he-who-must-not-be-named explains that *first you start with inequality, then you proclaim that inequality arises from natural law, then that any attempt to constrain the power of the rich constitutes a "distortion" to that natural law*). I was hooked.

"How did you find this guy?" I asked Dil, as I browsed the articles, many of which were accompanied with beautifully visualised data.

He laughed. "I joined an economics society in Hastings – we meet up once a month and discuss economic ideas. One of the other fellas kept coming up with these amazing insights but eventually confessed he was cribbing it all from Blair Fix."

I'd got a bit stuck on my *why aren't low house prices a policy goal?* report and I'm not sure my meeting with Chris in Hackney or Dil's conspiracy theory had really helped. I didn't know whether low house prices *should* be a policy goal, but I realised that I'd made a mistake in my approach – if I wanted to know whether *mainstream* economics made an error in its analysis of housing, I probably shouldn't be searching for answers from people and sources who were so steeped in the mainstream that they were soaked through with economic orthodoxy.

Blair Fix, by contrast, described himself on his website as an "economic heretic – someone who thinks that mainstream economics is largely ideology in service of the powerful". He seemed like just the kind of economist I needed to speak to.

In an article called "The American Housing Crisis: A Theft, Not a Shortage", Blair Fix used data to show that what has occurred in the last 50 years in America wasn't so much a failure to build houses, but rather was the massive redistribution of wealth away from the poor and towards the rich.

His data shows how much the average home costs, not in dollars, but as a multiple of different Americans' incomes. In this way, we can see how inequality has developed.

In 1970, the average American home cost 20 times the annual income of the poorest *eighth* of Americans. But today, that same home costs that same multiple of 20 times the annual income of the poorest *third* of Americans. Meaning almost three times as many Americans see the average house as *very* expensive compared to fifty years ago.

Plotted on a graph, these numbers look like this:

These numbers are even more striking at the bottom of the income scale.*

In 1970, only *one in a hundred* Americans would earn less than 1 per cent of the cost of an average home. Now *one in seven* Americans do – that's about 14 per cent of all Americans completely excluded from home ownership.

Fix concludes that the issue isn't necessarily a shortage of affordable homes – it's a shortage of decent wages at the bottom end of the scale.

"Politicians don't want to address this because it gets into the very politically charged arena of income distribution," Blair said to me, via Zoom, from what I think was his attic.

He had told me that he lives in a time zone called "Mountain Time", which I thought was Canadian slang, like "Moose Hour", but no, it's a real thing, and is so many hours behind London that I had to talk to him late at night, just before he went to work in the morning, as it were.†

"I notice you call yourself a *political* economist," I said, having read

---

* This graph first appeared in Blair Fix's article "The American Housing Crisis: A Theft, Not a Shortage".

† I appreciate that I'm in no position to sneer at the names of time zones, living as I do in one named after a surly London suburb.

through most of his articles by the time I arranged to speak to him, "but when you refer to theorists you don't like they're just 'economists'..."

He looked at me like he hadn't realised that he did that, then patiently explained what he described as the fundamental flaw of economics – that separating economics from politics was, in his words, "a lie from the start".

I nodded, perhaps a bit too eagerly. From the moment I'd started working at the think-tank all I'd seen was politics. The academic economists at my university were generally proudly left wing, the students heading for careers in finance all resolutely right wing. Politics seemed to drip from every pore of economics, yet so much economic literature shied away from it.

"I would say that *political* economist is a compliment," he said. "You have to explicitly recognise that economics is political. Human societies have always had ideologies. Historically they were religious or superstitious, with capitalism it's secular ... but that doesn't mean that ideology went away. Ideologies are designed more to shape your behaviour than describe the world as it actually is. And a lot of economics is still ultimately a big fiction, because we still have classes, and owners, who want to keep things the way they are."

It was refreshing to talk to another economist who, like Kanya, was sceptical about most of economics. He was adamant that what he was doing was science, whereas a lot of economics was, as he put it, a pseudo-science, at best.

We talked about where this artificial separation of politics and economics had come from, and he pinpointed none other than the economist John Bates Clark – the one who Blackbeard had described as Rockefeller's anti-Georgism attack dog.

"Clark was the one who created the idea of 'marginal productivity' – that workers and capitalists are paid in proportion to what they contribute to society. He was very explicit that this was an ideological project – he said in the introduction to his book, *if workers thought that they weren't paid what they produced, they would have the right to revolt* ... And he wanted to basically prove, and he used those words, *prove* that workers and capitalists were in a competitive market, so paid their marginal product. He wants to say to people, *listen, you have no reason to be unhappy, because you're paid what you contribute to society."*

"A lot of people believe that," I suggested.

"It's a very powerful argument. And it taps into very deep-seated human ideals of fairness. Most people would say that incomes should be in proportion to what they produce, but what does a doctor produce, or a lawyer, or a CEO?"

I found myself nodding. I wasn't sure I'd *produced* anything for almost the entirety of my career.

Like Joan Robinson had in the 1930s, Blair Fix had concluded that incomes are really about power dynamics. His research into how incomes are distributed across society reveals that *pay* is far less driven than you might expect by age, geography, education, IQ, or any measure of skill or productivity. Instead, the main determinant of your income is simply where you are in the "hierarchy". If you're the boss, you get paid more.

At first glance, that might seem obvious – *of course bosses get paid more*. But here's the key point: it doesn't matter if the boss is competent, intelligent, experienced or well-educated. The higher up the hierarchy they rise, the more they get paid, *regardless* of talent. This is certainly how I feel about most of the bosses I've ever had.

And what do those at the top of the hierarchy all have in common? It's power.

—

In the 1970s, the average CEO earned around 30 to 40 times the pay of the average worker at their company. Fifty years later, the average CEO is earning between 120 and 300 times more. That's a colossal increase.

The usual justification goes like this: if a particular CEO can increase a company's profits by $100 million compared to a less talented CEO, then paying them $30 million is still a good deal for shareholders. That sounds (almost) reasonable, until you look at the actual data.

Over the last 50 years, profit margins for large corporations have not increased. The CEOs are not outperforming their peers, especially their historical ones. If anything, they're getting worse.

Half of the profits made by the 500 largest listed companies in America today are made by just seven companies, all of which owe their success to technological innovation (and in some cases, monopolies).*

—

I mentioned to Blair Fix that productivity had risen enormously since the 1970s, but wages hadn't, and put my colleague Dil's idea that houses should be as cheap as possible to him.

"Sure," he said. "At the bottom of society, incomes have just collapsed – *that's* where the housing crisis is. The reason it's a crisis is because of income, not house building."

I asked him what he thought about the issue of money creation pushing up house prices.

"Ideally, you want either to give money to people who are poor, or put it towards specific programmes that are going to benefit underprivileged people," he said. "The worst-case scenario is what we have, that it's given to people who are already rich. There's nothing good, per se, about just creating money for no reason. What matters is always what you do with it."

Then I asked him what sort of reactions he'd had to his research.

He gave a sort of slightly bemused half-smile. "Well, it's very popular with the anarchist left..."

I got the impression that wasn't what he had intended. He views himself as a scientist – the idea that his research should be popular with people who hold a particular ideology is no more logical than a particular neuroscientist being admired by social democrats.

—

---

* Of course, *profits* and *profit margins* don't mean the same thing. A profit is just a dollar amount, but a profit margin is the profit amount as a proportion of revenue. Apple makes profits of around $30 billion per year, but has a lower profit margin than Games Workshop, the maker of Warhammer gaming figurines. So which company is better run? Yet Tim Cook, Apple's CEO, was paid $75 million in 2024, thirty times more than Kevin Roundtree of Games Workshop.

When British veterans of the First World War returned home, they were greeted with posters declaring that "you cannot expect to get an A1 population out of C3 homes".

During the war, the British military assessed fitness levels using a classification system with A1 at the top (hence being in "A1 shape"). If you were generally fit but needed a bit more training, you'd be A2. If you were the wrong side of forty and needed glasses, you'd be a B1, and so on. Meaning a C3 home had syphilis.

The posters were part of a campaign called "Homes for Heroes", which marked the beginning of a 60-year period in the UK in which the government saw the provision of housing as part of its remit.

In the first four years, over 200,000 new homes were built with government money and managed by local councils. New *garden cities* and *garden suburbs* filled with these "council" homes were developed, with an emphasis on quality – modern plumbing and plenty of open space.

After the Second World War, the building spree started again. Over a million new council homes were built by Clement Attlee's government in the years to 1951, and then between 100,000 and 200,000 homes every year for the next three decades. By 1979, when Margaret Thatcher came to power, over 40 per cent of the UK's population lived in council houses.

This is in remarkable contrast to the rest of the English-speaking world, particularly the USA, where public housing has a troubled history, often marred by racial segregation and failed projects. In 1980, just 1.5 per cent of Americans lived in publicly owned housing (though about another 10 per cent got some form of government-assisted rental support).

Margaret Thatcher's big idea was to introduce a "Right to Buy", with discounts of at least a third off the price of a council home offered to tenants. Thatcher is hardly remembered as a socialist, but this was one of the largest redistributions of wealth that Britain had ever seen.

In the short term, the scheme was enormously popular. Council houses were generally lived in by the poorest half of society, many of whom now found themselves, for the first time ever, owning their own home.

Some parts of Australia aped Thatcher's Right to Buy policies, and

New Zealand was in thrall to sweeping market-based reforms known as *Rogernomics* (named after our old friend, *Mr 2 per cent*, Roger Douglas); Canada significantly withdrew funding from public housing. President Reagan likewise introduced schemes that reinforced reliance on private markets to deliver housing.

In Continental Europe, meanwhile, many countries continued to maintain strong commitments to public housing and cooperative housing sectors, with some remarkable results.

In Vienna, Austria, to this day 60 per cent of people live in either government-owned (and rent controlled) buildings or in subsidised, non-profit, cooperative housing, built with government support. These buildings are often attractive and well-maintained, with rents based only on what it costs to maintain the building. And as rents are low, the Viennese have much higher disposable incomes, and as such Vienna consistently ranks as having one of the highest standards of living in the world.

This, to me, was the key point. If houses are cheap, rents and mortgages will be cheap, which will leave us all with more money for everything else.

The Iron Lady, as Thatcher was known, insisted that local governments use the proceeds from the sales of council homes to pay off their debts and cut local taxes. Being a firm believer in laissez-faire economics – a "let it be" approach that preached that governments should leave the markets alone and not interfere – she forbade councils from building new houses. Free markets would always deliver, and at the *correct* price.*

But homebuilders had another idea. Why build a house now, if suppressing supply will further boost prices? They could bank the land they own and reap profits by doing nothing.

As house prices rose, contrary to Thatcher's predictions, the number of new homes built actually *fell*.

Undeterred, her government then relaxed mortgage-lending rules so that

---

*   Ironically, given laissez-faire is a French phrase, Thatcher's contemporary, President Francois Mitterrand, was busy nationalising everything he could get his hands on in 1980s France.

people could borrow greater multiples of their income. *Right to Buy* effectively became a *Right to Borrow*. She copied America by making mortgage payments tax-deductible, further encouraging borrowing. With fewer new homes being built and more cash being given as loans to potential homeowners, houses became more expensive.

Rising prices reinforced the allure of property speculation. Easy money could be made by just buying a house, doing nothing with it, and then selling it at a profit. All this "investment" created further upward pressure on prices.

Local councils, incidentally, were still obliged to find homes for people who needed them. So they were forced to rent back the same homes they'd previously owned from private landlords, at rising market rents.

By the 2000s, housing had become less about shelter and more about speculation. As borrowing expanded and housing supply lagged, home ownership grew increasingly out of reach for many, while property wealth snowballed for the lucky minority.

—

I realised that everything I had learned about economics was coming together in my report about the perils of rising house prices.

There was the blind faith that free markets would provide the solution, even though decades of evidence showed that manipulation was more likely than equilibrium. There were the insane assumptions of high finance and the shrewd analysis of Hyman Minsky. There was Blair Fix with his simple graph showing just how bad the problem was.

And then there was the historic idea that started it all, that the economy was a contest between workers and landlords and capitalists, and of course Henry George's simple solution, being blindly ignored.

It seemed obvious that money that could have been used to invest in wealth creation, by, say, helping businesses expand, was instead being pumped into the giant pyramid scheme of rising house prices. After all, no *new* capital is created when you buy someone else's house.

Having grown up as a proud capitalist, I worried about all this – if capital doesn't create more capital, then surely capitalism has failed.

—

I titled the draft of my report "The Inequality Machine" and went to speak to Ioannou about how we could get some publicity for it. My colleague Dil had produced some wonderful graphics showing the change in house prices over the years, broken down by regions and local wealth levels. I'd done some highly speculative mathematics on what effect reduced house prices would have on economic growth, showing the huge increase in disposable income we'd all have if houses and rents were cheaper.

I was excited – here was a cause that, finally, I believed in. I was talking far too quickly.

"If you dig down into the economic justifications for ever-growing house prices, it always comes back to *debt*. Every financial crisis, every house price crash, is always, in at least some way, because people have borrowed too much. But this is crazy! If we only need ever-increasing house prices because banks lend too much money to people, then isn't the really easy solution here staring us in the face? Let's lend less money to people."

I'd printed out some of Dil's graphs and pointed at my favourites. "The 2008 financial crisis was largely caused by banks lending ridiculous amounts of money to buyers – like 120 per cent loan-to-value mortgages – and doesn't it seem weird that despite most homes being lived in for between eight and twelve years, many mortgages last for twenty-five or thirty years?"

He sat in his chair, pretty expressionless, which oddly made me more animated.

"So, when house prices fell and millions of people defaulted on their ludicrously big loans, how did Western governments respond? By encouraging more new lending. Look here – about three-quarters of all money created is due to new mortgages. That's hundreds of billions used to do nothing other than increase house prices, which makes it harder to get on the property ladder, so governments are then forced to subsidise housing.

And now they're talking about relaxing lending rules even further. What the hell is going on? If lending rules were tightened – say, mortgages limited to small multiples of income with ten-year payback periods – then houses would be much cheaper. All that money could be spent on new schools or hospitals or whatever instead."

Still he sat there, not really responding. He wasn't dead or anything – the hedge fund with the house price equation hadn't bumped him off – but he wasn't going, "Wow, yeah, so interesting" either. Or even, "What the hell are you talking about, you muppet?"

"I mean, sure, as a homeowner, I'm aware of that little devilish voice on one shoulder saying, *yeah, but look at what your house is worth now . . .*" (I was conscious that he was a homeowner too) "but that voice is a moron. I want my kids, and even your kids – though I'm less fussed about them – to be able to buy a nice big house without taking on preposterous debt. They will only be able to do that if house prices fall. I've got a list of politicians here who might be sympathetic to our cause . . ."

Ioannou didn't let me finish. He held up his hand, palm out, to indicate that I should stop talking.

"We've had an offer from a bank," he said.

"Huh?"

"They've realised how much free publicity Nationwide get with their 'house price index' reports and they want to muscle in on that territory. Only they don't have an in-house team to do it."

"So . . . what? What are you saying?" Though of course I knew exactly what he was saying, I just didn't want to hear it.

"The bank sells mortgages. They're not going to want to employ us to analyse house prices if we're mouthing off about how people should take out smaller mortgages and house prices should *fall*."

Dil asked me how my meeting with Ioannou had gone. I told him a bank had killed it.

Far from looking disappointed, he narrowed his eyes and said, "Of course. The cabal."

13

YOU ARE HERE

"If all the economists were laid end to end, they'd never reach a conclusion."
George Bernard Shaw, not an economist

As I'd expected, Blackbeard had started dating again. Actually, more than that – he now officially had a new girlfriend, and he invited me to meet her at one of the campus bars that was considered "classier" (because they served olives). She, too, was an economist – they'd met at a conference in Manchester and she told me that she had first noticed him when he started heckling a speaker. "At one point he was asked to leave," she said. "I rather agreed with what he was saying, though, so I followed him out."

Blackbeard had removed the pencil from his beard, again. He tucked his finger where it would be, anyway, as if it was muscle memory, then in a slightly abashed voice said to me, "I've told her about the book you're writing – that's why she was keen to meet you."

I'd semi-confessed my secret identity to Blackbeard. I'd decided by this point that I wanted to write about economics as a follow up to *Taxtopia*, given how both books could share a theme of cynicism about convoluted systems that just happen to benefit the already rich, and given how central Blackbeard had been to so much of what I'd learned, I'd figured I should get his permission to feature him as a character.

"Could you depict me as debonair and sophisticated?" he asked.

"I was thinking... more as a *pirate*?"

He looked touched. "I'd love to be a pirate!"

"I know."

I wondered why his girlfriend would be particularly keen to meet me, though, unless Blackbeard was just being uncharacteristically polite.

I nibbled an olive as she told me about a book she'd written on *depreciation*, which she'd attempted to get published, so far without success.

"It didn't go down well," she said. Blackbeard guffawed, though I'm not sure she was intentionally joking. He was clearly smitten.

Her name was Maya. She had an amazing bunch of braids on either side of her head that reminded me of Princess Leia, until she untied them and let her hair fall over her shoulders. I had a brief image that if she and Blackbeard ever had a child together it would have more hair than face.

I thought perhaps she was going to ask for tips on getting published, but then she suddenly put her hands on the table and fixed me with curiously eager eyes. "Are you going to write about MMT?" she asked.

I'd briefly mentioned Modern Monetary Theory, or MMT, in *Taxtopia*, but only really as a punchline to an outlandish justification for tax avoidance. But something about the way Maya stared at me made me hope that she didn't know that.

For advocates of the theory, it's something that could change the world.

The traditional view is that governments collect taxes in order to have money to spend on public services. If they don't collect enough money they will have to borrow the difference. In any one year this difference is called the deficit, and the cumulative borrowings are the national debt.

For centuries, politicians have fretted about this debt. They have repeatedly used it to justify austerity programmes, requiring tax rises and severe cuts to social security payments. President Thomas Jefferson warned that "There does not exist an engine so corruptive of the government and so demoralising of the nation as a public debt." President Hoover was more sarcastic: "Blessed are the young, for they shall inherit the national debt."

Ronald Reagan warned that "We must act now to protect future generations from an unconscionable burden of debt." He then tripled that debt by cutting taxes and raising defence spending. George W. Bush doubled the national debt, leading Barack Obama to describe national debt as "a sign that the nation cannot pay its bills". Obama then doubled the national debt again.

In fact, it's been doubled and tripled so many times that as I write this in 2025, the US government debt stands at $36 trillion (over $100,000 per person).

It sounds terrifying, but ... what does this debt actually mean? It means that the American government owes someone dollars, and the British government owes someone pounds, and the Japanese government owes someone yen. To which some economists – the modern monetary theorists – quite reasonably ask, so what?

So what if America owes $36 trillion? If the American government wanted to it could print a $36 trillion-bill with a picture of Donald Trump mooning Congress on it and pay off its debts in one go.

Indeed, half of Japan's 1.3 quadrillion yen debt is owed to – wait for it – the Bank of Japan! They wouldn't even need to print a bank note, they could literally just tap a couple of keys on a Central Bank computer and – ta-da! – half their debt is gone.

According to economist Stephanie Kelton, when we talk about national debt all we really mean is a record of how much money has been created by the government. After all, if one person is in debt, another person is in credit. That other person is *you*. For a government to pay down its debts it has to take money back from you. Kelton argues that this is the real role of tax. Governments don't collect tax to pay for schools and hospitals, they do it to reduce the amount of money in circulation.

If you've not come across this interpretation before, I'll give you a moment to scratch your head.

The logic is compelling: national debt is not the same as household debt, because a household can't just create more money, but the government can. Indeed, a government that issues its own currency can never run out of money.

When the government *spends* money it is *creating* that money. A government could, in theory, just keep spending without ever raising taxes.

Though of course there's a catch. If there was lots of spending without any taxation we would end up with severe inflation, as too much money would be chasing too few goods.

So, to control inflation, the government needs to raise taxes. Taxes are also useful, of course, to redistribute money to tackle inequality and to discourage certain behaviours, like smoking or polluting. But taxes, according to Modern Monetary Theory, are not needed to actually pay for stuff.

Blair Fix said that he didn't see why it was called a theory, rather than just "how money works", but that's not how everybody sees it. Former US Treasury Secretary Larry Summers called it "Voodoo economics".

It turns a lot of economic thinking on its head. A large deficit (being the difference between spending and taxation) is not a sign of a government being unable to pay its bills, but simply a sign that more money is being created.

The Modern Monetary Theorists argue that creating money out of thin air is a good thing, as when too little money is created it results in unemployment. It follows that whenever there's unemployment it's because deficits are too small. The government should be out there pumping money into the economy, not desperately cutting social security to pay down an inconsequential debt.

Indeed, the few times in history when governments have significantly reduced their national debts it has been a disaster.

Only once has the American national debt been fully paid off, during Andrew Jackson's presidency. Jackson raised taxes, sold land and vetoed spending bills to pay off the debt completely in 1835. What followed was the "Panic of 1837", the worst recession to hit America until the Wall Street Crash of 1929.

British prime ministers Gladstone and Disraeli ran budget surpluses from the 1870s onwards, coinciding with the "Long Depression" which lasted over a decade.

In Japan, the 1990s is referred to as the "Lost Decade", after the government raised taxes and cut spending in the wake of the bursting of an asset price bubble, sucking money out of the economy just as it needed it most.

Bill Clinton ran budget surpluses from 1998 to 2001, which took money out of the economy and contributed to the recession of the early 2000s.

And sure, sometimes countries have found themselves in horrendous debt spirals – Greece in 2009 is the most common example – but they weren't able to print their own money. Greece wasn't allowed to print euros. Most poorer countries borrow in American dollars, and *they* can't print dollars, but America can.

We even know exactly how national debts could be paid off: debt is owned by banks and other investors, so the government would print (electronic) money to buy the debt from them, resulting in the government owing the debt to itself. The government would then cancel this debt. The result is no government debt any more and banks that now have cash instead of bonds, so are no poorer. Everybody wins.

It seems like magic, so why are we not doing this? Somewhat counterintuitively, some Modern Monetary Theorists argue that printing enormous amounts of money in this way is likely to be *deflationary*, as bonds earn interest, but cash doesn't. So when the banks held bonds, they were earning income, which they could spend, but now that they only have cash they will no longer have that income, so will spend less.

I'm still scratching my head.

"Yeah, maybe I'll write about MMT," I said to Maya. "Do you think it's important?"

She pulled her hands off the table and folded her arms.

"It's the most vital idea in economics," she said.

A short while later, she excused herself to go to the loo. I took the opportunity to ask Blackbeard what he thought of MMT.

"I think it's guff," he said. "But if you tell her I said that I'll murder you in your sleep."

—

There seems to be a general view among economists that the financial crash in 2008 marked, if not a watershed moment, perhaps a chance to re-evaluate their discipline.

Bank of England governor Mervyn King's acknowledgement about economists' "collective failure of imagination" was taken to heart, and a greater diversity of ideas, such as Modern Monetary Theory, started to receive more attention.

In 2011, 70 Harvard University students walked out of their economics course in protest at an "overly conservative bias", which they argued "contributes to and symbolizes the increasing economic inequality in America". Their professor, Gregory Mankiw (who had served as the chairman of the Council of Economic Advisers for George W Bush) responded to the protest with an article in *The New York Times*. The article is, I think, fascinating.

Like Paul Samuelson before him, Mankiw has written an economics textbook, called *Principles of Economics*, that has dominated the teaching of economics worldwide (he's rumoured to have received $42 million from sales of the book). Indeed, if you studied economics any time in the last thirty years, you may well have studied from Mankiw's book.*

Mankiw made clear in his article that he thought the students were wrong to walk out. "The course I teach is a broad survey of mainstream economics. It includes ideas of many greats in the field, like Adam Smith, David Ricardo, Arthur Pigou, John Maynard Keynes and Milton Friedman. The material is similar to what you'd learn at most other universities" and that furthermore, his course was necessary as a "grounding for the study of economics as a social science".

He pointed out that, "like most economists, I don't view the study of economics as laden with ideology" and that "If my profession is slanted toward any particular world view, I am as guilty as anyone for perpetuating the problem."

Um... if I've got this right, students protested because economics courses perpetuated the ideology that only neoclassical economics was "mainstream" and that maybe the views of "great" economists like Milton Friedman had created inequality and instability on a gargantuan international scale, and

---

* Or, given its $280 cover price, maybe photocopies of his book.

the response from Harvard's most esteemed professor was to say, "those fools, what I'm teaching is *mainstream economic science.*"

But what if the mainstream is wrong? The entire history of economics, from mercantilism onwards, is the history of the mainstream being proved wrong. I don't mean that in a rude way – it's an absolutely wonderful thing. It means it can keep getting better. In the physical sciences, if someone finds a flaw in a theory, it's a cause for celebration. In economics, it leads to arrogant tossers posting on Reddit that someone *just doesn't get it*.

And what if economics *isn't* a science? Or worse, what if it's the kind of science where you only realise your mistake after you've blown up the lab?

I wasn't telling my students that orthodox economics is wrong, or not a science, or even that it's dangerous. I don't know the answer to these questions. But neither do economists, and yet a lot of them pretend that they do, despite the last few centuries of economics being a litany of failure. As the bestselling economist Thomas Piketty put it in *Capital in the Twenty-First Century*, economists must "set aside their contempt for other disciplines and their absurd claim to greater scientific legitimacy".*

One of the biggest shifts since 2008 has been economists' gradual embrace of a tool accountants have relied on since the 15th century: the balance sheet.

Hyman Minsky foresaw the 2008 financial crisis because he examined the economy through this lens, tracking assets, liabilities and changes in wealth. With balance sheets, you cannot ignore debt, whereas mainstream economics had largely treated debt as a side issue, until its sheer scale meant they no longer could.†

Contemporary "heterodox" economists like the Australian professor

---

* Actually, he was even more brutal, as he then added that economists "know almost nothing about anything". That seems a tad harsh.
† If you've never had to deal with a balance sheet, congratulations! What you've been missing out on is this: a balance sheet is a measure of what you own (your assets) and a record of how you came to own those things (perhaps by borrowing, or making a profit, or seducing investors).

Steve Keen and modern monetary theorist Stephanie Kelton highlight flaws in orthodox thinking by using balance sheets and simple double-entry bookkeeping – that one person's income is always another person's expense, and that one person's debt is always another's credit.

This got me thinking. What else could economists learn from accountants (other than our famous self-confidence and swagger)?

Have a five-minute conversation with any business's accountant and you'll hear about all sorts of things keeping them awake at night, like rent and interest payments, which barely feature in traditional economics.

Take one of economics' most analysed concepts – *capital*.

On my transition from accountant to economist, it was the concept that gave me the most headaches. It always seems to mean something different.

David Ricardo defined it as "that part of the wealth of a country which is employed in production, and consists of food, clothing, tools, raw materials, machinery, etc". Honestly, I don't see how food and machinery belong in the same category. An accountant would be jailed for fraud if they tried to pass one off as the other.

Then Karl Marx came along to declare that capital was more a "social relation" of "self-expanding value". Gee, thanks Marx, that definitely clears things up.

To financial economists, it usually just means *money*, or at a push, *wealth*. Neoclassical economists usually lump it all together in one single, homogenous, theoretical blob, called "K". And there's no end of other *capitals* – human capital, social capital, cultural capital, natural capital, you name it – all of them nebulous and unquantifiable.

I mean, for fuck's sake. I'm sorry to swear, but seriously? We've had economists arguing over capital, capitalists and capitalism for centuries without even agreeing what the hell they are arguing over? That's the kind of thing a toddler would do. If a word means different things to different people, what good is it? Wouldn't it be easier just to say exactly what we mean? Like "van" or "potato".

So here's an idea: why not do what accountants do, and avoid using the word altogether? In a set of company accounts, you won't find any "capital" in the records of income and expenditure, and it's not used to mean cash. Indeed, it isn't an asset at all. The only time it appears is at the very bottom of a balance sheet as a residual record of wealth, but normally it gets ignored entirely.

If we did that, then suddenly we would all be capitalists, because we could all agree that having some residual wealth is a good thing. That would then leave us to argue over everything else.

—

Let me take you back to where I began all this, just for a moment.

I was on a fake Zoom call in a side room at an American TV station. An assistant producer called Savannah-Rose had asked me to sound less British and I'd blown it by immediately using the word "tosh" (which in case you're wondering, means the same as "codswallop").

As Savannah-Rose nodded reassuringly, my interviewer had asked me why it was that the institute I worked for held a position that three-quarters of economists thought was wrong. What do you think I should have said?

Perhaps the truth – that I was paid to defend my think-tank's position?

Or another truth – that discourse and disagreement is essential in the pursuit of knowledge?

Or the biggest truth – that Ioannou just liked the publicity?

And do you think, were you in my shoes, that what you would have said would have been more left- or right-wing than what I said?

And what does your answer say about whether economics is ideologically driven?

—

One of the running gags in the history of economics is how the discipline keeps forgetting crucial things, then denying it was ever an issue when someone points it out. The classical economists somehow managed to ignore entrepreneurs; Henry George had to shout about land monopolies because no one else was; Joan Robinson noticed that bosses might use power to keep wages down (what a shock!); I love Robert Solow going, "Oh shit, we forgot to include *technology*"; and almost everybody except Hyman Minsky ignoring the role of finance.

A recent addition to this list is the role of *energy*.

In much the same way as the Industrial Revolution would not have been possible without easy access to coal, imagine the 20th century without oil – indeed, look at the impact that the sudden increase in oil prices in the 1970s had on economic thought. Everyone suddenly abandoned Keynes and chanted *All Hail Milton Friedman*, as if monetarism could pump crude out of the ground. Maybe what we really needed was cheaper energy?

In the last couple of decades, the American economy has pulled significantly ahead of Europe. Some people argue it's because there's too much regulation in Europe, or too much social security, or that Europe lacks the American culture of entrepreneurialism. All of that may be true, but want to know what else happened in this time? America exploited their shale oil and gas deposits. This kept energy prices low in America and turned the US into a net exporter of energy (which it hadn't been since the 1950s).*

Perhaps the most ridiculous example of this comes from a machine called MONIAC, built by an economist from New Zealand called Bill Phillips to physically demonstrate the movement of money around an economy.

He was inspired by a diagram in Paul Samuelson's famous *Economics* textbook (the one with the family tree that excluded Henry George). The diagram was a picture of what Samuelson called *circular flow*: that households receive salaries in return for providing labour to firms, which then make goods that are purchased with salaries; that banks lend and savers borrow; that governments spend and tax.

The machine, apparently made out of scrap from old Lancaster bombers, was at one point going to be called the *financephalograph* but came to be called MONIAC, or Monetary National Income Analogue Computer. Pumps and drains would shift water around different taps, depending on set levels of taxation and expenditure. In the days before actual computers, this was

---

* And luckily, this came with no environmental consequences. Oh no, wait ...

astounding stuff, and at least twelve MONIACS were made and distributed to economics departments around the world.*

What no one seemed to notice was that this machine, that could so magnificently demonstrate how Samuelson supposed the economy works, needed to be switched on.

This grand metaphor of the economy, reimagined as a madcap plumbing system, literally sat there useless unless someone supplied it with energy. Which, if you think about it, seems like a delicious joke – economists had built a model of the economy but forgot the thing that makes it move.

The Welsh economist Ely Devons observed that "if economists wished to study the horse, they wouldn't go and look at horses. They'd sit in their studies and say to themselves, 'What would I do if I were a horse?' " It's hard not to see something similar going on here. Rather than look at what, besides labour, businesses spend their money on (rent, interest payments, energy bills), economists constructed models of the economy that assume wealth creation needs just labour and capital. Weird.

The cynic in me thinks that perhaps it's not so weird. If we don't analyse land or finance or energy bills, then it's the landowners, bankers and oil companies that benefit from our ignorance.

—

Most of the developments in economics since 2008 have been extremely positive. Economists like Thomas Piketty, Emmanuel Saez and Gabriel Zucman have brought the study of whether inequality is a *drag* on growth (and not just a social issue) back into the mainstream. Nobel prizes have been awarded to economists focused on what can be empirically proven to alleviate poverty and spur development in poorer regions, rather than what we might theorise would.

Behavioural science, once a fringe pursuit of left-field economists even

---

* It's lucky that it wasn't called the financephalograph, as that literally translates as *writing finance with a phallus*. Although, given the machine worked by pumping fluids, maybe Phillips knew what he was doing.

while it was being exploited by marketing executives in real-world businesses, is now taught as a vital part of understanding how the economy works.

Where once esteemed economists like Robert Lucas could blithely claim in 2003 that the "central problem of depression prevention has been solved", in 2010 the term *credibility revolution* was coined to describe a growing insistence on evidence. Instead of elegant but untethered theories, economists now increasingly test ideas using randomised control trials, actual data and natural experiments – in other words, they've started doing the things real scientists have been doing since roughly the Age of Enlightenment.*

And at long last, humanity's impact on the environment is being taken seriously within the profession. For decades it was treated as someone else's department – the ecologists' problem, not the economists'. But now ideas like sustainability and the principles of "circular economics" are being nudged slowly towards the centre of the discipline. The question is no longer just "how fast can the economy grow?" but "can it grow without destroying the planet?" Which feels like a fairly important question to finally have on the agenda, at least if you're attached to, say, breathing.†

However, not every development since 2008 has been positive. After the financial crash, governments around the world saw their national debt levels soar, and not everyone was towing the "don't worry about it" line that the Modern Monetary Theorists were throwing around.

Two Harvard professors called Carmen Reinhart and Kenneth Rogoff published an influential academic paper called "Growth in the Time of Debt"

---

* A natural experiment is one that takes place outside of a controlled lab environment, so seeing how people *actually* behave, rather than how 20-year-old college kids behave when bribed with pizza to fill in a survey.

† The environmental economist Kate Raworth (who promotes the idea of circularity – effectively "reuse and recycle") goes further, and asks if maybe we should consider if we need the economy to grow at all. In her book *Doughnut Economics*, she quotes the ecologist Edward Abbey, who points out that "growth for the sake of growth is the ideology of a cancer cell." (I somehow doubt that will be the slogan of the next G7 summit.)

in 2010. In the paper, Reinhart and Rogoff compared national debt levels to economic growth for 44 countries over the last 200 years. Their conclusion was a sharp rebuke to the Modern Monetary Theorists.

Far from not worrying about their debts, there was actually an empirically provable link between high debts and low growth. More specifically, there was a threshold rate: on average, if a country had debt levels equal to 90 per cent or more of their GDP, their economic growth rates *halved*.

This was music to the ears of Republicans in America and Conservatives in the UK, and economically right-wing parties elsewhere, who had long argued for the need to reduce government spending. The Republican Party's budget proposal in 2012, which advocated cuts to the funding of healthcare, student grants, renewable power, infrastructure projects, libraries, and even grants to disabled people and neglected children (as well as income tax cuts for the rich), cited just one academic paper in support of its argument: Reinhart and Rogoff's "Growth in the Time of Debt".

In the UK, in 2010, more than 20 leading economists (including Kenneth Rogoff) wrote to *The Sunday Times* to argue that the government needed to do more to reduce government spending and raise taxes.

George Osborne, who became the UK's Chancellor of the Exchequer in May 2010, duly ushered in an "Age of Austerity", featuring huge cuts to welfare spending (particularly disability and housing benefits), a decade-long pay freeze for public sector workers, the halving of local governments' budgets, the tripling of university tuition fees and a reduction in per-pupil school spending. Taxes were increased on discretionary spending (though cut for the very richest).

The same story repeated elsewhere. In Italy, Greece, Australia, Spain, Portugal, Ireland and Canada, governments argued that *debts needed to be cut*. And the way to cut them was to reduce spending and raise taxes (except on the rich, of course).

But a few years later, something curious happened. A young graduate student named Thomas Herndon decided to examine the data for himself. Nobody had previously thought to actually check the workings in Reinhart and Rogoff's "Growth in the Time of Debt". The original paper hadn't been peer-reviewed, indeed only its conclusions had ever been published. These were the conclusions that had helped usher in an international age of austerity.

What Thomas Herndon found was that there were basic, almost embarrassing, errors in the spreadsheet. Some data was being accidentally left out. Significantly, the key calculation was meant to find an average for 20 countries, but Australia, Austria, Belgium, Canada and Denmark had been mistakenly excluded. (I suspect anyone who has ever written a spreadsheet will have made similar mistakes, though probably not with global financial consequences).

Even more weirdly, a single bad year in 1951 for New Zealand, caused by striking dockworkers, was given equal weight as 20 years of British debt-fuelled economic growth.

When Thomas Herndon and his colleagues corrected these errors, they found almost no correlation between debt and economic growth.

Which suggests that the Age of Austerity was a mistake. As *New York* magazine put it, Herndon had "just used part of his spring semester to shake the intellectual foundation of the global austerity movement".

So really there was no need make education, health, housing and disability support worse, after all.

Economic growth during George Osborne's era as chancellor was lower than in the previous decade, and lower than countries that tried stimulus packages rather than austerity.

—

Blackbeard had never invited me round to his house before. It was a small, ivy-covered, thatch-roofed cottage in a village with a green and a pub and a medieval church, about a 20-minute drive from the university. I had expected it to be like his office – cluttered and messy with old books gathering dust, but it was immaculate. The windows were clean, the carpets hoovered, the shelves were orderly and the table was laid. But then, of course it was like that, as he was trying to impress Maya, his new girlfriend.

She greeted me at the front door and welcomed me in. "We're having a roast!" she said, with great enthusiasm.

I was there because I'd told Blackbeard that I wanted his help writing the conclusion to my book. He'd taken this task seriously – entire roast lunch seriously.

As the meat would need another hour, he suggested that the three of us go for a walk. There was a somewhat overgrown lane that wound out of the village and up a nearby hill. He claimed that from the top we would be able to see the central tower of the university, but he may have been having me on. At one point we paused at a large map, on which there was a red circle with the words "YOU ARE HERE" helpfully written on it.

"How do they know?!" asked Blackbeard, giggling like a schoolboy. It was wonderful to see him in such a good mood.

At the top of the hill, he rested his hands on his hips as he pretended to admire the view while really trying to catch his breath.

"I think I've worked it all out," he said, narrowing his eyes, pretending the thought had just occurred to him. I smiled sideways at him, not quite sure what he was going to say next.

"Yeah?"

"Yes. It's all the fault of the Treaty of Westphalia," he said it matter-of-factly, as if identifying a blockage in my plumbing.

I couldn't help but laugh. It was such a ... wacky thing to say.

"Go on ..." I suggested.

"The Treaty of Westphalia ended the Thirty Years' War in 1648, right?" He checked that I was nodding in appreciation, appropriately, and that Maya was not looking at him like he was completely mad. "It was the first time that powerful nations agreed to leave each other to their own devices. It established the idea of state sovereignty – it's the origin of *nationalism*."

He was excited about his interpretation of history, and clearly pleased to have gone further back than Adam Smith and *The Wealth of Nations*, which is where most economic histories start. The problem with economics, as Blackbeard saw it, could be seen in Adam Smith's title. Why were we analysing the wealth of *nations*?

"Everything is done in *national* terms. Taxation, spending, balancing the books, trade treaties, deregulation, the whole works, it's all set at a nation-state level. So even when economists allow a little bit of *morality* to creep back into their thinking, it's still always about redistributing wealth within the borders of their own country."

He paused for breath again. A little bit of me worried that he was going to have a heart attack, which would probably mean I wouldn't get to eat any of the roast. But he was just unfit. "Look at migration, we've got it the wrong way round. The problem isn't migrants wanting to move to rich countries – of course they do! The problem is that there are so many crap countries in the world. I mean, seriously, how many countries would you actually want to live in?"

"Quite a lot . . ." I said, having recently chatted to a friend who'd spent a year in Sri Lanka.

"I don't mean as a rich expat – I mean, as an averagely rich person in that country . . ."

"Oh, okay, maybe twenty countries?"

"Exactly – out of two hundred countries in the world you'd be happy being an average person in just ten per cent of them. There's your problem."

"So what . . ." I asked him, "you think we need another Marshall Plan?"

"Too right. Once we're all on a roughly equal setting we can have free trade galore, free movement all over the world, no more wars, no one starving and six times as many scientists to build the robots, or whatever. What do you reckon?"

I quite liked it as an idea, though obviously I couldn't tell him that, so I shook my head, called him a hippy, and pointed out that another Marshall Plan is already underway.

—

George C Marshall is the only army general to ever be awarded the Nobel Peace Prize, having convinced America to rebuild the destroyed infrastructure of Europe after the Second World War.

By the 1950s, America had transferred around $34 billion to European countries (the Soviet Union was even invited to receive some of the funds, but declined). For comparison, the entire tax take of the American government was around $38 billion in 1947.

The plan was meant to deal with three issues: most of Europe was in ruins, the Soviet Union was eager to expand westwards and American industrial capacity had soared beyond the capacity of the American people to buy its goods. Restoring Europe would halt the communists and create a permanent market for American exports.

The plan worked, and by the early 1950s Western Europe was largely back to its pre-war levels.

In November 2022, the European Union held a launch party for a programme dubbed *Marshall Plan 2.0*.

Almost 80 years after the original plan, the same issues had resurfaced – an impoverished continent too poor to buy Western goods while a communist aggressor eyed it for political influence, only this time the continent was Africa, and the communists were Chinese, not Russian.

The European Union proposed to spend €300 billion over six years, on "smart investments in quality infrastructure, respecting the highest social and environmental standards, in line with the EU's values and standards". They called the initiative "Global Gateway".

The intentions were good, even if the name sounded like an airport waiting lounge. But getting the 27 member states of the European Union to coordinate was a challenge. Impact assessments and environmental reports dragged on for far longer than construction would take. Anti-corruption conditions were like refusing to pay for a Saharan railway if there was a danger of getting sand on the tracks. And someone had the bright idea to host the launch party, which was already one year late and cost €387,000, *virtually* in Facebook's Metaverse (one journalist claimed that when he attended, only five other people were there).

An internal review by the European Commission in 2024 warned that Global Gateway had fallen flat as "efforts are spread too thinly". Nowhere near the original €300 billion has been invested. In short, Global Gateway is not the new Marshall Plan that I was referring to as being underway.

For that, we have to look to China.

In 2013, China launched their own investment plan, called *One Belt One Road*, to build ports and railways and other infrastructure throughout Asia,

Africa and South and Central America. Where Europe offered billions, China planned to spend trillions.*

Many Western governments viewed (and still view) the Chinese plan with suspicion. Ports were designed with dual civilian and military use, Chinese-financed mines have given China control over key minerals and resources, Chinese money has encouraged recipient nations to side with China in disputes.

Some critics saw the deals as "neo-colonialist" – China was extracting resources from poorer nations by exerting its financial clout. The infrastructure plan was for a "hub and spokes" – meaning all roads would lead to China, rather than facilitating trade between other nations.

There were fears of "debt-trap diplomacy", as local infrastructure could be seized by the Chinese government if interest payments weren't made. All the same, autocrats welcomed funding without having to pretend to care about pollution or human rights.

Though, of course, it's not quite "no-strings". Recipient countries have to accept the Chinese policy of "non-interference", which is the diplomatic way of saying *don't concern yourself with other countries' internal affairs*. China does not regard Taiwan as a separate country, remember, so an invasion of Taiwan would be an "internal affair" in Xi Jinping's eyes.

By contrast, the European Global Gateway scheme requires democratic accountability with sustainability at its core. Where China is funding coal power stations, Global Gateway finances solar plants. Global Gateway monitors and acts to prevent corruption; China has been accused of exporting organised crime.

—

We sat on a bench at the top of the hill, looking over the village to the countryside beyond.

---

* The Chinese authorities now usually refer to the plan, in English at least, as the Belt and Road Initiative. Confusingly, the "belt" refers to roads and the "road" refers to sea-lanes.

"Imagine if Global Gateway *worked*," said Blackbeard. "Think what the future would be like. Your grandkids could be studying at the prestigious Mogadishu University, or performing at the Kabul Opera House, or whizzing on high-speed trains to Yangon to go surfing for the weekend, or designing high-tech materials in Kinshasa."

I liked the sound of that.

He had a dreamy tone to his voice that I hadn't heard before, as he continued, "Here's a test: imagine that some global law was passed that decreed that in exactly ten years' time, all national borders would be abolished. And not just that – imagine if everyone would also be given an instantaneous lift to anywhere they wanted to live in the world. And now, with that on the horizon, where would economists tell us we should be investing? I'll eat my beard if they don't suddenly say we should pump money into the poorer parts of the world."

I was about to say that I thought it was an interesting thought experiment (I'd propose calling it the *Blackbeard Test*), when Maya suddenly exploded (in a romantic sort of way).

"What absolute claptrap are you on about?" She took a deliberately over-the-top intake of breath and then shook her head slowly, side to side. "First off, what kind of Eurocentrist attitude have you got that it's *our* little European kids who get to joyride around the world? Kabul doesn't need us imposing Wagner on them, they've got six thousand years of Afghan culture to celebrate. And what is this meant to prove, exactly? We'd need to overthrow corrupt regimes at gunpoint, otherwise they'd steal the aid. Is that what you want? Stop with the bloody hypotheticals, that's the last thing we need in economics right now."

"Claptrap?" gasped Blackbeard, in mock outrage. "I'll tell you what *is* claptrap..."

As they argued, I felt my phone buzzing. Henrí had taken our kids to see her parents, who live not far from Blackbeard's village. She had sent me a message, asking how my lunch was going. Then she'd added:

Solved the world's problems yet? X

Blackbeard and Maya had started vigorously citing different developmental economists to back up their claims. Maya was calling him a "typical naive pinko". They looked like they were about to tear each other's clothes off.

So I messaged back.

Not yet

NOTES

One of my favourite popular economics books is *Doughnut Economics*, by Kate Raworth, mostly because it's about doughnuts.

But I have one major gripe with it. It's not that the doughnuts are metaphorical, I can just about cope with that. Rather, for a book that is all about economies working in harmony with nature, the last 70 pages of it – being a fifth of the entire book – is made up of academic notes, references, acknowledgements and an index. That book was an international bestseller and must have chalked up hundreds of thousands of sales. That means her publishers must have printed and schlepped around the world maybe thirty-odd million pages that no one was ever going to read. That's enough pages to fill a good couple of trucks, which is hardly harmonious with nature.

Let's be honest, if you want to fact-check anything in this book, you're going to google it or ask ChatGPT, aren't you? And unless you're one of about a dozen or so people who'll get thanked in person, you don't care in the slightest about the *acknowledgements* in a book. When authors thank their wives or agents or children for *being there for them* I usually feel a bit nauseous. Indeed, one of the books I read as prep for this one even had an entire page about the music the author was listening to as he wrote. What a tosser.

Instead, here are some notes that are designed to be readable. Think of them as extra bits that I thought were interesting but didn't really fit in the main narrative.

I've mostly been listening to Enya.

Introduction

Boy, do I love that quote from **Joan Robinson**. She has been described by British Chancellor of the Exchequer Rachel Reeves as "the most famous economist not to be awarded the Nobel Prize".

Joan Robinson herself rejected the theories of neoclassical economics and embraced Keynesianism, and is most celebrated for her work on theories of economic growth and for identifying *Monopsonies* – a type of market with just one powerful buyer.

Her book *Economic Philosophy* had an enormous influence on this book. In it, Robinson argues that there is a constant battle within economics between those who view the discipline as a science and those who recognise it as ideology. She rejected many of the ideas of classical and neoclassical economics, argued that most of the "scientific" ideas are metaphysical at best, and concluded that the task of economists is to fight against the idea that the only values that matter are the ones that can be measured in monetary terms.

Though, in later life, she dove headfirst into the ideological pool and went full Marxist, praising Kim Il Sung of North Korea as a "messiah rather than a dictator" and writing in 1964 that "sooner or later the country must be reunited by absorbing the South into socialism." In her defence, North Korea was more prosperous than South Korea until the late 1960s, and she probably didn't know about the North's concentration camps. Today, South Korea is about sixty times richer than North Korea, so she definitely got that one wrong.

Her student Amartya Sen, who would himself go on to win the Sveriges Riksbank prize, described her as "totally brilliant but vigorously intolerant". She died in 1983.

You'll often see references to when famous people died in non-fiction books. It's for the benefit of the libel lawyers who give the book the all-clear before publication. Dead people can't sue for libel.

I haven't really been listening to Enya, sorry.

I've googled it and only found one medical school with a student society named after **Galen**, so perhaps his influence on young doctors is less widespread than I feared. As well as his views on the four humours and the origins of semen, he believed that women got hysterical if they didn't have sex. I tried to write a joke about this but struggled to find one that didn't make me sound like a 14-year-old boy. Talking of which, my son thought the cure to my *not being able to sit down* issue was to get a *bottomectomy*. Anyway, all is fine now. Indeed, I'm sitting as I write this.

The observation about English translations of **Xenophon**'s *Oeconomicus* describing "servants" instead of "slaves" was made in Professor Jane Whittle's paper, "How free was wage labour in England 1500–1700? The case of servants". She highlights that many Medieval and Early English translators would also translate "slaves" as "servants", as the elite would view slaves and servants as having a similar function and status. Many Tudor scholars argued that servants should be as obedient to their masters as their masters were obedient to God.

Chapter 1

John Kenneth Galbraith worked as an economist for the administrations of Presidents Roosevelt, Truman, Kennedy and Johnson and at one point was America's ambassador to India. He was a prolific author and is a goldmine for cynical quotes about economics: "under capitalism, man exploits man; under communism it's just the opposite"; "the only function of economic forecasting is to make astrology look respectable"; "It is a far, far better thing to have a firm anchor in nonsense than to put out on the troubled sea of thought"; and so on.

I understand that many children's publishers lament that young boys aren't reading as much as they used to, but then they go and offer them books about making friends with unicorns or how to understand their feelings. Seriously? Don't you think 10-year-old boys would prefer to read about super-powered pre-teens engaged in a battle royale?

Oh well, back to the drawing board. My next kids' book will be called *Feely the Magic Horse*.

The **East India Company** was a British trading corporation founded in 1600 that ended up ruling large parts of India. Backed by a private army, it exploited India's resources, imposed brutal taxes, and is largely responsible for both the Bengal Famine of 1770, which killed millions, and for starting the Opium Wars with China.

You can read about the investigation by *The New York Times* into the **funding of think-tanks by foreign governments** on their website. The article was published on 6 September 2014 and was titled "Foreign Powers Buy Influence at Think-tanks". You can read about Brookings president John Allen resigning in 2022 in most online newspapers.

The TV show featuring the **inflatable hippo's anus** got as close to being made as a TV show can be before the TV channel that would have funded it ran out of money. As I write, there's a possibility that another channel might fund a drama series based on *Taxtopia*, but it sounds like it will be more serious (so is unlikely to feature the inflatable hippo).

The **Clark Center for Global Markets** runs weekly polls of dozens of leading economists asking them whether they agree or not with certain statements about economic issues. You can see the results of these surveys at kentclarkcenter.org

Chapter 2

The quote from **Charles Darwin** comes from his own journals, written in 1836 after seeing the way slaves were treated in South America.

You may know that economics is sometimes referred to as the "dismal science" – I used to think that this was meant in comparison to more reliably predictive sciences, like physics or chemistry, but it isn't.

The term was actually coined in 1849 by the Scottish philosopher Thomas Carlyle as a contrast to what he called "Gay Science" (which sounds so much more fun) in a tract called "Occasional Discourse on the Negro Question". Yup, it turns out the phrase has racist roots.

Carlyle had been taken in by Thomas Malthus's faulty mathematics about population growth, which Carlyle described as a "dismal science" – dismal in that suffering was inevitable.

He argued that a consequence of Malthus's calculations was that it was necessary to *reintroduce slavery* (which had, by then, been banned in Britain), since more food was needed. He viewed this as *morally right*. For one thing, he argued, the conditions aboard slave ships were not nearly as bad as was often reported. And didn't slaveowners treat their slaves "like family"? A distressing number of people at the time seemed to have agreed with him.

Some historians interpret Carlyle even less favourably – that what he found so dismal was the idea that classical economics would not distinguish between different races.

One of my favourite examples of the folly of **mercantilism** is what is sometimes known as "reverse alchemy". When the Spanish discovered gold in their colonies, they used it to build cathedrals and palaces in Spain (turning gold to stone). In fact, so much gold was brought to Spain that prices for goods increased five-fold between the early 1500s and the mid-1600s (as there was now a lot more gold but no extra products being made). Wages for the average Spaniard didn't increase as quickly as prices rose, so most Spanish people actually got *poorer* due to the import of gold.

Speaking of gold, I laughed out loud recently when I read that Bitcoin entrepreneur Paolo Ardoino had described gold as "natural Bitcoin", and that he was planning on investing in it. But the more I thought about it the more reasonable a comment it seemed. Most gold trading these days doesn't involve physical bars being handed over, but only new ownership records being inserted into a spreadsheet . . . exactly like Bitcoin. Both investments rely on a collective hysteria that other people will continue to buy them, both allow anonymous purchases outside of government control, and both are shockingly bad for the environment (Bitcoin uses as much electricity as Argentina, gold mining produces as much CO_2 as Bangladesh).

Given I've also read about impoverished gold miners in Africa trading Bitcoin (as local banking systems exclude them), it seems we're now in a weird system where Bitcoin miners buy gold, while gold miners buy Bitcoin, and neither contribute much to the wealth of the world – indeed, arguably they reduce wealth, due to the environmental damage they cause and their facilitation of money laundering.

I sold all my crypto holdings after reading Zeke Faux's *Number Go Up*.

Adam Smith's **The Wealth of Nations** is an absolute tome and pretty hard going. More fun is the American satirist P J O'Rourke's analysis of it, *On the Wealth of Nations*.

As an aside, after failing to notice that he'd put bread and butter in a teapot, allegedly Adam Smith then declared "this is the worst cup of tea I've ever met with."

By contrast, Ricardo's **On the Principles of Political Economy and Taxation** is an easy read. It's free online. The units of wine and cloth I included in a footnote are the exact same numbers he used. Most economists buy his argument about comparative advantage, indeed the economist Paul Krugman wrote a lengthy article in which he compares comparative advantage to the theory of evolution, and expresses his exasperation that anyone wouldn't accept Ricardo's theory, arguing that only "poseurs" and people "with a desire to be intellectually fashionable" would reject its fundamental truth. Krugman spends a great deal of the article wondering if too many people just don't understand the maths (yes, this is the same Krugman who also said that economists "went astray because they mistook beauty, clad in impressive-looking mathematics, for truth").

Not everyone agrees with Krugman. The economist Steve Keen points out that one of Ricardo's assumptions is that labour and capital can move from one type of production to another, but how, asks Keen, does a wine press convert into a spinning jenny?

More pointedly, Ricardo's friend John Mallett said of Ricardo that "he meets you with ... a mind made up, his opinions in the nature of mathematical truths ... his entire disregard of experience and practice ... makes me doubtful of his opinions on political economy".

The University of Texas economist **James Kenneth Galbraith** does great work analysing inequality and other economic issues, and is the son of John Kenneth Galbraith. And given that Professor **Matt Watson** has written a book called *False Prophets of Economic Imperialism*, I'm pretty sure he was being sarcastic about Ricardo.

The *Acknowledge, Bridge, Control* technique for media interviews is usually paired with a D for either *Dangle* (as in "we've just released a report on this, and the results are fascinating") or for *Drive the point home*. Once you're familiar with it you'll hear politicians using it every bloody time they're asked a question. "Well, it's interesting you ask about my scuffle outside a sports bar, because many people have been asking me about the urgent need to slap sense into the housing market, and our new policies will deliver real benefits this year."

Chapter 3

I do wonder if **Paul Samuelson** was joking when he said that the economy performs better if we don't understand it, given that he wrote the *Economics* textbook. Though given that most of the neoclassical theories in his book have been disproved, it might have been a *mea culpa*.

I almost went with a quote by Jacob Viner, whom Samuelson selected as one of seven "American Saints of Economics". Viner once claimed that "economics is what economists do", which is often quoted admiringly by other economists yet strikes me as Exhibit A for the allegation that there's too much arrogance in economics.

I lost thirty hours of writing time to **INSET** days. So if you think any lines in this book could have been a little sharper, or any facts better researched, feel free to blame Baron Baker of Dorking, the education minister who introduced them. It's not just the kids missing an entire term of school, or the millions of lost productive days as parents take time off to cover for the teachers, but surveys show that teachers themselves think they don't get much value from these "training days". I bet they don't shut schools for an entire term in China, just sayin'.

Madeleine Dean brandished a **banana** and challenged Commerce Secretary **Howard Lutnick** over tariffs during a House Appropriations Committee hearing on 5 June 2025.

In the film *Ferris Bueller's Day Off* there is a scene where some schoolkids are bored to stupefaction by a lesson on **Reed Smoot**, while Ferris drives round in a Ferrari with his girlfriend. Their teacher doesn't even point out that Smoot's sidekick Willis Hawley's name has at least two rude words in it, the amateur.

One big advantage of **John Maynard Keynes**'s idea for an international currency – the *Bancor* – was that it wouldn't rely on gold. For much of the 19th century, a "Gold Standard" had enabled most currencies to be exchanged for set amounts of gold. This had the positive effect of stabilising prices for long periods of time, which helped trade, but the disastrous side effect that entire economies could be ruined if they ran out of what is, let's be honest, just a particularly heavy type of metal.

Britain abandoned the Gold Standard in 1931, the Australians abandoned it in 1932, the Americans effectively stopped converting dollars to gold in 1933 and the French followed suit in 1936, so by the Bretton Woods conference most country's currencies were backed by *nothing*, which allowed governments to print more money whenever they needed it. For countries that needed a lot of money (and didn't have much gold), a monetary system that didn't depend on gold was *ideal*.

Decrypted communications and witness testimony from defectors suggest that **Harry Dexter White** did indeed pass secret documents to the Soviet

Union, though these were mostly about America's economic plans rather than, say, classic spy stuff like the blueprints for nuclear submarines.

The European Union has recognised that goods made outside its borders are often cheaper as they are made in more environmentally damaging ways, so it has imposed an import tariff called the Carbon Border Adjustment Mechanism on imports created by pollutive industries, in order to level the playing field and encourage good environmental stewardship abroad.

This is actually similar to something proposed by Benjamin Franklin – in the 1700s there was so much farmable land available in America that American businesses had to offer quadruple the hourly wages that European workers received to entice people to be employees rather than farmers. But that meant that American goods were more expensive to manufacture than foreign goods, so fearing that US businesses would be undercut by products made with cheap foreign labour, Franklin proposed tariffs on products made in places where labour was cheap.

The World Trade Organization also deals with a long list of trade disputes related to the "dumping" of subsidised goods abroad. For instance, the EU has introduced import taxes on Chinese electric vehicles, on the grounds that it's not a fair trade if the Chinese government is subsidising those industries, which it is. (China responding by putting import taxes on European brandy – which is not subsidised).

Chapter 4

If you want to read more about the West's trade with awful regimes, I strongly recommend the Pulitzer Prize-winner Anne Applebaum's *Autocracy, Inc: The Dictators Who Want to Run the World*.

A more niche but also interesting read is Thane Gustafson's *The Bridge: Natural Gas in a Divided Europe*, which quotes the French phrase more fully as *une épouvantable usine à gaz*, which the author translates as "a frightful town-gas plant". Apparently, there were 700 of these plants in France, "most of them primitive and wheezingly inefficient."

For the harrowing stats on **Chinese slavery** have a look at walkfree.org. Walk Free is an international human rights groups that compiles the world's most comprehensive data set of modern slavery.

You can read **Bloomberg Economics**' estimate of the cost of a war with China at bloombergeconomics.com (it's behind a paywall, though there's a free summary on the United States Institute of Peace website: usip.org); comparing wealth and income levels in different countries is a real challenge for economists, especially in communist dictatorships which often produce deliberately false economic data, or refuse to publish such data at all. There's also the issue of fluctuating exchange rates and the effective purchasing power of local currencies. Still, economists do try – in 2023 the United Nations, for instance, estimated average wealth to be higher in Cuba than China.

If China is so desperate to absorb Taiwan, why don't they invite the Taiwanese government to run China? I mean, China started off with far greater resources and a much bigger population, but today Taiwan is – per person – much richer, freer and more successful. It seems like an obvious solution, if Xi Jinping simply wants what's best for the Chinese people.

Chapter 5

Joseph Stiglitz is the sort of economist that people queue round the block for at book signings and has parties thrown for him by prime ministers and presidents (though not Trump, whom he described as "the ultimate idiot nephew"). He's wonderfully rude about financiers, arguing that their products were only innovative because the products were stupid, and he's scathing about bankers who pushed people into taking out bigger mortgages when interest rates were low (as which was the only direction interest rates could go in?). The most recent book of his I've read (and nicked the best bits of) is called *The Road to Freedom: Economics and the Good Society*.

You can read Guido Fawkes's analysis of whether Chancellor **Rachel Reeves** really was an economist at: order-order.com – look for an article called

"Rachel Reeves bank economist myth busted" published on 24 October 2024.

Heteroskedasticity is a statistical issue where data becomes more variable while still seeming to fit on a straight line. For instance, imagine you were measuring the heights of kids in a classroom – if they were 90cm, 100cm and 110cm, you would plot their average as 100cm. If next year they were 100cm, 120cm and 140cm, you would plot their average as 120cm, and conclude that *on average* each kid has grown 20cm. But the kids' heights have become much more spread out. Heteroskedasticity shows that sometimes drawing simple straight lines through data points won't always give you a complete picture.

A **liquidity trap** is a situation where interest rates are so low that people hoard cash, rather than invest or spend it, which can hold back government efforts to stimulate the economy by lowering interest rates further.

I can just about manage a Mill's Mess, but have never quite mastered **juggling** four balls at once. Hat's off to you if you have. Apparently, if you juggle before sitting an exam you're more likely to pass it, as it gets your brain buzzing the right way to think clearly. Though I've also heard the same being said about staying hydrated, so please don't rely on this for your next test.

After New Zealand introduced the world's first **minimum wage** laws in 1894, Australia followed in 1896, Canada in 1918, Japan in 1947, India in 1948 and in fact almost every other country introduced minimum wages before the UK did, except Russia and Ireland, both of which held out for a few more months before joining minimum wage club. (Though technically, most Scandinavian countries, Switzerland and Italy don't have minimum wages laws, but they have pretty equivalent provisions.)

Out of rich countries, only Portugal has a lower minimum wage than the US.

David Card, who co-wrote the book *Myth and Measurement* about minimum wages, co-won the Sveriges Riksbank Prize in 2021.

Scott Galloway, of New York University's Stern School of Business, argues that had minimum wages risen in line with "productivity gains" (meaning the extra amount of stuff workers produce) since their peak in 1968 they would now be $25/hr.

One of the most interesting theories for why wages (especially minimum wages) stopped being linked to productivity in the 1970s is that women started joining the workforce in large numbers. The theory goes that this suppressed wages, as more people were competing for jobs (and because women were systematically paid less), and pushed up house prices as two-income households could borrow more than one-income households could.

Continuing that theme, although India has now overtaken China as the world's most populous nation, China still has more people in work, thanks to its far higher rate of female participation in the labour force. If as many women in India worked as in China, India's economy would already have overtaken China's.

You can read Steven Levitt's "Using Big Data to Estimate Consumer Surplus: The Case for **Uber**" online. It came out in 2016 and (I think) is still the biggest attempt to actually find a demand curve in reality (or at least, the biggest that's been published – I'm sure similar studies have been kept private by the companies that commissioned them). It's a very clear and easy to follow paper, though it understandably tries to put Uber in the best possible light.

In 1956, a marketing guru named Wendell R Smith wrote a pioneering paper called "Product Differentiation and Market Segmentation as Alternative Marketing Strategies" that paved the way for the widespread adoption of something called *price discrimination*. This is the practice of selling the same good to different people for different prices – in other words, to convert a **consumer surplus** into a *supplier* surplus.

This is why airlines or train operators might charge different prices for the same seat depending on whether they're selling in advance, or with a return flight (especially with a Saturday night stopover, which indicates it's not business customer), or to a student (who is more likely to get a coach instead).

It's why online retailers have been accused of charging Apple users more than PC owners and why this book costs more in the UK than in India. It's also why, as consumers, we shouldn't always celebrate hugely profitable companies – that profit may well have previously been our "consumer surplus".

There are hundreds of online videos and essays explaining the **theory of supply and demand** and how they result in **equilibrium prices**, which is depressing, given how flimsy the theory is. For a systematic deconstruction, have a read of Steve Keen's *Debunking Economics* or watch Jonathan Nitzan's *Skating on Thin Ice* on YouTube. In short, supply and demand curves are unmeasurable, equilibriums are unobservable, supply and demand may not be independent, demand doesn't always slope downwards nor supply slope upwards.

The **Sonnenschein–Mantel–Debreu Theorem** demonstrates that demand curves could be all sorts of wacky shapes, even if everyone was perfectly rational (which they're not) and that market forces will not result in stable, unique equilibriums. It's a *very* mathematical theorem, so unless that's your thing, probably just move right along.

None of this says that supply and demand don't affect prices, it's just that there's nothing neat and predictable about any of it, let alone stable equilibria.

The failure of supply and demand to reflect reality was understood from the very beginning. William Stanley Jevons, who if you remember had kicked off the use of mathematics in economics, had talked of "comparative statics" – snapshots in time. But many other economists said that wasn't good enough. Keynes recognised that it was what lay between these snapshots that was interesting. Joan Robinson observed in 1962 that "a model applicable to actual history has to be capable of getting out of equilibrium; indeed, it should rarely be in it."

Even Hayek was aware of the limitations of the concepts underpinning his belief in free markets. In his Sveriges Riksbank award acceptance speech he acknowledged that the failures of economists were due to their propensity to imitate science, "an attempt which in our field may lead to outright error". Though this was probably a dig at Keynes, whose theories had been dominating politics right up to the 1970s (when Hayek got his award).

Another famous economist to lament the failure of economics to explain change was **Thorstein Veblen**, who is most well-known for coining the terms *conspicuous consumption* and *conspicuous leisure*, a good 111 years before Instagram launched. He claimed that the upper classes were only good at looking important rather than doing anything useful and famously used old boxes for furniture and rarely changed his clothes. Despite this, there is a story that the dean of the University of Chicago once fired him for having too many affairs with his colleagues' wives.

Chapter 6

A **production frontier** (or sometimes production possibility frontier) is the hypothetical maximum output of an economy ... which is fine, but every explanation of such a frontier always begins with something like "imagine an economy that produces only two products". Ah yes, that famous two-product economy, where everyone owns sombreros and apples and *nothing else*.

The **Phillips Curve** is a supposed trade-off between inflation and unemployment that has now largely been debunked but is still used by central banks to forecast inflation.

The **Ricardian Equivalence** equation is not really that complicated. It merely represents the intertemporal budget constraint, which states that the present value of lifetime consumption must equal the present value of lifetime resources, so given a lifetime utility of consumption today and discounted future utility, in order to maximise lifetime utility an individual will choose to balance their utility across both periods, subject to their budget constraint. *Obviously*.

It's possible to read the newspaper reports of the funeral of **Henry George** online. I got a lot of detail from the *New York Sun* and *The New York Times*, and the addresses themselves can be accessed via the Library of Congress (loc.gov). The great hall of Grand Central Palace on Lexington Avenue has since been demolished and replaced with a skyscraper. The bust had been made by his son, Richard – he made quite a few of them and I found one on an auction site going for $150.

If you want to read any of Henry George's books, they're also all available online as they're way out of copyright. There are good guides on where to start at henrygeorge.org. *Progress and Poverty* is very readable but he doesn't half take a while to get to his point (I laughed when I read a review on Amazon that said, "Once in a while he stumbles upon a good question such as, 'What is the meaning of life?', but he just keeps rambling and never tries to answer it.") There's a modernised version by Bob Drake that's easier to read, as well as a few hyper-abridged versions floating around.

Karl Marx was apparently sent six copies of *Progress and Poverty* from friends of his saying "Karl, you've got to read this new book, you'll love it!" He really didn't love it, though he gave a copy to Engels.

Land and Liberty: Henry George and the Crafting of Modern Liberalism by Christopher England is very good, too, and has a lot of interesting biographical flourishes. Henry George lends himself to biographies (of which there are several), as he has a certain Forrest Gump-style connection with many of the major people and events of the late 19th century.

Tammany Hall got its name from a Lenape chieftain known for his peaceful relations with early English settlers, and who became a symbol of noble "native" virtue and democratic ideals. When American colonists rebelled against British rule, many local societies named themselves after this chieftain, whom they romanticised as an American patron saint. So it's ironic that the Tammany Society of New York, later referred to by their meeting place, was a violent anti-democratic society.

I understand that there are currently five **dwarf planets**, with Pluto being the most famous one. They are not proper planets because they haven't cleared their orbits of other material. One of them is shaped like an egg.

The pub really is called **The George**, but good luck finding it, as there are over 200 pubs in England also called The George. Sadly, the pub is named after *King* George, rather than *Henry* George.

I can't find any pubs named after economists (except the Red Lion, famously named after James Red Lion, Cambridge School economist and winner of the Sveriges Riksbank prize in 198— Oh, no, wait, sorry).

Chapter 7

Comparing historic wealth levels to modern ones is tricky, as none of the comparisons are quite fair. I've compared **Rockefeller's wealth** to the size of the US economy, though most people were so poor in those days that the economy was much smaller than today. Some historians just try to use cumulative inflation figures, but that doesn't really work out either – suppose a loaf of bread used to cost 10 cents and a dock worker used to earn a dollar a day. Does that mean that bread was expensive or dockworkers were poor? If you fancy playing around with this, I recommend the website measuringworth.com.

Anyway, Rockefeller was preposterously rich. You can go on a guided tour of Kykuit, his forty-room mansion in New York State, if you want to get a feel for Gilded Age living.

Millicent Fawcett is also famous for being a leading suffragist, sister to the first woman in Britain to qualify as a doctor, and mother to the first woman to come top in Cambridge's maths exams. Yup, one of *those* families.

You can read her book *Political Economy for Beginners* for free online. She ends each chapter with a quiz – I realised too late that Hans Rosling's global bestseller *Factfulness* also contains quizzes, as does Daniel Kahneman's *Thinking, Fast and Slow*, and number-one bestseller *Murdle*, so maybe quizzes are the secret to bestsellers (though *Murdle*'s not even tangentiality related to economics). In case you want a quiz:

What is Hollywood star Millie Bobby Brown's full first name?

What do Americans call what the British refer to as a "tap"?

If you want to read more about the conspiracy theory that the Robber Barons deliberately financed economics departments to suppress Henry George's arguments for land taxes, try Mason Gaffney's "Neo-Classical Economics as a Stratagem against Henry George", which you can read online as part of *The Corruption of Economics*. All of Gaffney's work is available at masongaffney.org.

I tried to interview Gaffney to corroborate Blackbeard's version, but discovered that he had died in 2020. I spoke instead to someone who knew him, who said he was "very nice", which is great to hear, but didn't really give me the colourful detail I was hoping for.

The list of **Robber Baron-funded institutions** goes on: Johns Hopkins University was founded by railroad magnate Johns Hopkins, Cornell University by industrialist (and owner of 500,000 acres of New York State) Ezra Cornell, Vanderbilt University by shipping magnate Cornelius Vanderbilt.

Andrew Carnegie (who owned at least 28,000 acres of land) founded what became Carnegie Mellon in 1900 (the *Mellon* bit comes from the Mellon Institute of Industrial Research, founded in 1913 by industrialist and banker Andrew Mellon, who would later become the US Treasury Secretary, advocating tax cuts for the rich).

There were, of course, many reasons for the ultra-wealthy to found universities, and some were genuinely and simply philanthropic – I can well believe that George Eastman (of Eastman Kodak photography fame) wasn't trying to bend the public ear when he founded the Eastman School of Music, for instance.

Funnily enough, **Karl Marx** refers to the elite controlling ideas several times in his work, using phrases like "false consciousness" and "mental production". In 1846, Friedrich Engels and Marx co-wrote *The German Ideology*, in which they argue that the ruling ideas of any society are the ideas of its ruling class, meaning that what people consider "common sense" is shaped by those in power to maintain their dominance.

I once had a lovely afternoon beer with two friends from university outside a pub in the very upmarket neighbourhood of Primrose Hill, in London. One of my friends almost spat out his drink as he clocked the sign on the house opposite. "Oh my God, that's Engels' house!" he squealed. He thought it hilarious that the principal sponsor of Marxism lived in what is now a £10 million house.

Not all Robber Barons were against Henry George, by the way. One minor industrialist, the businessman and politician Tom Loftin Johnson, who had made his fortune monopolising tramlines in several big American cities, was so convinced by Henry George's arguments that he did the opposite of what the rest of the Robber Barons were doing. He paid his lawyer the equivalent of about $20,000 to analyse *Progress and Poverty* as if it were a "legal question". He explained to his lawyer that his conundrum was simple: "I must get out of the business, or prove this book is wrong."

The lawyer, who in fairness was not an economist, could not convince his client that Henry George's ideas were mistaken, and Tom Loftin Johnson, on the advice of Henry George himself, stepped back from his business interests to go into politics. On the campaign stump, he argued against the wicked ways of Streetcar Barons, and pointed out that he should know, because he was one. He recognised that public transportation in many cities was a natural monopoly so he argued that public transit should be in public ownership. It was a message that hit home, and Tom Loftin Johnson was elected first as a member of Congress and then the mayor of Cleveland, Ohio. Today, you can visit a bronze statue of him reading *Progress and Poverty* in Cleveland Public Square.

The **Knights of Labor** never really recovered from the Haymarket Massacre. More specialised industry-specific unions took their place, and they shut their headquarters in 1917 and formally disbanded in 1949.

Millie Bobby Brown's full first name is Millie. Yup, it was a trick question – there are very few famous Millicents.
 Americans call taps "faucets".
 There's probably a reason I didn't include more quizzes.

The hugely influential economist Joseph Schumpeter – so influential that *The Economist* magazine named a column after him – wrote that **Léon Walras** was "the greatest of all economists". (Though, unfortunately, no one seems to have liked his romantic fiction. I feel his pain – I once wrote a truly terrible novel about teenage romance that no one ever read.)
 A detail that is often (and perhaps deliberately) overlooked is that Walras was an ardent supporter of land taxes. He went even further than Henry George, arguing that land should be nationalised, and that the rents from land would be sufficient to support the nation, meaning no other taxes would be needed. And these nationalised land rents, unlike taxes on goods or capital or labour, would not harm the economy.
 The Economist column Schumpeter focuses on business stories. Schumpeter himself believed that entrepreneurs knocked markets out of equilibrium, and that economic development then followed a series of waves: two Kitchin waves formed a Juglar, two Juglars made a Kuznet and three Kuznets made a 54-year Kondratiev. And I know that sounds like I'm making it up – I once joked about how ridiculous this was in a seminar, and an apprentice oil trader interrupted me to swear that Kondratiev waves were true.

While discussing **William Stanley Jevons** and **Léon Walras** with a psychiatrist friend of mine, she remarked that they lived in a time when many parents were absolutely horrid to their kids. She was reading a book about the history of parenting that included old advice like *Never hug your child. If you must praise them, a handshake is preferable.* It got me wondering if the ream of economists who tried to explain people's behaviour mathematically was because of their own emotional repression. I wondered if there was a psychiatric or neurodivergent history of economics waiting to be written, then quickly realised that I was well out of my depth, not least because of my own emotional repression. I can't shake the thought, though...

You can read **Alfred Marshall's** 900-page *Principles of Economics* free online, too. I wouldn't, though.

The **John Bates Clark Medal** is awarded by the American Economics Association to the economist under 40 who has most successfully used the phrase *deathless soul jelly* in an academic paper. Or maybe it's to whoever made the biggest contribution to economics...

Chapter 8

I was a little bemused to be called a Marxist. I mean, Marx thought all value ultimately came from labour, but that's demonstrably not true. If it was true, then art would be valued by how long it took to paint, fine wines would never appreciate in value (as no labour has been added), and sticking a Gucci label on a handbag would do nothing to its price. Far more significantly, Marx's vision was of a "dictatorship of the proletariat", but history has shown that all Marxism leads to is a "dictatorship of the dictator".

In every country in which Marxism has been introduced, the effect has been murderous horror – more than 30 million people died due to the famines and purges under China's Chairman Mao, perhaps 20 million died in the Soviet Union due to Stalin's Great Terror, a quarter of Cambodia's population were murdered by Pol Pot's communist regime. I don't think that saying *billionaires don't pay much tax but poor people pay loads* is quite in the same league.

Andrew Leigh's book is *The Shortest History of Economics*. Apparently, the longest economics book ever written is *Lehrbuch der Nationalökonomie*, a five-volume German work containing 3,969 pages.

The Harvard history professor who suggested that Adam Smith thought the invisible hand was just an ironic joke is Emma Rothschild. She married Amartya Sen, who is the economist I quoted a few pages back as a student of Joan Robinson. Small world. You can read her full article, "Adam Smith and the Invisible Hand", in the *American Economic Review*.

Incidentally, should you be stuck for something to do on a rainy day in London, you can visit the embalmed body of utilitarian philosopher **Jeremy Bentham** at University College. His head, though, is kept in an undisclosed location, ever since it was stolen as a prank by students from rival Kings College.

Decoy pricing gets me every time I take my car to the carwash. A Platinum wash costs £40, but the Gold wash only costs £15, and Silver costs £10. Compared to the Platinum wash, £15 seems a perfectly reasonable price to pay for two minutes of foamy water and those weird slappy tentacle things. Coffee shops do something similar with their size options (and this can work both ways, sometimes pushing you to buy the expensive option, because it's only a *bit* more than the middle one).

    Freemium pricing is what online games do – *Candy Crush* is free... until you run out of lives.

    I was rather tickled that on the cover of a book called *The Capitalist Manifesto* by Swedish historian Johan Norberg there is, as part of the cover art, a "fake" discounted price sticker – the sort of peel-off price you used to see a lot in the old days, with a new, lower price stuck over the older, higher one. *The Capitalist Manifesto* argues that *everything* would be better if there were no restrictions on free markets or free trade, on the grounds that in a free market, consumers will rationally move their spending power to the product that grants them the highest utility. And yet here *on the cover* was a demonstration of how people are irrationally tricked by fake discounts, which suggests governments need to intervene with laws to prevent rip-offs.

The Capitalist Manifesto is a very readable book if you want to read more about why free markets may be the solution to everything. It wobbles a bit about environmental degradation and enriching China, and oddly he's all for governments financing universities, which is an outrageously communist idea.

I have no idea if Kanya's fat-penned supply and demand diagram makes sense, but in a world of nonsensical two-dimensional economic diagrams, I'm not sure that matters.

The fact that economic theories don't have to be true as long as they *sound* clever has been noted by economists themselves. Ronald Reagan's advisor David Henderson delivered a lecture series for the BBC called "The Unimportance of Being Right". The economist Samuel Brittan agreed: in a report on whether there was such a thing as an economic consensus, he wrote that "it is much more important for a paper to be competent than for it to be right".

Shareholder value maximisation appears all over the courses at my business school. I hate it with a passion. Among other problems, it's also a root cause of ugly architecture – why spend money on making a building *that everyone has to look at* attractive? How does that help shareholders?

American Airlines justified removing an olive by claiming that only 40 per cent of their customers ate the olive. I suspect that far fewer than 40 per cent of people read the notes at the back of non-fiction books, but here we are.

If you want to read the pamphlet produced by **Henry Ford** for his employees, look for "Helpful Hints and Advice to Ford Employes (sic)" – it's available at thehenryford.org. It's got some great photos. Cynics argue that it wasn't really altruism, but an attempt to reduce training time, strikes and absenteeism, and deprive his rivals of workers.

Don't just google "Henry Ford pamphlet", though, or you'll be directed to a four-volume set of antisemitic books called *The International Jew*, which Ford backed financially. Ford later claimed to recant his antisemitic position, but historians disagree about how sincere he was.

Fortune magazine's article about **Elon Musk** "subsidy harvesting" was published on 19 March 2025.

Chapter 9

If you would like to **see the cat**, in a *literal* sense, go to: henrygeorge.org/catsup.htm

You can watch *Thames Wallah* on YouTube.

The statistics on how much of England is owned by aristocrats are taken from the book *Who Owns England?* by Guy Shrubsole. The 30 per cent owned by aristocrats has barely changed in centuries. Another 17 per cent is owned by "oligarchs and bankers".

The **School of Philosophy and Economic Science** was founded by British MP Andrew MacLaren as the Henry George School of Economics in 1938. In the 1950s, it incorporated transcendental meditation and the ideas of Russian mystic George Gurdjieff into its teaching, and by 1961 had enough members to fill the Albert Hall; in the 1970s it founded schools for children which in the 1980s were described by the *London Evening Standard* newspaper as having a harsh discipline regime. The newspaper also described the School of Economic Science as a cult. By 2006, an inquiry report found that there had been "a real change in the ethos and conduct of the schools ... [witnesses] speak of them as happy places where there appears to be a relaxed atmosphere between pupils and teachers."

As well as economics in a sane society being Georgist, **Aldous Huxley** wrote that politics would be "Kropotkinesque", which was a term I had to look up. It's the idea that instead of central government control there should be a system of self-organising communities. Apparently, it's a form of "anarchist communism", which by coincidence is how I refer to the culture at my kids' playgroup.

All the characters in *Brave New World* are named after famous historic figures, like "Darwin Bonaparte" and "Benito Hoover". There's also a *Henry* and a *George* ...

I read one claim that **Friedrich Hayek** had only two friends. I don't know if that's true, but I wouldn't be surprised, given his miserable view of human nature. Somewhat ironically, for someone who literally set up a society to influence governments, he thought that it was arrogant to think economies could be organised from the top down. I guess organising to be unorganised doesn't count.

The **Hoover Dam** was actually given the go-ahead before the Wall Street Crash, and was originally called the Boulder Dam. It was the biggest dam in the world when it was built, but isn't even the biggest in America any more, and nowadays wouldn't make the top 50 biggest dams in the world.

I have a bit of a soft spot for the University of Chicago economist **Frank Knight** (the one who objected to the Mont Pelerin Society being named after catholic aristocrats), simply because he once said "never waste any time you can spend sleeping", which is a sentiment I can wholly get behind.

You can join the **Mont Pelerin Society** or find out more about them at montpelerin.org. Their statement of aims includes a clarification of what is meant by *liberal*.

In terms of the same word meaning different things to different people, I'm still struggling to understand what Americans mean by "**middle class**", a term that comes up in a lot of economic analysis. To me, it means watching rugby union, having National Trust membership and my friends teasing me that my toddler's favourite food is camembert, but isn't necessarily anything to do with wealth. I think Americans just mean *not that poor, not that rich*, which in fairness is probably a more useful economic indicator than owning a Le Creuset set.

I asked the **Institute for Economic Affairs** if I could take one of their economists out for lunch to get their side of things and they never even acknowledged my request. Maybe it went to their junk folder?

They recently lost a legal battle over claims that they were a "hard-right lobby group". If you would like to judge for yourself, their website is: iea.org.uk.

You can learn more about the **Foundation for Economic Education** at: fee.org.

The full title of the **Sveriges Riksbank Prize** is the Sveriges Riksbank Prize in Economic Sciences in Memory of Alfred Nobel. The prize is administered and awarded by the Royal Swedish Academy of Sciences, which must grate with those economists who don't consider economics a science (or don't believe in royalty). Oxford University economic historian **Avner Offer** co-authored *The Nobel Factor: The Prize in Economics, Social Democracy, and the Market Turn*, which explores how the prize helped free-market liberalism to push social democracy aside.

The first Sveriges Riksbank Prize was given to two economists for making economics more mathematical. The second prize was given to Paul Samuelson, the man whose book *Economics* had done more than any other to raise the profile of neoclassical economics (and bury Henry George).

The **Earth** takes 23 hours and 56 minutes to rotate once on its axis. In that time, it will have completed just under one 365th of its orbit of the sun, so will have to rotate for another 4 minutes for the sun to be in the same position in the sky again.

Chapter 10

You won't normally read that the **Chinese Civil War** was between Communists and Georgists, either because of just how utterly Henry George has been erased from history, or because it's a bit like claiming that the American Civil War was between industrialists and traditional agrarians – I mean, yeah, *I suppose*, but there were bigger arguments at stake. In the Chinese case, the civil war was mostly between communists and anti-communists, it just happened that the anti-communist leader had proposed Georgism as an alternative. Few people who did the actual fighting would have been familiar with Henry George.

So if you'd rather stick to your boring, conventional narrative from your well-researched and documented history book, written by an expert who's spent their prestigious academic career researching this topic, telling you that the war was between communists and nationalists, then be my guest.

I read a brilliant summary of Taiwan's economic history in a book about the Asian Economic Miracle (the high growth period from the sixties to the nineties) but I can't for the life of me remember the book's title. I must have it somewhere in my house, but I've just spent 20 minutes looking for it and I'm at a loss. Maybe I left it at my parents' house? I bet this never happens to Michael Lewis.

The question of where money comes from is, astonishingly, not something that all economists agree on. And a shocking number of economic theories simply ignore money as if its existence and use is insignificant.

For most of the 20th century, textbooks taught that the money supply grows because the same "note" was endlessly recycled: deposited by a saver, then lent to a borrower, who spent it, which created another depositor, and so on, in a phenomenon known as the money multiplier.

This money multiplier features in a famous scene in the Christmas movie *It's a Wonderful Life*, in which George Bailey, the owner of Bailey Brothers Building and Loan, is assailed by his customers, who demand the return of their deposits during a run on the bank. Desperately, George Bailey explains that he doesn't have the cash in his safe, as it's "in Joe's house and the Kennedy house and Mrs McLaine's". In other words, one person's deposit is another person's loan.

In reality, every time you borrow money, that money isn't coming from some big stash of cash kept in a bank vault (virtual or otherwise), nor is it in Joe's kitchen extension, it is simply "created" at a key stroke. The Bank of England finally acknowledged that this is how money is created only in 2010, but then I guess analysing where money comes from isn't that important for the, erm, Bank of England.

Ironically, when *It's a Wonderful Life* was released in 1947, the FBI issued a statement claiming that the film was communist as it "represented rather obvious attempts to discredit bankers". You can watch the clip I'm talking about from *It's a Wonderful Life* on YouTube.

My favourite Christmas movie is *Die Hard*.

Before 2011, most economic textbooks would also tell you as a fact that people in ancient societies bartered with each other. Then anthropologist David Graeber published *Debt: The First 5,000 Years*, which made the point that there's absolutely no evidence for this, and it doesn't even make sense as a theory.

I read one article that complained that money isn't created out of thin air, but is rather created from future income. That alone perhaps demonstrates how some economists are willing to convert mathematical calculations into a deranged perception of reality. I mean, if I pulled a rabbit out of my hat and said, "Actually, I haven't made it appear from nothing, I summoned it from the future!" you would think I was either quite mad, or genuinely a wizard.

I mention how economists are afraid of **wage–price spirals**. Interestingly, a comprehensive study of data across a wide range of economies going back over 60 years was conducted by six economists at the International Monetary Fund in 2022, and found evidence of wage–price spirals in only a small minority of cases. Strangely, politicians ignore this evidence when opposing pay rises for public sector workers.

You can read the report at imf.org. The paper is called "Wage–Price Spirals: What is the Historical Evidence?"

Snapdragons are *technically* a **firework**, but it's not like Blackbeard was launching rockets at his students (I assume).

I told the "I've a joke about **trickle-down** economics, but you won't get it" joke to a friend, who looked puzzled for a moment then said, "Try me."

The phrase "trickle-down economics" was invented by the American comedian Will Rogers in the 1930s in response to Herbert Hoover's tax cuts for the rich. (Will Rogers is also famous for saying "no man is great if he thinks he is".) The phrase was revised in the 1980s as a criticism of Reagan's tax cuts for the rich. No economist advocating tax cuts for rich people ever dares use the phrase nowadays, preferring instead to talk about the "size of the pie", as in "a smaller slice of a larger pie is still a larger slice of pie", which isn't, geometrically, guaranteed to be true.

If you do like bad economics jokes, how about:

"How many free-market economists does it take to change a lightbulb? None, if it needs changing, the market will change it."

Or

"What do an economist and a plumber have in common? They both deal with gross domestic product."

You can probably see why I left them out of the main text.

The Indian government guarantees paid employment for up to 100 days per year to people in rural areas. Like Roosevelt's New Deal, most of the work is on infrastructure projects, such as building new roads or irrigation channels or afforestation programmes. It's only if the government can't offer suitable work that unemployment benefit gets paid instead – a recognition that paying someone to do *something* is better than paying them to do *nothing*.

You can read Keynes's original essay online, in which he predicts we'll be working a **15-hour week** by 2030. Search for "Economics possibilities for our Grandchildren". It's not the easiest read, though he does trace Britain's prosperity to a single event – Francis Drake stealing Spanish gold. And at one point he refers to people who love money for its own sake as possessing a "somewhat disgusting morbidity".

The **North Sea oil fields** were split between the United Kingdom and Norway, but the two countries took a very different approach to their management.

Norway set up a state-owned fund to manage their oil wealth. Rather than chase short-term profits, as British oil businesses did, they deliberately slowed production when prices were low and then sold more when prices rose. Instead of financing tax cuts, the oil revenue was invested in both domestic and international companies, and foreign commercial property – including parts of Regent Street in central London and Times Square in New York (neither the British nor American governments own any of Karl Johans Gate, the nearest equivalent in Oslo). Forty years later, the Norwegian Sovereign Wealth Fund is the largest such fund in the world, worth over $300,000 per person in Norway, and is mostly used to fund Norwegians' pensions.

I appreciate that Norway benefits from having a smaller population than the UK, so had the UK set up a similar fund it would only be worth around £25,000 per person now. But still, where's my £25,000?

John Williamson wrote "A Short History of the **Washington Consensus**" for the *Peterson Institute for International Economics*, in which he makes a number of frank criticisms, including, "We have since been made very conscious that it matters a lot how privatization is done: it can be a highly corrupt process that transfers assets to a privileged elite for a fraction of their true value."

Chapter 11

The **time value of money** has more names than probably any other concept in finance. It is often referred to as a discount rate, or r, but depending on what you're using it for can also be (hold your breath) the cost of equity, the cost of debt, the risk free rate, the cap rate, the cost of capital, the WACC, the hurdle rate, the required return, the DCF rate and the IRR, Kd, Ke, K, i, and TVM. Whatever it's called, it's pretty much a guess.

A great book on the rise of hedge funds and the role that **Alfred Winslow Jones** played is *More Money than God* by Sebastian Mallaby. And just in case you don't subscribe to *Institutional Investor* magazine, you may have missed their annual ranking of the 25 highest-earning hedge fund managers, which recorded them collectively earning over $25 billion in 2023, so an average annual pay packet of $1 billion each. The ranking has been collated since the year 2000; Jim Simons of Renaissance Technologies made the list every single year until his death in 2024.

Matt Taibbi referred to **Goldman Sachs as a great vampire squid** in an article titled "The Great American Bubble Machine", published in *Rolling Stone* magazine on 5 April 2010.

The professor who referred to **Nordhaus**'s recognition by the Sveriges Riksbank as *the Nobel Prize for Climate Catastrophe* was Jason Hickel, a professor at the Institute of Environmental Science and Technology at the Autonomous University of Barcelona. You can read more at foreignpolicy.com.

One of the biggest reports into the possible effects of climate change is the Stern Review, a 700-page analysis by London School of Economics professor Nicholas Stern, commissioned by the UK government. Stern used a discount rate of 1.4 per cent, which suggests we should pay about £25 today to avert £100 of damage a century from now.

The examples of the damage caused by **private equity** could fill an entire book. Here are just a few:

The seafood restaurant chain Red Lobster filed for bankruptcy in 2024 after being locked into overly expensive leasing deals to rent their *own* restaurants, following a private equity deal that was financed by selling their own property and renting it back. At the time, their CEO claimed the bankruptcy was due to their offer of $20 "all-you-can-eat shrimp", but that's obviously ridiculous – they weren't legally obliged to offer unlimited shrimp.

The car rental company Hertz, encouraged by their new private equity owners, borrowed billions of dollars (using their own fleet of cars as collateral) then paid a $1 billion dividend to those private equity owners. Shortly afterwards they, too, filed for bankruptcy (though were eventually able to continue trading).

The Carlyle Group bought the nursing home chain HCR ManorCare, mostly using borrowed money that HCR ManorCare would have to pay back, rather than the Carlyle Group. The private equity firm then sold most of the nursing homes to recoup their initial investment, forcing the company to pay half a billion dollars a year in rent to occupy the properties they once owned (which I rather feel should be called "doing a Red Lobster"). Carlyle also did a Toys "R" Us and extracted $80 million in advisory fees. To cope with the new financial pressure, ManorCare desperately cut costs and laid-off staff.

According to research from the National Bureau of Economic Research, the private equity takeover of nursing homes in America has led to 20,000 premature deaths over a 12-year period (see nber.org/papers/w28474). I should stress that this statistic was not about any one particular private equity firm.

You can read more about **Thames Water** in any of hundreds of damning articles, but more fun is to watch the short film made by campaign group

Led by Donkeys called *Water privatisation is a con*, which they projected onto the headquarters of Thames Water in 2023. The video is on YouTube.

The **Paul Krugman** line is from a 6,000-word article he wrote for *The New York Times* in 2009 about how economists had so massively failed to foresee or prevent the 2008 crash. In the article, he talks about widening fault lines in the profession, accusations of "schlock economics", "discredited fairy tales" and the "intellectual collapse" of the Chicago School. His article concludes that economists will have to learn to "live with messiness".

Or rather, it *should* have concluded that economists have to live with messiness, instead it then banged on for several more pages about babysitting cooperatives. I guess no one at the *Times* was willing to tell the Sveriges Riksbank winner to edit down his work.

I was amazed when I sold the TV rights for my last book – I mean, it's a book about *tax evasion*. But then Hollywood made a film out of Michael Lewis's *The Big Short*, and that was about **collateralised debt obligations**.

If you want a whole book on how mad the finance industry is, I recommend *Other People's Money* by the economist John Kay (who I *think* is not the same person as Steppenwolf frontman John Kay).

And easily my favourite book on the history of finance is James Owen Weatherall's *The Physics of Finance*, but then I'm a big fan of books about both physics and finance.

If you want to check out **Teodorin Obiang**'s seized yacht, there are pictures at the Stolen Asset Recovery Initiative website star.worldbank.org. Obiang has also had his $100 million French home seized by the French authorities, been sanctioned by the UK and Brazilian governments, given a suspended sentence by a French court, and reached a settlement with the US in which he surrendered his Malibu home, a Ferrari and other assets worth $34 million (though he was allowed to keep his Gulfstream jet and Michael Jackson's crystal-encrusted glove, which he'd bought for $275,000).

He didn't have to explain how he was able to afford these things on his official $100,000 salary.

University of Missouri professor **Michael Hudson** has written extensively about the problems with the financial sector, and has not just his own website (michael-hudson.com) but, should you want to give him some money (because the banks aren't about to), his own Patreon too (see patreon.com/michaelhudson). He says that "the financial sector essentially makes its money not by being part of the production and consumption economy but by siphoning off as much money from the production and consumption economy as it can", and points out that Americans are spending over 40 per cent of their incomes on housing today, up from 25 per cent in the 1940s, 1950s and 1960s.

If you want to know more about **Charles Ponzi**, there's a great book called *Ponzi's Scheme* by Mitchell Zuckoff. Or if you want a shorter summary and subscribe to *International Banker* magazine, they had a good bio in September 2021.

In brief, in the summer of 1919 Charles Ponzi was a dead-broke former convict struggling to make a living in Boston. He stumbled across what in the financial world is known as an "arbitrage opportunity". At the time, it was possible to buy "International Reply Coupons", which were a form of pre-paid postage, so that you could, say, write to your grandmother in Italy and include a coupon that could be exchanged for stamps in Italy, so that she could write back to you in America. What Ponzi realised is that the prices of the International Reply Coupons and the Italian stamps were not the same – it would be possible to buy a coupon for ten cents and use it to buy stamps worth fifteen cents, which could then be sold. It was an opportunity to make risk-free profits.

Except, of course, it wasn't. Coupons weren't sold in bulk, so someone would have to queue up in a post office, buy as many coupons as they could, somehow transport them to Italy, queue up to buy stamps, sell the stamps, then bring the cash back to America. That little logistical obstacle didn't stop Ponzi persuading a handful of his friends to invest $1,250 in the scheme.

But confounding rational expectations, within a few months Ponzi had managed to pay them $750 of interest on their investments. Word spread of his successful enterprise, and another eighteen investors put $100 each into his scheme. Within a month of depositing their cash with him, these new investors also received market-beating interest payments. Soon people were clamouring to invest in this fantastic arbitrage opportunity, so much so that Ponzi had to hire a large office and employed a team of people to collect deposits.

In February 1920, he received $5,000 from investors, in March another $20,000, by May another $400,000, by June over $2,000,000. And the phenomenal returns kept flowing to the investors, most of whom *reinvested* straight back into the scheme. People remortgaged their homes and threw in the life savings. It's said that three-quarters of Boston's police force had bought in. By July, he was receiving over $1,000,000 per day. And these were 1920 dollars, when a new car might cost $1,000 and the grandest homes would have cost less than $100,000.

By the end of July, the *Boston Post* newspaper had started to investigate, and calculated that for Ponzi's scheme to work he would need 160 million International Reply Coupons, but only 27,000 had ever been printed. More than that, the US Postal Office said that the coupons were not being bought or sold in large quantities anywhere in the world.

So where were the "profits" coming from? It was simple. There weren't any. Ponzi simply paid interest using new investors' cash, or even by using the investors' own cash. Take just that original $1,250 that got the ball rolling – the $750 in "interest" that Ponzi had paid was really taken from the initial investment. Had his friends asked for all their money back, they would have exposed his scam, because after the "interest" payment he would only have had $500 remaining (or actually less, as he spent a lot of it on himself).

The bursting of Ponzi's scheme caused such financial chaos that six banks collapsed in its wake.

After the scheme collapsed, Ponzi received two three-year jail sentences (with a complicated legal break in the middle), but once released for good set up a scam to sell swampland in Florida and soon ended up in prison once more.

Ponzi's original scheme looks quaint next to Bernie Madoff's more recent iteration – Madoff began his own Ponzi scheme in the 1970s, and by 2009, when he was finally convicted, had stolen almost $65 billion from duped investors.

One of the reasons **Hyman Minsky** was largely ignored by mainstream economics (up until he was proved right) was that he didn't like to express his ideas using mathematical equations. Instead, he would use interlocking balance sheets – rather like how accountants see the world.

The moral is *listen to accountants more*.

I'm only 50:50 on whether **ten thousand trequadragintillion** really is a one with 127 zeros after it. It seems unlikely that we would have a word for a one with 123 zeros (trequadragintillion) but have to add ten thousand in front of it to get to 127. Then again, it's not a number I use very often, so maybe it doesn't matter?

Along with *International Banker* magazine, I also never miss an issue of *The Reykjavik Grapevine*, which reported on the number of jailed **Icelandic bankers**. You can read it at grapevine.is. They also have some very interesting articles like "Hey, remember when those whaling ships were sunk?" and "It's Always Fun On Arnarhóll".

You can listen to **Ellen Brown**'s podcast *It's Our Money* at itsourmoney.podbean.com. She's also got a lot of books out about alternative medicine and the menopause, which I'm afraid I haven't (yet) read.

Chapter 12

Although I started this chapter with investment advice from **Mark Twain** he was apparently absolutely appalling at investing himself; he passed on the opportunity to be an early investor in Bell Telephone and instead put all the profits from his book sales *and* his wife's inheritance into a typesetting machine that never turned a profit.

Prior to **Liz Truss**, the shortest-serving prime minister was George Canning, who served for just under four months. Unlike Liz Truss, he wasn't kicked out by his own party, he simply died.

Although a few commentators noted during Truss's brief premiership that she was the first accountant to become prime minister, no one seemed to realise that her particular accountancy qualification required no tax knowledge whatsoever.

The moral is *only listen to accountants more if they are tax accountants.*

I claimed that the **extra £10 billion borrowing costs** inflicted on Brits by Truss's budget would allow police numbers to double, afford free school meals, buy the *Mona Lisa* and fix potholes. Here are my workings:

There are about 34,000 police officers in London, earning around £40,000 on average, so a crude doubling of police numbers would cost £1.36 billion. *The Guardian* newspaper estimated giving free school meals to every school child would cost a bit under £5 billion. I suspect you could pick up the *Mona Lisa* for a cool billion, leaving around £2.5 billion for the potholes (which in truth is at the lower end of the estimated repair bill). Alternatively, you could build a little over 20 miles of High Speed 2, the world's most expensive railway.

The New Zealand Finance Minister **Roger Douglas** is still alive. I should stress that *I* don't think he was a fuckwit, or a bastard. I'm just reporting what I was told (and, um, said). Like Reaganomics, he cut taxes on the rich, raised them on the poor (by introducing sales taxes) and privatised state-owned businesses. His father and grandfather were also members of the New Zealand parliament.

The **stats on British and American wealth** are from a Global Wealth Report compiled by UBS. Iceland is top of the list for median wealth (with $413,000 per person), Switzerland is top for mean wealth (with $709,000). Haiti is bottom on both measures, with a median wealth of just $207.

One economic historian I spoke to referred to the housing markets as "a machine for inequality", and clearly the phrase stuck with me.

If you want more on that theme there's a great book by *The Observer* newspaper's architecture critic Rowan Moore called *Property: The Myth that Built the World* that examines how our system of property ownership "threatens the freedoms and stability it was meant to sustain". It's also got a really lovely tactile cover, which I appreciate is a less intellectual thing to say, but it does.

The UK government pays around £16 billion a year to private landlords on behalf of claimants of housing benefit, enough to build around 100,000 homes each year and then give them away for free. Or at least it would be enough, if only they didn't have to buy the *land*, which is super expensive and in private hands, usually because someone's ancestor killed people on behalf of the king.

I once pitched my agent a book about interest rates, which he rejected on the grounds that it sounded "really boring". Meanwhile, the historian Edward Chancellor wrote *The Price of Time: The Real Story of Interest*, which got rave reviews, sold really well and won the Hayek Book Prize (a $50,000 award given by the Manhattan Institute, a think-tank founded alongside the Institute for Economic Affairs).

I also like *The Price of Money* by Rob Dix, *The Price of Inequality* by Joseph Stiglitz, *The Price of Civilisation* by Jeffrey Sachs and the *The Price of Salt* by Patricia Highsmith.

Chapter 13

If you want more of a feel for **Modern Monetary Theory**, probably the most accessible place is Stephanie Kelton's book *The Deficit Myth*. I've been to a couple of MMT conferences and the speakers often seem giddy with excitement, like explorers who have just discovered a new country. I tried to explain the theory to my mum – that taxes don't pay for things, they just take money out of the economy to prevent it overheating when the government spends too much.

"But either way the government needs to tax us to pay for things, then?" she asked.

"Um, yes," I said.

"So what difference does it make?"

That seems like a reasonable point. I guess the main takeaway is that we shouldn't worry as much as we do about government deficits.

US Treasury Secretary **Larry Summers,** who called Modern Monetary Theory "Voodoo economics", was one of the economists who advised on the privatisation of Russian state industries following the collapse of the Soviet Union and on the repeal of the Glass–Steagall Act in the run-up to the 2008 financial crisis.

You can read Harvard's own account of their economics students walking out of **Gregory Mankiw**'s lecture in Harvard's own newspaper, *The Harvard Crimson*, from their 2 November 2011 edition. Once upon a time, their paper was called *The Magenta* but changed its name to *Crimson* with an apologetic acknowledgement in 1875 that it had all been a misunderstanding: "magenta is not now, and . . . never has been, the right color of Harvard".

Gregory Mankiw's response is in "Know what you're protesting" in *The New York Times* edition of 4 December 2011.

Interestingly, Cornell Professor Robert H Frank has shown that studying economics at university makes students less likely to cooperate with others, suggesting that exposing people to the assumption in much of modern economics that we're all self-interested sociopaths makes us more likely to become self-interested sociopaths.

David Ricardo's attempt at **defining capital** is even shoddier than I made out. He begins his opus by stating that every product is derived from "labour, machinery and capital". But 89 pages later he says that machinery *is* capital. So which is it?

And I'm still struggling with food being capital. Like, a yoghurt is capital? Really?

His main point was that "capital is that which gives effect to labour", which suggests that Ricardo's vast wealth *wasn't* capital, as his houses, estates and piles of money weren't "giving effect to labour".

Yet Ricardo clearly considered himself a capitalist, and remember he said that the produce of the Earth will be divided between "landowners, labourers and capitalists".

Imagine if instead he'd said what he really meant: "How should the produce of the Earth be divided between rich people, poor people and other rich people?" Then his conclusion of "we should give more produce to rich people" would be more obviously suspect.

I'm not the first person to suggest we stop using the word "capital" in economic analysis. In the 1950s and 1960s, the **Cambridge Capital Controversy** was a long-running debate between economists like Joan Robinson and Piero Saffra in Cambridge, England, and Paul Samuelson and Robert Solow in Cambridge, Massachusetts that centred over whether the Americans' definition of capital was based on circular reasoning.

At the heart of the debate was whether the profits earned by capitalists were a consequence of mathematical laws or were determined by social and institutional constructs. Eventually, the Americans acknowledged that their own mathematics was faulty, but then more or less carried on as they had before.

If you would like to see a real-life **MONIAC** machine, they are on display in the Science Museum in London, the Reserve Bank of New Zealand Museum in Wellington, Istanbul University and Cambridge University, with more modern replicas elsewhere.

On the subject of energy, the pioneer of mathematical economics William Stanley Jevons recognised a problem: that as we become more efficient at creating energy, we actually use more of it, rather than less. A modern LED lightbulb uses a fraction of the energy of an old incandescent one, but does that mean that we now use less electricity? Not a bit – I've just counted and I've got 22 lights on in the room I'm writing this in (it was triple that when my Christmas tree was still up). As petrol engines have become more fuel-efficient, we've responded by buying bigger cars. As food became cheaper, we over-bought it and chucked more away.

This is now known as the **Jevons Paradox**, and has serious environmental implications, for instance that owners of energy-efficient homes sometimes use more energy, rather than less, as it becomes easier to heat their homes rather than put a jumper on.

The European Commission said that, actually, 300 people had "logged in" during their **Global Gateway launch party**, though didn't say how long they stayed for. However long it was for, that's still over €1,000 per guest.

If you want any more, please follow me on X.com (@rebelaccountant) or watch my videos on xvideos.com.

And if you do know what my real identity is, please keep it secret.

Thank you for reading.

RAISING READERS
Books Build Bright Futures

Dear Reader,

We'd love your attention for one more page to tell you about the crisis in children's reading, and what we can all do.

Studies have shown that reading for fun is the **single biggest predictor of a child's future life chances** – more than family circumstance, parents' educational background or income. It improves academic results, mental health, wealth, communication skills, ambition and happiness.[1]

The number of children reading for fun is in rapid decline. Young people have a lot of competition for their time. In 2024, 1 in 10 children and young people in the UK aged 5 to 18 did not own a single book at home.[2]

Hachette works extensively with schools, libraries and literacy charities, but here are some ways we can all raise more readers:

- Reading to children for just 10 minutes a day makes a difference
- Don't give up if children aren't regular readers – there will be books for them!
- Visit bookshops and libraries to get recommendations
- Encourage them to listen to audiobooks
- Support school libraries
- Give books as gifts

There's a lot more information about how to encourage children to read on our website: **www.RaisingReaders.co.uk**

Thank you for reading.

---

[1] OECD, '21st-Century Readers: Developing Literacy Skills in a Digital World', 2021, https://www.oecd.org/en/publications/21st-century-readers_a83d84cb-en.html

[2] National Literacy Trust, 'Book Ownership in 2024', November 2024, https://literacytrust.org.uk/research-services/research-reports/book-ownership-in-2024